The Works of Gordon Haddon Clark
Volume 15

Books by Gordon H. Clark

Readings in Ethics (1940)
Selections from Hellenistic Philosophy (1940)
A History of Philosophy (co-author, 1941)
A Christian Philosophy of Education (1988 [1946])
A Christian View of Men and Things
The Works of Gordon Haddon Clark
Volume 1 (1998 [1952])
What Presbyterians Believe (1956)[1]
Thales to Dewey (1997 [1957])
Dewey (1960)[2]
Religion, Reason, and Revelation (1995 [1961])
William James (1963)[2]
Karl Barth's Theological Method (1997 [1963])
The Philosophy of Science and Belief in God (1996 [1964])
What Do Presbyterians Believe? (1985 [1965])[1]
Peter Speaks Today (1967)[3]
The Philosophy of Gordon H. Clark (co-author, 1968)
Biblical Predestination (1969)[4]
Historiography: Secular and Religious (1994 [1971])
II Peter (1972)[3]
The Johannine Logos (1989 [1972])
Three Types of Religious Philosophy (1989 [1973])
First Corinthians (1991 [1975])
Colossians (1989 [1979])
Predestination in the Old Testament (1979)[4]
I and II Peter (1980)[3]
Language and Theology (1993 [1980])
First John (1992 [1980])
God's Hammer: The Bible and Its Critics (1995 [1982])
Behaviorism and Christianity (1982)
Faith and Saving Faith (1990 [1983])
In Defense of Theology (1994)
The Pastoral Epistles
The Works of Gordon Haddon Clark, Volume 15 (1999 [1984])
The Biblical Doctrine of Man (1992 [1984])
The Trinity (1990 [1985])
Logic (1998 [1985])
Ephesians (1985)
Clark Speaks from the Grave (1986)
Logical Criticisms of Textual Criticism (1990 [1986])
First & Second Thessalonians (1986)
Predestination (1987)
The Atonement (1996 [1987])
The Incarnation (1988)
Today's Evangelism: Counterfeit or Genuine? (1990)[5]
Essays on Ethics and Politics (1992)
Sanctification (1992)
New Heavens, New Earth (First and Second Peter) (1993 [1980])
The Holy Spirit (1993)
An Introduction to Christian Philosophy (1993)
Lord God of Truth & Concerning the Teacher (1994)
William James and John Dewey (1995)
God and Evil (1996)[6]
Philippians (1996)
Ancient Philosophy (1997)
In Defense of Theology / Evangelism and Emotion
The Works of Gordon Haddon Clark, Volume 14 (1999)
What Christians Believe
The Works of Gordon Haddon Clark, Volume 2 (1999)

1. Revised as *What Do Presbyterian Believe?* (1965) and *What Christians Believe* (1999)
2. Combined as *William James and John Dewey* (1995)
3. Combined as *I & II Peter* (1980) and revised as *New Heavens, New Earth* (1993)
4. Combined as *Predestination* (1987)
5. Reissued as *Evangelism and Emotion* with *In Defense of Theology* (1999)
6. Chapter 5 of *Religion, Reason and Revelation*

Gordon Haddon Clark
A. D. 1902-1985
The Bible alone is the Word of God.

THE PASTORAL EPISTLES

The Works of Gordon Haddon Clark
Volume 15

The Trinity Foundation

The Pastoral Epistles

Published by The Trinity Foundation

ISBN: 1-891777-04-1 (hardback)
ISBN: 1-891777-05-X (paperback)

Contents

First Timothy

Chapter One

1:1, 2

Paul, apostle of Christ Jesus, by the command of God our Savior and Christ Jesus our hope, to Timothy, legitimate son by faith: grace, mercy, and peace [from] God the Father and Christ Jesus our Lord.

In the epistle to the Galatians it was necessary for Paul to defend his status as an apostle in the face of pointed opposition. Timothy did not need the spirited defense given in *Galatians*. Nevertheless Paul mentions, if he does not stress, his apostolic authority to make clear the divine imposition of the following commands. Futhermore, in *2 Thessalonians* 3:17, Paul states that his signature is "a distinguishing mark in every letter." Of course it is theoretically possible that someone could have forged his signature. But how likely is it, when you today receive a letter from a well-known friend, that the letter is a forgery?

There are no apostles today.

Paul was an apostle by the command of God. Unlike some other places where Paul refers to his being chosen or predestinated to his office, this verse simply indicates that God commanded him to be an apostle. There are no apostles today; but even ministers, though of lesser rank, must be commanded or called. They are stewards of God's wisdom and grace. Now, no man can appoint himself to the office of steward. Hence, if a young man desires the office, he must seek the divine appointment at the hands of a presbyterial ordination. This matter will become clearer in a later verse.

One may note in passing that God is here called Savior. This title is usually applied to Christ. But here Christ is called our hope. *Hope*, as other New Testament passages show, does not signify our subjective hoping. *Hope* designates the thing hoped for. Subjectivizing these terms and failing to understand their objective meaning results in misconstruction of the divine message.

Timothy is the addressee. He is called a legitimate son. I do not think that Timothy, at first an illegitimate child, became legitimate by his faith. One might indeed say that before Timothy believed the Gospel, he was not a son at all, and then by believing he was born a son. Here it is perhaps better to use the English preposition *in*. The sense would be that Timothy was a true or legitimate son in the sphere of faith. The greeting that follows needs no explanation. Its three-fold form, "grace, mercy, and peace," rather than the two-fold form in *Philemon*, has no particular significance. There is no reason to suppose that *Philemon* is a forgery because its form is two-fold, nor, what is more frequently the case, to suppose that if Paul were the author of *1 Timothy* he could not have used the three-fold form.

Paul did not furnish us with a literary style worthy of imitation. His sentences are usually grammatical, but they are long and complicated.

1:3, 4

As I urged you to remain in Ephesus, when I was leaving for Macedonia, that you might command certain [persons] not to teach heterodox doctrines, nor to pay attention to [or, concern themselves about] myths and endless genealogies, which give rise to [mere] speculation rather than God's administration in [or, by] faith;

Paul did not furnish us with a literary style worthy of imitation. His sentences are usually grammatical, but they are long and complicated. The present sentence begins with verse 3 and continues to the end of verse 7. In fact, this sentence is not strictly grammatical, unless we mentally supply an obvious apodosis: "as I have urged you . . . so you urge your people." In the interest of a more English version, translators often break up these lengthy complications into shorter sentences. I shall try to reproduce the original style, and everyone will be glad that ministers in the pulpit will not use it.

The historical situation envisaged here seems to have been Paul's departure from Ephesus to Macedonia. There are a few other historical notes in these epistles. One may try to fit them into the account of Paul's missionary journeys in *Acts*, but the result will prove unsatisfactory. If the time of the events in *Acts* is the same time as that of the hints in *1 Timothy*, there is not enough detail to fit everything together. One must remember that *Acts* omits many things Paul did. One must also remember that detective stories depend on the absence of some facts and the non-factual arrangement of others. In the present case it is more likely that the events here given come from a time after the end of *Acts*.

Conzelmann makes the most of these difficulties. He suggests that *Acts* 19:22 "could be based on an error." Either *Acts* or *1 Timothy* presents us with "a legendary feature." Paul could not have had time to visit Ephesus again between the first and an imaginary second imprisonment. *1 Clement* 1:5 knows only of one imprisonment, and besides it is not a reliable document. Then, too, why did not Paul give these instructions to Timothy when he was with him?

They were fellow travelers. Paul had no need to write this epistle. "Schleiermacher, who inaugurated the criticism of this epistle . . . emphasized the difficulty which lies in the artificiality of the situation" (15, 16). Dear old Schleiermacher; where is my Jewish graduate student?

After Paul's historical allusion to his leaving for Macedonia he gives his first instruction to Timothy: Timothy is to stay in Ephesus in order to combat certain persons who were teaching heterodox theology. One might ask, who were these persons, and what did they teach? Who and how many there were, we do not know. From verse 20 we assume that Hymenaeus and Alexander were their leaders. What they were teaching is more clearly stated. First, however, let us note that Paul's main concern was the true doctrine. Correct theology has first place. Today some seminary professors would insist that a young minister's first duty is to be a marriage counselor. Theology, doctrine, intelligible teaching are held in low repute now. But it was not so with Paul.

Timothy is to stay in Ephesus in order to combat certain persons who were teaching heterodox theology.

Paul's main concern was the true doctrine. Correct theology has first place. Today some seminary professors would insist that a young minister's first duty is to be a marriage counselor.

The first word in verse 4 is "nor." This might indicate that the heterodox doctrine was one thing and the myths and endless genealogies were something else. If this is the correct understanding of the word *nor,* we have no information here as to the nature of the false teaching. The *nor*, however, could be less adversative; in which case the myths and genealogies would give content to the reference.

Even so, it is difficult to make certain what Paul referred to. Many New Testament scholars like to find here, and in other places, such as *Colossians* and *1 John*, references to gnosticism. Gnosticism was a wide-spread heresy of the second century. It almost engulfed and destroyed Christianity. No doubt it had its roots in the first century. But it is not clear that the apostles knew anything about it. If John's writings were late, though one is not forced by any evidence to date them late, he might have begun to recognize the developing gnosticism. At any rate, gnosticism had something that could be called a genealogy. From God's secret mind, there developed a series of spiritual beings called eons. A pair of eons, male and female, gave birth to another pair; and these eons explained both the creation of the physical universe and the process of salvation for fallen humanity. But there were only thirty eons; and thirty is hardly endless.

Perhaps one can say that although the number of eons was not infinite, the discussions they engendered were endless. Paul could therefore just possibly have had gnosticism in mind, but I doubt that he did.

It is much more likely that the myths and genealogies are Jewish. Conzelmann produces a little evidence from the Qumran material:

> For the man of understanding, that he instruct and teach all the sons of light concerning the succession of the generations of all the sons of men, all the spirits which they possess with

> their distinctive characters, their works with classes, and the visitation with which they are smitten, together with the times when they are blessed.

No doubt the Qumran material shows that the Jews or some of them gave mythological interpretations to the Old Testament genealogies; but more to the point are some verses in these epistles themselves. Verse 7, just below, shows that these false teachers thought that they were interpreting the Law, and we can suppose that this means the law of Moses. *Titus* 1:14 explicitly refers to Jewish myths. *Titus* 3:9 also refers to the Law. If anyone wishes to hold that these Jewish teachers also had been influenced by some proto-gnosticism, he cannot be proved wrong. Alford's judgment (302, column 2) is just:

We are still very much disturbed by "strange doctrines." One of the strangest doctrines is that doctrine is not of much importance.

Christianity cannot survive without correct doctrine.

Justification and an understanding of it inevitably produce sanctification. If faith without works is dead, that faith is not faith at all.

> It is plain that any transitional state from Judaism to Gnosticism will satisfy the conditions here propounded, without inferring that the full-blown Gnosticism of the second century must be meant, thus calling in question the genuineness of the Epistle.

Today we are not disturbed by gnostic or Jewish myths and genealogies; but we are still very much disturbed by "strange doctrines." One of the strangest doctrines is that doctrine is not of much importance. Yet in this epistle the very first instruction that Paul gives to Timothy is to condemn and silence the teaching of other or different doctrines. Since Paul repeats this note several times as the letter continues, we may conclude that Christianity cannot survive without correct doctrine.

This contrasts with the usual modern emphasis. Pious but uninstructed ministers frequently enough denounce doctrine and stress Christian living. Faith without works is dead. Now, it is true that moral behavior is important. There are Biblical commands that we must obey; and this epistle will give us some. But it is also true that a true Christian life depends on true doctrine. Justification and an understanding of it inevitably produce sanctification. If faith without works is dead, that faith is not faith at all—not saving faith: It may be the use of Christian language without realizing its meaning, or it may be outright hypocrisy. But this is no excuse for slighting the doctrines of the Trinity, the atonement, the resurrection, and the several points mentioned in this epistle.

No doubt Paul could have given many reasons for opposing heterodoxy. Here he satisfies himself with one short phrase: The myths and genealogies give rise to useless speculations. Since an interpreter has some obligation to apply Scriptural principles to the situation in his day, we ought to ask whether there are religious controversies today which do no more than encourage useless speculation. In a few places Calvin seems to say that discussions of the Trinity can become useless. He thought that the Schoolmen had carried their fine spun theories too far. Calvin, however, did not advocate an end to discussions on the Trinity.

Today there is so little interest in the basic Christian doctrines that this particular admonition from Paul is mainly inapplicable. One might find a better example among the dispensationalists with their pre-post-mid-tribulation rapture and other smaller details. Even if some of their views happen accidentally to be true, they so lack Scriptural support that discussion is useless. I remember one minister who in 1927 identified Mussolini as the Antichrist and dismissed Hitler as an insignificant figure who merited no attention.

However, in this age there is on the whole so little discussion of doctrine that Paul's remark does not apply to very much. More discussion, at the very slight risk of uselessness, is preferable. While I should encourage debate on the Trinity, and the two natures of Christ, the loudest debate at the present time centers not on theological niceties but on plain and simple moral principles. Of course I am interested in the Trinity; but we must bend every effort to confound the liberal politicians and the United States Supreme Court in their advocacy and defense of homosexuality, promiscuity, and the resulting abortions. There is also the Internal Revenue Service and its taxing married couples more heavily than unmarried couples living together. If only the church today had nothing more to worry about than useless genealogies! Hence the first part of Paul's reason for opposing these false doctrines may not apply to other false doctrines.

Heresy and heterodoxy do not produce sanctification.

God administers his household by means of faith.

God guards his church by true doctrine.

The following phrase, however, applies to all doctrines in all ages. Heresy and heterodoxy do not produce sanctification. They do not further "God's administration in [or, by] faith." The *New American Standard* says, "God's provision which is by faith." The *King James* has "godly edifying which is in faith." The Greek word is *oikonomian*, economy or administration. In *1 Corinthians* 14:26, after four or five references to *edification*, the Apostle gives us the exhortation, "Let all things be done for edification." The word *edification* in *1 Corinthians* 14 is not the same word as the *administration* in *1 Timothy*; but they both refer to the well-being of a household.

There is, however, a difference of opinion concerning the grammatical construction of the sentence. The verse may mean that God administers his household by the gift of faith. Or it may mean that Paul and Timothy exercise stewardship over God's house in or by their faith. But "exercising stewardship" is an almost impossible translation of *oikonomia;* and *parechousin oikonomian* is a very strange use of the verb, which means *offer, grant, show, supply, cause,* or *bring about.* Hence we understand the verse to say that these genealogical debates give rise to, cause, or bring about mere speculations and do not bring about or further God's economy which is advanced by faith. God administers his household by means of faith. False doctrine is the contrary of faith. God guards his church by true doctrine. Therefore, each minister today, and each communicant member to the best of his ability, must be alert to discourage heterodoxy and to build up the body of Christ by the truth. The truth is obtained by studying the Scriptures.

1:5, 6

But the aim of the command is love from a pure heart, a good conscience, and a sincere [unhypocritical] faith, from which some have deviated and turned away to vain [useless] argumentation,

The "command" here probably is not the first commandment of verse 3, at least not directly. Paul commanded Timothy to stay in Ephesus in order that Timothy should command the Ephesian Christians to avoid false doctrine. The second command could be the reference; it is Timothy's command to the Ephesians. Incidentally, the *American Standard Version* is incorrect in translating it "our command." In a sense it is Paul's command (unexpressed in verse 3) that Timothy repeats; but the word *our* is not in the text. One commentator wants to identify the command with the commands of the Mosaic legislation. He defends this interpretation by noting that the false teachers were Jews; but even so, he acknowledges that Paul more likely had "the Christians' moral obligations" in mind. Of course, Paul has the Mosaic Law somewhat in mind, and he also has the Christians' moral obligations in mind. This will become perfectly clear in the next three or four verses. But the remainder of the epistle will show that morality, narrowly conceived as simply overt action without a theological basis, is not the whole of Paul's interest. At any rate, the "command" is the command that Timothy must give to the Ephesians.

The aim, goal, or purpose of Timothy's commanding the Ephesians is to produce in them "love from a pure heart, a good conscience, and a sincere, unhypocritical faith." Changing the order of the words slightly, we shall first consider the term *heart* and then *love*. Many commentators and ministers explain the term *heart* as "the core and center of man's being, man's inmost self." This is singularly unenlightening. The core of an apple is not appetizing; the center of a city is often a slum; and maybe man's inmost being is his stomach. To explain Scripture, or any other subject of some difficulty, metaphors, similes, and analogies, all of which can be understood in a dozen different ways, should give place to intelligible, literal language. When Scripture speaks of the heart, it usually does not mean the organ in one's chest that pumps the blood. One should examine all or many of the Old Testament verses wherever the word occurs. In eighty percent or more of these instances, the context describing the functions shows that the intellect or man's mind is intended. Maybe ten percent mean volition. Another ten percent signify the emotions. Hence the actual usage very nearly identifies the heart with the intellect. *A pure* heart, then, is most probably an unhypocritical mind.

Each minister today, and each communicant member to the best of his ability, must be alert to discourage heterodoxy and to build up the body of Christ by the truth.

Many commentators and ministers explain the term heart as "the core and center of man's being, man's inmost self." This is singularly unenlightening.

To explain Scripture, or any other subject of some difficulty, metaphors, similes, and analogies, all of which can be understood in a dozen different ways, should give place to intelligible, literal language.

Next, the term love should be examined. It is interesting to note that love is commanded. One of my college students, a girl of brilliant mind and attractive appearance, seemed to be "in love" with one of the boys. She was upset, almost unconsolable, when he had to leave the college. But after two months she was positively uninterested in him. Although the boy was now a thousand miles distant from the college, someone kept the girl informed of his state of mind, for on one occasion she reported, with a trace of insouciance in her voice, "He hasn't gotten over me yet." Suppose now a professor or stupid counselor had commanded her to love the boy again. Ridiculous; she could not have done so, even if she had tried. Love, romantic love of this sort, cannot be commanded. Or suppose you command a boy to love a certain girl. Now, it may be that he could date her and find her lovable. But it is also possible that he might find her so unattractive that he could not bring himself to date her, even once. A boy might find a girl a pleasant conversationalist, and he could admire some of her mental or even physical qualities without in the least being romantically affected. This is true even when the boy is not in love with some other girl. Love cannot be commanded.

Love, romantic love of this sort, cannot be commanded.

Many ministers love to preach about love. I hear the theme with distressing frequency.

But Timothy commands the Ephesians to love. Love, then, is something volitional, not emotional. Many ministers love to preach about love. I hear the theme with distressing frequency. It is all the more distressing because the sermons do not explain the difference between Christian love and the love of either the Christian Scientists or the love of Joseph Fletcher. The sexual anarchy and licentiousness of the present age desperately necessitate information on a love it little knows. The Scriptures explain and define this voluntary, non-emotional love in several places, though not in this one verse. The reader may occupy himself profitably trying to find these other passages.

The purpose or goal of Timothy's command also includes a good conscience. Though there may seem to be little difference between a good conscience and a pure heart, perhaps the mention of both could be based on a certain ambiguity in Hellenistic Greek. As in modern French also, there is just one word for conscience and consciousness. In fact, the emergence of the meaning of moral judgment hardly antedated the time of Paul. The Stoics were introducing this meaning. Hence, someone reading "a good conscience" might think of a person who fairly well knew himself, his strengths and weaknesses. The idea of morality would intrude only slightly, if at all. Now, Paul certainly had morality in mind. Could it not be therefore that he added "a pure heart" to indicate the meaning of a good conscience? Well, however the linguistic situation may have been, Paul certainly had moral considerations in mind.

But he also has something else in mind. For love flows, not only from a pure heart and a good conscience, but also from a sincere faith. If there is any significance in the order in which these three are mentioned, faith would seem to be the most fundamental. In *1 Corinthians* Paul says that the greatest among faith, hope, and charity, is love. But though greatest, love cannot exist without faith. Faith is the source of love. One must know the doctrine first. If an immature Christian (of any age) wants to learn how to love, the pastor may well tell him, Study the doctrine of the Trinity, the perseverance of the saints, but especially the atonement. If the young Christian achieves some understanding of the atonement, he begins to know something about love. Since the original author of all Scripture is the Holy Spirit, it is permitted to quote John as an interpreter of Paul. His first epistle several times connects the atonement with love. John wrote, "In this is love . . . that he loved us and sent his Son to be a propitiation for our sins." This theology makes this love Christian love. Emotional love gets along much better without theology.

Though greatest, love cannot exist without faith.

If the young Christian achieves some understanding of the atonement, he begins to know something about love.

The word *which* in the phrase "from which" in verse 6 is plural. Hence the reference is not to faith alone but to all three. The heterodox have deviated and turned away from love, a good conscience, and a sincere faith. Their belief in non-Christian doctrines has ruined their consciences and their pure hearts. In their case, though not necessarily in all other situations, their departure from the faith had resulted in their occupation with useless debates. This does not mean that all debating is useless. Peter and Paul, by example as well as by precept, encourage useful debating. Not only is there the familiar recommendation to engage in apologetics, but there are frequent examples of the apostles' engaging in argumentation. But when the argument descends to the level of mere semantics, or to trivialities, and thus avoids the real issues, it becomes *mataiologian,* useless verbiage. The following verse explains the example.

Peter and Paul, by example as well as by precept, encourage useful debating.

1:7

wishing to be teachers of the Law, but understanding neither what they say nor the things they so confidently assert.

This verse indicates that the false teachers were Jews rather than Greek gnostics. Alford notes that these Jews were not guilty of the sins Paul condemned in *Romans*. There was a large group of Jews in the Ephesian church, of whom some had ambitions to be teachers of the Mosaic law. But their education was deficient. Presumably their I. Q. was also, for they did not understand the meaning of the Old Testament text. They did not even understand the meaning of the words they themselves used. The first requirement of the Christian life is to understand. One cannot believe the Gospel without understanding it. One cannot obey the moral commands without understanding what they mean. That is why the *Westminster Larger Catechism* explains the Ten Commandments in great detail. *2 Peter* says clearly that everything that conduces to piety and godliness comes to us through the understanding of theology: the knowledge of God.

Everything that conduces to piety and godliness comes to us through the understanding of theology: the knowledge of God.

But these men in Ephesus did not have the requisite knowledge or intelligence.

With this the complicated sentence comes to an end, and with it the paragraph also.

1:8

We know that the Law is good, if one uses it lawfully,

If anyone, contaminated by mysticism or deflected by a mistaken method of evangelization, thinks that the previous comment emphasizes knowledge too greatly, the first words of this verse should give him pause. Paul is able to argue conclusively to Timothy on the ground that "We know." If Paul had not previously in his other epistles explained the nature and uses of the Law, he would have had to do it here. But relying on his earlier teaching and Timothy's studying, he can appeal to a well-known thesis: The Law is good. Of course good things can be used wrongfully. So Paul says the Law is good if a person uses it lawfully. In *Galatians* Paul had said that the Law is a schoolmaster, or domestic slave, to lead us to Christ. In *1 Corinthians* 5:1 he condemns one man and the laxity of the whole congregation for having violated a law of *Leviticus*. *James* 2:3 also appeals to *Leviticus*. It will be well if the student now searches the Scripture for other references to the Law.

Paul is able to argue conclusively to Timothy on the ground that "We know."

1:9, 10

knowing this, that the Law was not given for [the sake of] a just man; but for the lawless and undisciplined, the impious and sinners, the unholy and profane, those who strike their fathers or mothers, murderers, pornographers, homosexuals, slave-dealers [kidnappers], liars, perjurers, and if anything else opposes sound teaching . . .

First, a minor point on the translation. Some versions have patricides and matricides instead of "those who beat their parents." The latter is better, because: (1) the next word is *murderers,* and this includes patricides, so that it need not be separately mentioned; and (2) Paul probably has in mind *Exodus* 21:15, "He that smites his father or mother shall surely be put to death." And perhaps (3), patricide and matricide are fortunately rare.

With respect to the verse as a whole, it is not necessary to suppose that the false teachers whom Paul is denouncing were guilty of all the particular sins here enumerated. In fact, it is unlikely. As shown above, their fault consisted in failing to understand the Law, and especially its purpose or purposes. Rather than accusing them of murder, homosexuality, or slave-dealing, we may better picture them as self-righteous and conceited. In contrast with their ignorance, Paul and Timothy know the intended function of the Law. These false teachers lacked understanding. Thus the passage puts considerable emphasis on knowledge, for once again, only a line below, Paul appeals to knowledge. He is not here referring to his or Timothy's knowledge, but rather to "someone" who uses the Law lawfully. The Christian ideal is not that the pastor alone should have knowledge, but that every Christian be well instructed. The particular piece of knowledge indicated in this context is that the Law was not given for the sake of the righteous. If Adam had not sinned, and if we always did by instinct what is right, there would have been no need of the Mosaic law. Unfortunately, there is none righteous, no, not one. Therefore we all need the Law.

In this connection Donald Guthrie (*The Pastoral Epistles,* 61) appears to be seriously mistaken. To quote:

The Christian ideal is not that the pastor alone should have knowledge, but that every Christian be well instructed.

> Since its supersession by the gospel, the Decalogue still retains its value as an external instrument of justice, but for the *righteous man* (*dikaios* here being used in its widest sense, but probably intended to represent the Christian) it can no longer apply as a positive standard of conduct.

The Ten Commandments are a positive standard for the heathen, but not for the Christian. This is antinomianism with a vengeance.

In other words, a non-Christian, parricide or kidnapper, is obligated to avoid profanity, to keep the Lord's Day, to refrain from adultery, while a Christian need pay no attention to these commandments. The Ten Commandments are a positive standard for the heathen, but not for the Christian. This is antinomianism with a vengeance. Paul applied the Levitical law in Corinth; and the *Shorter Catechism* says, "The moral law is summarily comprehended in the Ten Commandments."

The basis of Guthrie's antinomianism is the phrase, "the Law was not given for a just man." This he interprets to mean, "*dikaios* is being used here in its widest sense, but probably intended to represent the Christian." On the contrary, *dikaios* is probably used in its narrowest sense and is intended to be an *ad hominem,* sarcastic reply to the false teachers. They studied the Law, but on their own basis, on their own conceited claim to have achieved sinless perfection, the law does not apply to them, and their study was useless.

That the Law does not apply to Christians is false because, first, Christians are not sinless; and, second, the context is clear: The Law is good, if one uses it lawfully. This implies that it may be used lawfully in the present circumstances—circumstances present to the Ephesian church, and by implication to Christians today. As Calvin so perspicuously saw, "It was not the apostle's intention to set out all the functions that the Law fulfills; his argument is rather *ad homines,* to those with whom he was dealing."

Equally unacceptable is Conzelmann's attempt to use this "catalogue of vices" as an argument against the Pauline authorship. He regards this as a "popular list of crimes, intended to have the effect of posters . . . a widespread form of presentation . . . not referring to actual contemporary events. . . ." In the next column he adds, "We are dealing with a Hellenistic transformation of Jewish ethics . . . an adaptation of Hellenistic-Jewish *parenesis* [advice, exhortation]" (23). There is more to the same effect in his pages, if anyone wishes to study them.

The list of sins here mentioned overlaps the Decalogue, but the language and form do not follow it exactly. It is simply a list, arranged in a balanced literary style, its technical incompleteness obviated by the final phrase: anything else that opposes sound teaching.

The reference to "sound teaching" is interesting, especially because it follows the earlier mentioned heterodoxy. In our twentieth century, among evangelicals, a division has been made, or overemphasized, between theology and morality. The popular division is not Pauline. Of course, some very conservative Christians recognize that morality, in the sense of action and even of motive, is as much theology as is the doctrine of the Trinity. But many more despise "doctrine" and vigorously want to be "practical." However, practice is always the practice of a theory. If the theory is that one can answer each moral question independently, and that "abstract" principles are far removed from reality, the result is inconsistency. Christian living is not chaotic; chaotic living is not Christian. Hence we must pay close attention to sound doctrine. Moral teaching is as much a matter of intelligible and intellectual propositions as is the doctrine of the atonement. The popular "practical" man is the most impractical of all. Murder is a sin *because* God forbids it. Leave out God, repudiate theology, and one will feel free to murder anyone, including innocent unborn babies. Abortion is wrong *because* the Godhead consists of the Father, Son, and the Holy Ghost. All this is

Practice is always the practice of a theory.

Christian living is not chaotic; chaotic living is not Christian.

Moral teaching is as much a matter of intelligible and intellectual propositions as is the doctrine of the atonement.

1:11

according to the Gospel of the glory of the blessed God, which [Gospel] I myself was entrusted [with].

The *New English Bible* merits first place in the department of terrible translations: "the Gospel which tells of the glory of God in his eternal felicity." Old English is much better.

Paul declared himself innocent of the blood of all men because he preached the whole counsel of God.

In our times liberal theologians have attempted to make a distinction between the Gospel, or *kerygma* as they call it, and all other material in the Bible. They seldom, if ever, define the contents of this *kerygma*. It seems to be very narrow and restricted. Last century, if I am not mistaken, the Darbyites distinguished between the Gospel and "church doctrine." Fundamentalists generally accept some such distinction. But that is not the Pauline and New Testament view. Paul declared himself innocent of the blood of all men because he preached the whole counsel of God. It is strange that professedly evangelical preachers, preaching not to heathen as Paul did, but to people who have been raised within the church, should restrict themselves to a deeply truncated message. Such poverty did not characterize the apostles, nor the Protestant Reformers. Would that the seriously devout Christians of today spend some time studying the major sixteenth and seventeenth century authors. There they will find the Gospel of the glory of the blessed God.

The word *blessed* here is the same word as that in the beatitudes. But clearly the blessedness of God is superior to any blessedness man can have. On this lower level it can refer to any ordinary human happiness. God's blessedness, on the other hand, consists in all his divine attributes: omniscience, omnipotence, and so on. Further study of the doctrine of God, as expounded in the better works on systematic theology, would give further knowledge and understanding of this phrase.

It is a privilege, but also a great responsibility, to be entrusted with the preaching of this Gospel.

Would that the seriously devout Christians of today spend some time studying the major sixteenth and seventeenth century authors. There they will find the Gospel of the glory of the blessed God.

1:12, 13a

Thanks I give [or, grace I have] to him who strengthened me, Christ Jesus our Lord, because he considered me trustworthy, having put [me] into [his] service, [even though] I was formerly a blasphemer, a persecutor, and an upstart.

With regard to verses 13 and 14 it is interesting to note that one commentator (other than Conzelmann) says, "it is very difficult to believe that Paul himself wrote them"; while another regards them as "thoroughly typical of Paul."

The strengthening mentioned here is not to be restricted to the cases of severe persecution related in *2 Corinthians* 11:23 and the verses following. The sense of the passage requires a reference to Paul's ministry as a whole. The Lord considered Paul trustworthy to be an apostle, and this judgment of the Lord was attested by his inducting Paul into his service. The participle is second aorist and I think "having put" is the best translation. It is second aorist middle, which allows us to say, "having put me in service for his own interests." The induction or ordination is the evidence that God knew that Paul would prove trustworthy. Because he had been a persecutor, it took some time of service before the Christians could think him trustworthy.

1:13b, 14

But I received mercy because in ignorance I did it in unbelief, and the grace of our Lord superabounded with faith and love [as they are] in Christ Jesus.

The last half of verse 13 presents us with difficulties. Were Paul's persecutions of the Christians forgivable because he did them in ignorance and unbelief? No doubt in *Romans* 10:2 the apostle describes his own state of mind as well as that of the main body of Jews: "They have a zeal for God, but not in accordance with knowledge." Yet, if so, why should not God have considered them trustworthy also? Does it not seem that a sin committed in ignorance is no sin at all? Even today Arminians incline to that opinion. Guthrie interprets *2 Timothy* 1:3 to mean not merely that Paul, when an apostle, but Paul, when a persecutor, had a clear conscience before God. But even though Paul had had such a conscience, one could not discover the fact in *2 Timothy* 1:3. The word *forefathers* there does not refer to Paul as a young man having a father and grandfather, but to ancestors like Abraham, David, Isaiah, and others. Even if God pitied the young Paul, Guthrie cannot be right in maintaining that "this misguided pre-christian career had been the object of pity rather than judgment in the sight of God" (64). If this were so, it were better not to take the Gospel to the heathen, for in their ignorance God would pity them, but if they heard the Gospel and rejected it, God would condemn them. C. K. Barrett, though not very orthodox, supports in this instance a better interpretation:

> This verse, superficially read, suggests that Paul's sins were pardoned because he acted ignorantly, . . . If this were the full meaning [or even a part of the meaning] it would not merely be inferior to but inconsistent with the doctrine of the New Testament as a whole.

The New Testament is far from basing salvation on meritorious ignorance.

Since, then, grace is unmerited favor, it does not follow that God will, much less must, forgive other ignorant people.

Then whatever difficulties remain Barrett dismisses on the ground that "it is very difficult to believe Paul himself wrote them."

Barrett is right in asserting that the New Testament is far from basing salvation on meritorious ignorance. What we need, however, is some indication in the passage itself that the epistle is consistent with the New Testament. Strange to say even Conzelmann defends this consistency, much as he rejects the Pauline authorship: "The explanation which the author thus gives for the possibility of pardon does not mean that he denies the role of grace in the conversion [of Paul]." On the contrary, "grace has been abundantly rich." Far from exculpating or attenuating the guilt of ignorance, Paul only a few lines below characterizes himself as the foremost sinner of all. Hence the context itself forbids any interpretation that would make it contradict the rest of the New Testament. Since, then, grace is unmerited favor, it does not follow that God will, much less must, forgive other ignorant people. We have already seen the epistle's stress on knowledge, and there is more to come. Paul's justifying faith was a gift of God's superabounding grace.

1:15

Trustworthy [credible, faithful] is the word and worthy of all acceptation [there is no need here to improve the King James translation] that Christ Jesus came into the world to save sinners, of whom I am first.

The pastorals contain five "trustworthy sayings," two of which are introduced by the added phrase, "and worthy of all acceptation." The most detailed and most scholarly study of these five sayings is George William Knight III's *The Faithful Sayings in the Pastoral Letters*. Some use of this *Academische Pröfschrift* will be made here, but his lengthy linguistic investigations are mostly beyond the scope of this commentary. As to the term *saying* [*logos*], Knight concludes that Paul, though the author of the epistles, did not originate the sayings, but that they were well-known sayings of popular origin.

The term *trustworthy* is explained by the phrase "worthy of all acceptation." This phrase can be interpreted in two different ways: (1) worthy of full acceptance; absolutely, entirely, completely acceptable; (2) worthy of acceptance by everybody. Though there are reputable commentators who vigorously defend the latter extensive meaning, the former intensive meaning seems better. Paul is describing the saying; he attributes to it the characteristic of credibility. He does not seem to have in mind the people who do or may believe it. The emphasis is on the proposition, not on the populace. Therefore, it is the characteristic of the proposition to be worthy of all acceptation—full, complete acceptance. Of course, if it is so worthy, all people ought to believe it. But the subject of characterization is the saying itself.

The Earth is the locus of God's redemptive activity.

The saying itself is, "Christ Jesus came into the world to save sinners." This refers to his incarnation and states its purpose. Since every baby is born into the world, some commentators take the term *world* to mean the physical universe, or at least the planet Earth. Others wish to understand *kosmos* as a moral or spiritual world—the sinful human race. It is indubitable that Christ came to save sinners; but this does not validate the translation of *kosmos* as the sinful race. One must not inject into a single word all the explanations given in other contexts. Why should not Paul say that Christ came to *Earth* in order to save sinful men? This is the flaw in Hendriksen's statement,

> The fact that this divinely anointed Savior "came into the world'"indicates not merely a change of location, a "descent" from one place to another (from heaven to earth) but a change of state and of moral and spiritual environment (77).

One of the greatest of all Christmas hymns, in its original language, rather than its English dilution, is

> Minuit, chrétien, c'est l'heure solonelle,
> Où l'homme-Dieu descendit jusqu'à nous,
> Pour effacer la tâche originelle
> Et de son Père arrêter le courroux.

Of course; but the word *kosmos* does not mean all this. Christ had this purpose in coming, but he came to Earth. That the Earth is the locus of God's redemptive activity is absolutely true, but it is an additional truth not found in this single Greek word, Earth. Hendriksen stretches the word *kosmos* too far. Yet the main thought of the saying is not the historical event of his coming, but its purpose:

> Peuple, à genoux! Attends ta délivrance,
> Noël, Noël, Voici le Rédempteur.

Minimize the *kosmos, world,* but cram all the soteriology you can into *harmatōlous sōsai, to save sinners.*

Sōsai is aorist. It probably refers to a single act in past time. This would be the crucifixion. But if anyone demur, he is at liberty to take salvation in its full extent and condense it literarily into a single whole.

Then Paul adds to "sinners" the phrase, "of whom I am chief." This, of course, is not part of the saying, but rather an expression of Paul's own gratitude for God's grace.

But is this quite true? Was not John Newton the chief of sinners?. Or maybe King David? No, rather each of us must regard himself as the chief of undeserving sinners and praise God's mercy and grace.

Was not John Newton the chief of sinners? Or maybe King David? No, rather each of us must regard himself as the chief of undeserving sinners and praise God's mercy and grace.

1:16

But this is why I received mercy, [namely] that in me first Christ should show forth all his longsuffering, as an example for those who would later believe on him to life eternal.

Although our secret sins may have made us as great sinners as Paul was, and possibly worse, Paul's sin of persecution was public and dramatic. Few people, at least in the Western world, have engaged in such a vigorous persecution of Christians. Even in ancient Rome, though its persecutions were tremendous, possibly no one Roman officer was as fully motivated as the unconverted Paul. Surely at that time the Christians could hardly have regarded Paul as a likely convert. But to show forth the extent of his *makrothumia* (patience, forebearance) and to make, not Paul, but this case of God's longsuffering, an example to future generations, God converted Paul. At the present time, when nearly everyone rejects the idea of total depravity and ignorantly believes in the essential goodness of human nature (shades of Stalin and Idi Amin!) God's example in this case means little. But if there be a more realistic person who thinks he is too evil for God to save, the faithful preacher may use this verse to emphasize God's longsuffering and omnipotent grace. There is therefore no reason to be surprised that Paul in adoration now burst forth.

Nearly everyone rejects the idea of total depravity and ignorantly believes in the essential goodness of human nature.

1:17

To the King of ages, incorruptible, invisible, the only God, [be] honor and glory for ever and ever, Amen.

For the very reason that this is a paean of praise, many devout Christians tend to overlook its meaning. But surely God does not want unthinking adoration. Nor should we desire to ascribe empty words to him. Perhaps we are conscious of the connotation of the title "King." And "ages" can mean all of world history, or, more likely, all of world history and of the age or ages to come. This is why the *King James* says, "King eternal." It is pressing the text too far to translate *aiōnon* as eternal. The Bible implies in several places that God is immutable and eternal; and theologians have explored the meaning of eternity and God's relation to time; but another verse would afford a better occasion to discuss this interesting subject.

Hence let us consider the word *incorruptible. Romans* also uses the term. And *invisible* is found in *Colossians* 1:15 and *Hebrews* 11:27. What do these two terms mean?

For the very reason that this is a paean of praise, many devout Christians tend to overlook its meaning. But surely God does not want unthinking adoration. Nor should we desire to ascribe empty words to him.

The corruption in the word *incorruptible* is not the deplorable dishonesty in the federal government. Pauline corruption is not so much moral as basically physical. In Greek philosophy the word usually means "passing out of existence." In Greek science *phthora* is the process of aging in living things, their liability to deterioration and especially their death. Presumably the Greeks viewed their gods, even though physical, as incorruptible. Most often they did not consider the question. Spirits in Hades or Tartarus seem never to pass out of existence. What the worshippers of Baal thought, I cannot say: Probably they too did not think. With this Greek and Hebrew background it seems best to understand Paul as basing incorruptibility on the fact that God is incorporeal. The well-remembered *Children's Catechism* asked, "What is God?" The answer was "God is a spirit and has not a body like men."

In the long run, Christians are optimists.

During the lifetime of Paul there was no great need to insist that in addition to bodies the universe also contained spirits. The heathen had gods and demi-gods, spirits, demons, penates, and furies in great abundance.

Today the educated public allows no spirits at all. The large majority of psychologists, philosophers, zoologists, and physicists adopt some type of behaviorism. Only body is real. There is no soul, no mind, no god or devil. Then if sociologists and political scientists be added, the processes of change are considered good instead of bad. In spite of the horrors of this century, many people still believe in the optimistic nineteenth-century theory of progress. Man is essentially good and change is to be welcomed.

This is not the Christian position. To be sure, the Christian believes that God will bring good out of evil; that the massacres, the holocausts, the Communist genocides will be ended by Christ's return. In the long run, Christians are optimists. In the near term, however, Christians are deep-dyed pessimists. So they sing

Change and decay in all around I see;
O Thou that changest not, abide with me.

Strange, I have not heard a sermon on the incorruptibility or the immutability of God for years. In one community the theme of the sermons and Sunday School lessons was the fruit of the Spirit for four seasons within two years. But the immutable God remained in the background. On Reformation Day they allowed an old timer to preach on justification by faith alone—a theme most of the young people had never heard before. Then they went back to the fruits of the Spirit. These are indeed parts of the Christian message, but I think we ought to pay some attention to the nature of the Spirit whose effects they are.

The second word was "invisible." Bodies are visible. No doubt numbers—two, three, four—are invisible also. This might put numbers and mathematics nearer to God than zoology is. But numbers, though invisible and incorruptible, are not spirits. They are not the King of the Ages. But the King of the Ages is indeed incorruptible and invisible. If we have sense organs in Heaven (the New Testament indicates that some organs will be missing—our stomachs, for example), and if we have eyes and visual perception, still we shall not see God. God is invisible. When mystics indulge their literary flair and speak of the beatific vision, they can only mean intellectual interpenetration, a union of minds, and not bodily contact. For God is a spirit and has not a body like men. To him be honor and glory for ever and ever, Amen.

If we have sense organs in Heaven (the New Testament indicates that some organs will be missing—our stomachs, for example), and if we have eyes and visual perception, still we shall not see God. God is invisible.

1:18

This command I set before you, son Timothy, according to the previous prophecies concerning you, that by them you may fight the good fight,

The first noun in the verse means a command, and it connotes a rather strict command. The *American Standard Version* translates it correctly, but it is a bit strange that this version did not translate it so in verses 3 and 5. It is the same word, and therefore justifies the translation above.

Paul therefore sets before Timothy a strict command. Timothy was obligated to obey it. But what precisely is "this command"? It might refer to the command in verse 5; but there is too much intervening to make a direct reference plausible. The wording is a little awkward, but it is more natural to consider the last phrase of the verse as the command: Fight the good fight. Of course the nature of the good fight can partly be found in the earlier verse.

Paul then mentions previous prophecies concerning Timothy. The *New English Bible* has "that prophetic utterance which first pointed you out to me." The idea is that God used some unidentified person to lead Paul to Timothy and appoint him as his successor. There are two difficulties with this interpretation. First, the text does not contain the words *to me.* Second, Blass and Debrunner cite this verse as one in which *proagousas* means *previous. Hebrews* 7:18 uses this word in the same sense. The situation is not very clear. Something similar comes up in 4:14.

The command then is, Fight the good fight. The words "by them" can mean "under the guidance of" the prophecies, or something like "encouraged by them." The conditions of the fight are partly described in the next verse.

1:19

having faith and a good conscience, which some pushing aside have suffered shipwreck with respect to the faith,

In much that passes today for Christian devotion, the objective message is minimized and a psychological state of mind receives the emphasis.

Once again Paul emphasizes faith. Sometimes it is difficult to tell whether the word *faith* denotes the activity of believing (for *faith* is the noun whose verb form means *believe)* or whether it refers to what is believed. Since here the following words are "a good conscience," the subjective meaning might appear proper. Nevertheless, the objective meaning is strong at the end of the verse. Paul used the article: *the faith.* Of course those who suffered shipwreck ceased to believe, if ever they did; but they suffered shipwreck with respect to New Testament theology. They put aside the Pauline doctrines and taught a different message. In much that passes today for Christian devotion, the objective message is minimized and a psychological state of mind receives the emphasis. What is needed is a widespread understanding that the Gospel is good news—it is information that must be intellectually understood and voluntarily accepted. Without the good news there is no good news at all.

1:20

of whom is Hymenaeus and Alexander, whom I have handed over to Satan in order that they be taught not to blaspheme.

The verb before the name Hymenaeus is singular; the *whom* is plural.

In *1 Corinthians* 5:5 Paul berated the Corinthian congregation for not excommunicating the man who had married his stepmother. Paul himself then, by apostolic authority, did what the Corinthians ought to have done. He handed the man over to Satan for the destruction of his flesh. Although this phrase can refer to death, in this case it probably means sickness. As the apostles could heal the sick, so they could sicken the healthy. The purpose was to produce repentance so that the offender might be restored, or as Paul says in *1 Corinthians* 5:5, that his spirit might be saved in the day of the Lord Jesus. We can hardly suppose that the man could be saved at the day of judgment, unless he had lived to repent.

Ministers today do not have the apostolic power to heal or to cause sickness. And few churches excommunicate anybody, for few churches operate on New Testament principles. Even devout Christians have strange ideas.

Once when teaching *1 Corinthians* in a Sunday School class, and when this chapter came up, I referred to *2 John* 10. I might have also referred to the weaker verse of *Romans* 16:17. A lovely lady protested that if we have nothing to do with such a person we cannot win him back to the faith. Therefore we should not do what John tells us to do. Such was her pragmatic judgment.

But the lovely lady suffered from a deficient understanding of spiritual affairs and the procedure and purpose of these judgmental actions. Jesus himself in *Matthew* 18 gives the principles of ecclesiastical procedure in such cases. The man charged with an offense is to be brought before the session; if found guilty and if he does not repent, the Christian is to treat him as a heathen and a publican. In the situation in which Jesus was speaking, this meant, for one thing, complete ostracism.

We are to refuse him entrance to our homes.

Now the purpose of this is to redeem the offender. We are to refuse him entrance to our homes, for there is no point in further conversation. We spoke privately to him first; then the church spoke to him officially; and there is nothing left to do.

Does this ostracism or excommunication produce repentance? Well, of course, not always. But sometimes. There was another lovely lady, a widow, who wished to marry again—nothing wrong in that—but she wished to marry a non-Christian. The pastor spoke to her and made clear the New Testament requirement to marry in the Lord. The pastor even spoke to the man, who did not much like what he said. The woman married. The church excommunicated her and forbade her from taking communion in any church whatever. Strange as some people may think it, she obeyed—not because she had come to hate communion, but because of the prohibition. The marriage turned out disastrously. The man divorced her. She genuinely repented and was restored to the full rights of communicant membership. Unfortunately, most churches do not care to obey the New Testament commands.

Chapter Two

2:1, 2

Accordingly, I urge first of all that supplication be made, prayers, intercessions, thanksgiving for all men, for kings and all who are in authority, that we may lead a quiet and peaceful life in all piety and holiness.

The conjunction *accordingly* bases the following on the preceding. Although the letter is addressed to Timothy, its purpose is to establish ecclesiastical custom. It is not Timothy as an individual who is urged to make these prayers, but rather his church. This congregational, rather than personal, reference is further supported by the second half of the chapter. The practice of praying for our rulers and officials is mandated in the Episcopal prayer books, but often forgotten in fundamentalist churches.

Although the letter is addressed to Timothy, its purpose is to establish ecclesiastical custom. It is not Timothy as an individual who is urged to make these prayers, but rather his church.

Because of the phrase "for kings and all who are in authority," one gathers that Paul has in mind certain classes of men rather than each human being individually. It would be difficult, virtually impossible, for the early Christians ever to pray for all rulers individually. There was the Emperor, then the many subordinate kings, governors, consuls, and military officers. The context concerns classes of men rather than individuals.

There may be some slight variation in meaning among the various types of prayer mentioned here. The term *prayer* is clearly general; but some prayers are only petitions, and some only thanksgivings. But as petitions and thanksgiving are frequently included in congregational prayers, there is no point in insisting on any differences among these terms.

A further reason for understanding these prayers as public prayers for classes, rather than private prayers for individuals, is the purpose Paul assigns to them. The government has the power to make our lives uncomfortable. In the Roman Empire then, and now in totalitarian nations, the government harasses and persecutes Christians. When the North Koreans invaded South Korea they killed all the Christians they could find. The purpose of these prayers, therefore, is to implore God to stay persecution and allow his servants to live in peace and quiet. Obviously God has not always so willed. But he instructs us to pray for such a blessing. Americans have had much more freedom than citizens of other countries; but we are fast losing our heritage. We too should pray that God restrain the bureaucracy.

2:3, 4

This is good and acceptable before God our savior, who wishes all men to be saved and come to knowledge of truth.

The purpose of these prayers, therefore, is to implore God to stay persecution and allow his servants to live in peace and quiet.

If verse 4 needs considerable explanation, verse 3 needs very little. One point only need be mentioned: The phrase "God our savior" does not seem to envisage Jesus Christ directly; it more plausibly refers to God the Father. This plausibility is supported by the sense of verse 4.

The difficulty in this latter verse is considerable. If God wills the salvation of all men, and if some are not saved, then God is not omnipotent. Something thwarts his will. Since the New Testament clearly indicates that in fact some men are eternally lost, we either must say that the Bible contradicts itself or face the difficulty with omnipotence. One evangelist, on several occasions, told his audience, as many had come to the front at his invitation, that not even God could help them now. They were on their own.

The difficulty must be faced. First, it is not necessary to translate *thelei* as *wills.* Arndt and Gingrich, a well known lexicon, gives the first meaning of *thelō* as *wish* or *desire*. Among other citations is *John* 9:27, "Why do you *want* to hear it again?" Another instance where *thelō* cannot possibly mean *will* is *Galatians* 4:20, "I *wish* I were with you now." Granted, the verb sometimes means *will* or *resolve.* But it does not have to. In fact, it is used of things other than human beings. *Acts* 2:12 asks, "What does this mean [wish to be]?" The same phrase occurs in *Acts* 17:20. Using the more common weaker meaning of *thelō* may not completely remove the difficulty; but it makes removal easier and makes it harder to deny the divine omnipotence that inspired the psalmist to write, "Whatsoever the Lord pleased, that did he" (*Psalm* 135:6).

Since the problem involves the self-consistency of the Bible, the reality of Hell, as well as the nature of God, we ought to consider what other commentators have said about this verse.

Henry Cowles published a set of commentaries in the 1880's and 1890's. It is clear that I do not agree with his translation of *thelō;* but in spite of the handicap he imposes on himself, he insists that God did not decree the salvation of all the human race. To quote:

> Verse four declares explicitly that God wills to have all men saved. The verb he uses is not a mere future tense of the verb *to save*, but is a distinct verb having the sense of desiring; willing in the sense of an act of will; being pleased to do. There is no occasion to press this verb to the sense of an absolute decree or purpose made and executed irrespective of human agency—other verbs and never this being used for a purpose or decree which God forms and must execute. But it may, and indeed must, involve the real desire of his heart to save all men, and his will to have all appropriate means used to secure this result.

The one who says most (nearly five columns of dense print) and who is most to the point is the great Baptist theologian, John Gill.

Cowles really evades the problem. He says that the verb does not indicate an absolute decree, yet he adds that it is God's real desire to save all and it is his will to have all appropriate means used to secure this result. In the case of God, all appropriate means would of necessity secure the desired result. But this is universalism. Does Cowles really reject universalism? If he does, "appropriate" becomes a weasel word.

Donald Guthrie also evades the problem. He says that it is hard to reconcile what is said here with what Paul says elsewhere. But he offers no solution. A reader cannot tell whether Guthrie accepts universalism or not. Some other commentaries say even less.

The one who says most (nearly five columns of dense print) and who is most to the point is the great Baptist theologian, John Gill. Much as I disagree with the immersionists and independents, I would urge everyone to study his book, *The Cause of God and Truth,* and even his tremendous (almost a thousand pages of double columns) volume, *A Body of Divinity.* There were giants in the Earth in those days. Since many people would think it tedious to quote all five columns, seventy-five lines to the column, I shall summarize with a few verbatim passages.

> These words are often used to oppose God's decree of reprobation and in favor of universal redemption. . . . The salvation that God here wills . . . is not a mere possibility of salvation for all, . . . nor a proposal of sufficient means, . . . but a real, certain, and actual salvation.

Indeed this is clear from the final phrase of the verse.

> The will of God . . . is not a conditioned will . . . for if this was the case, none might be saved; and if any should, salvation would be of *him that willeth and him that runneth,* and not *of God that sheweth mercy. . . .* It is his ordaining, purposing, and determining will, which is never frustrated, but is always fulfilled. . . . The *all men* whom God would have to be saved are such whom he would also have *to come to the knowledge of the truth. . . .*

> By *all men* whom God would have to be saved, we are not to understand every individual of mankind. . . . for it is his will that some men should be damned. . . . Moreover, if it was the will of God that every individual of mankind should be saved, then everyone would be saved; for *who hath resisted his will?* . . . Nor should we pray for such as have sinned *the sin unto death*. . . . Certainly the apostle's meaning is not that the saints should give thanks for wicked men . . . nor for heretics and false teachers. . . . The phrase is therefore to be taken in a limited and restrained sense, for some only, as appears from verse 2, for kings and *for all* in authority. . . . It is better by *all men* to understand some of all sorts, as Austin [Augustine] did long ago, and is the sense in which the word *all* is to be taken in many places; as in Gen. 7:14; Matt. 4:23, 24; Joel 2:28; and is the meaning of it in ver. 1, and well agrees with the matter of fact; since Christ has redeemed some of all nations. . . . I rather think that by *all men* are meant the Gentiles, who are sometimes called the world, and every creature. [Here Gill goes to some length on Jewish exclusivism toward the Gentiles. Then he concludes:] Since these words cannot be understood of every individual man, they cannot be thought to militate against God's righteous decree of reprobation, nor to maintain and support universal redemption.

By all men whom God would have to be saved, we are not to understand every individual of mankind.

Certainly the apostle's meaning is not that the saints should give thanks for wicked men . . . nor for heretics and false teachers. . . . The phrase is therefore to be taken in a limited and restrained sense, for some only.

John Gill never avoided difficult passages, and his conclusions are never ambiguous.

The final phrase of the verse, which Gill used to show that Paul was talking about actual salvation, and not just an Arminian chance of salvation, is, "and come to the knowledge of the truth," though the Greek text is without the articles. Once again, therefore, we note Paul's emphasis on knowledge and truth. Kierkegaard would have us believe contradictions, sacrifice the intellect, and rely on infinite passion. This religion of experience is not Christianity. God is truth, and they that worship him must worship him in spirit and in truth. The Gospel is revealed information.

2:5

For God is one; one also [the] mediator of God and men, a man Christ Jesus.

The conjunction *for* connects verse 5 with the immediately preceding phrase. A truth that we must know is that God is one, or, if you wish, there is one God. There is not one God for the Jews and another, or many, for the Gentiles. Similarly there is but one mediator. No man comes to the Father except by Jesus Christ.

Jews today do not cause much trouble for Christians as they did before A.D. 70. But Roman Catholics practically make the Virgin and the pope a second and third mediator. One must come to God through the priesthood. Chicago is largely a Roman Catholic city.

Once a few years ago there was a city-wide Catholic demonstration or celebration of some sort. In those days the street cars carried advertising placards along the top edges of their sides. Presumably it was only accidental, but there I saw a placard, put up by some evangelistic group: There is one God and one Mediator, the man Christ Jesus. The prelatical system bars direct access to the Father and to the Son. This is also a truth, an item of information, which Christians should understand. Chicagoans should come to understand it too.

Neither God per se nor man per se could mediate. The God-Man could and did.

Only a brief note can be included on the term *mediator.* It means a go-between. Two parties are enemies, and a mediator reconciles them. But since Christ is God, God in his own right *(auto theos),* how can he be a mediator? He is one of the parties. Nor could a man be the mediator, for man is the other party. Here is a situation never found in cases of labor relations or international disputes. In these there is always someone who belongs to neither party. The only possibility in the divine-human encounter cannot be a neither-nor; it must be a both-and. One may note that the text does not say, "the man," but "a man," or, even better, simply "man." The emphasis is not on the individual person, Jesus, but on the fact that the mediator is a human being. He was also divine. The God-Man bridges the gap. Neither God per se nor man per se could mediate. The God-Man could and did.

2:6

Who gave himself a ransom for all, the testimony in (*to*, or, *for*) *[its] own times.*

The word *antilutron* condenses the doctrine of the substitutionary atonement. *Anti* means "instead of." Combined into one word with *lutron* in this verse, in *Mark* 10:45 it is an independent preposition: "a ransom of many." But first let us consider something much more difficult, though much less important.

The second phrase in the verse is hard to translate. I have given it word-for-word as much as possible. The *King James Version* has "to be testified in due time." This does not make much sense. Of course, neither does my translation, but at least it does not change a noun into a passive verb. The *New English Bible* is horrible: "so providing at the fitting time proof of the divine purpose." Imagine getting all that out of these four Greek words! There are absolutely no words in the verse corresponding to "divine purpose." The *Revised Standard Version* says, "ransom . . . the testimony to which was borne at the proper time." But what meaning can be attached to a "testimony to the ransom?" Is not the word *testimony (marturion)* in apposition to the word *ransom?* Sometimes a one-man translation is better than those made by a committee. Weymouth is not at all bad: "redemption price . . . a fact testified to at its own appointed time." But this faces the difficulty that the ransom seems to be the testimony itself. *Testimony* seems to be in apposition to the word *ransom,* as indicated just above. There is not another witness to testify to it. Rather, it is a witness or testimony to something else. Meyer seems confused. He says that *marturion* is in apposition to the previous verse—one mediator. This is entirely implausible. Then he says that it refers to the "proclamation of the deed." He writes,

> it is to be regarded as in apposition to the thought contained in the previous verse. . . . This does not mean, however, that *to marturion* [the witness] denotes Christ's gift of himself . . . for *marturion* is not the deed itself, but its attestation, the proclamation of the deed.

Christ's death itself was the testimony to the people of that day.

Meyer thus identifies the testimony or witness with the preaching of the Gospel. But this results in the peculiar translation: Who gave himself a ransom for all, the preaching of the Gospel in, at, or with respect to its own times.

Sometimes unbelieving scholars produce good exegesis. Since they do not believe what the Bible says, and since they are unperturbed by contradictions, they can, if they wish, pay close attention to the words. Conzelmann here concludes that

> the Testimony *(to marturion)* stands in apposition to "to hand over, to sacrifice oneself" *(didonai)* implied in "who gave himself" . . . "In its own (determined) times" *(kairois idiois)* . . . is a term referring to the history of salvation, a phrase which originally meant the time determined by God in his promises.

The meaning then would be that Christ's death itself was the testimony to the people of that day. If the plural *times* remains embarrassing, it could be construed to mean that Christ's death then is still a testimony to the truth of the Old Testament prophecies.

Often the most difficult phrases to exegete are those of lesser importance, and the important material is easy to understand. The last four words of the verse could be omitted without great loss; the first phrase is indispensable: "who gave himself a ransom for all." The doctrine here alluded to is the doctrine of the vicarious or substitutionary atonement, the sacrifice of Christ on the cross. His death is called a ransom. At the moment of writing this, the Ayatollah Khomeini, dictator of Iran, is holding fifty Americans as hostages, whose release is to be paid for by America's sending the Shah back to Iran for execution. It is his life for theirs, or theirs for his. He must die if they are to live. He can ransom them. This would be a substitutionary sacrifice.

A note may well be added concerning the preposition *huper,* though the point is no recent discovery. Modernists used to argue that the substitutionary idea in *anti* in *Mark* 10:45 was dropped by Paul's use of *huper.* *Anti* is clearly substitution. *Huper* merely means "for the sake of," indicating some sort of benefit, not necessarily and perhaps excluding substitution. Such a distinction was regular in classical Greek, but the distinction disappeared in Hellenistic Greek. One need not go outside the New Testament to see this. *John* 11:50 says, "It is good for you that one man should die *huper* the people." Caiaphas meant that otherwise the people would die, for he adds, "that the whole nation should not perish." If Christ were permitted to proceed, the Romans would destroy all the Jews. Similarly, Philemon 13 uses *huper* in an obviously substitutionary sense. One may also note that *ransom* in Timothy is not just *lutron,* as it could be in ordinary Greek, but *antilutron, a* substitutionary ransom.

Christ was not an unwilling victim.

Destructive critics are not always good interpreters. Here Conzelmann says, "It is pointless to ask to whom, in the author's opinion, the ransom is to be paid." Well, hardly. When one ransoms a prisoner, it is necessary to pay the ransom to him who can release the prisoner. To send the Shah to the Prime Minister of Great Britain would not please Khomeini, and he would not release the hostages. Paul envisages the prisoners of sin as subject to the wrath of God. Therefore, the ransom must be paid to God. This is not pointless.

The word *all* occurs again. It does not again say "all men"; and hence it could possibly mean all the elect. But in view of its obvious repetition of the word in verse 4, it must mean "all men." That this is not universalism, John Gill has already made clear.

Another phrase worthy of note is "gave himself." Christ was not an unwilling victim. In Gethsemane he knew how terrible his death for sin would be. Yet he voluntarily submitted to the will of his Father. He gave himself. Pilate had no power of his own to execute Jesus. Jesus could have asked for legions of angels to rescue him. But he died voluntarily. He gave himself.

2:7

to which I myself was appointed a herald and apostle—I speak the truth and do not lie—a teacher of the Gentiles in faith and truth.

It is clear from the *Acts* that Paul did not appoint himself to be an apostle. As the Gospels indicate, no one can make himself a steward of another's household. The owner appoints the steward. But if this is so clear in Paul's case, it might not be so clear, and it might not be the case at all, in other instances. Some men, from good or bad motives, might assume the office of minister on their own initiative. This does not mean that a young man should not seek the office. He may apply for it. But unless he is ordained by the presbytery, as will be made clear later on, he has no warrant to preach the Gospel.

Is it strange that Paul is so adamant in insisting that he is speaking the truth? Did not Timothy know that the Lord had appointed Paul? Why the phrase, "I speak the truth and lie not?" In Galatia Paul's apostleship had been challenged. There it was natural for Paul to insist on his right to preach the Gospel, and to insist also that what he preached was indeed the Gospel. But here? Well, the situation, though not the same, made it wise to use strong words. Not for Timothy's sake. Paul was not writing a simple personal note to Timothy. Through Timothy he was giving ecclesiastical instructions for ages to come. Since the church was the means for proclaiming the Gospel, and since the church received the Gospel from Paul, Paul was more than justified in asserting his authority. For if Paul had not been an apostle, his message would not have been God's message. That it was the Gentiles to whom Paul was sent gives at least some support to the previous point concerning all classes of men. And since most who will read this commentary will be Gentiles, we may all be thankful that he was so sent.

What he taught was faith and truth. Perhaps grammatically *faith* and *truth* are not the direct object of a verb implied in the noun *teacher.* Yet the *New English Bible* translates it "to instruct the nations in the true faith." The translation is not literal, but the sense is good; for if Paul taught the Gentiles *in* or *by* his own faith and truth, still that faith and truth are what he taught the Gentiles. Even Meyer, who explicitly denies that faith and truth are the direct object, soon arrives at the same meaning.

Why the apostle used both words, faith and truth, may be hard to guess. If the faith is the truth and the truth is the faith, there seems no need to mention both. Of course one may suppose that Paul aimed at clarity and completeness. But the motive could have been, especially if Paul had twentieth century conditions in mind, the realization that some faiths are not true. Many seminaries today teach that Paul did not tell the truth. His insistence that he does not lie, and that his message is true, is evidence that the Bible claims inerrancy.

Many seminaries today teach that Paul did not tell the truth. His insistence that he does not lie, and that his message is true, is evidence that the Bible claims inerrancy.

2:8

Accordingly, I desire the men everywhere to pray, lifting up holy hands without wrath and wrangling.

The instruction that people should pray in church, after verses on the mediator, the atonement, and even on Paul's apostolic authority, seems like a collapse into triviality. Doesn't everyone, even unbelievers, assume that people pray in church? But the matter is not quite that simple. The text says "the men." There are two words for *man* in Greek. *Anthropos* means people, men and women, human beings. But *andras* (plural here) not only means men as distinct from women, but is preceded by the article: "the men." In a moment Paul will speak of the women.

There are several matters to be considered here. Since the subject seems to be prayer, we may first see how this verse might apply to everybody who prays, and then come closer to Paul's main thought.

The context requires us to understand that the subject is prayer in church, not prayers at home. Nor does it mean that Paul wishes men to pray in every place: Philadelphia, Chattanooga, and Berkeley, California. Rather, it means that the men, wherever they are in church, should pray as here directed. Paul is speaking about churches everywhere and in every age. Several commentators wish to understand the verb *boulomai* as a royal command (compare Guthrie, 74). Meyer's American editor (111) contrasts it with *thelō,* which has a weaker meaning. This, I believe, is exaggeration. *Boulomai* simply means *wish* or *desire.* Instead of finding special meanings in the Greek verbs, it is better to note who does the desiring. As a commentator I desire people to read my commentaries. But when an apostle desires something, the force has a different ranking.

The subject is prayer in church, not prayers at home.

One should also note that the apparent break between verses 7 and 8 is not so sudden as it first appears. The opening verses of the chapter have already introduced the subject of prayer, to which the soteriology is grammatically subordinate, or, shall we say, parenthetical.

Paul therefore desires that in every place of worship the men should lift holy hands in prayer. Devout worshipers have used various postures as they prayed. Some kneeled, some lay prostrate, some stood and raised their hands to Heaven. In Presbyterian churches it is or used to be customary for the minister to do the latter during the invocation. But surely Paul is not forbidding other postures.* Rather, the emphasis lies in the desirability that the hands be holy and that the prayer be without wrath and wrangling.

Presumably the word *diologismos* means wrangling. As a Greek word it means consideration, reasoning, or debating, frequently, even usually, in a good sense; but it also means evil machinations, doubting, disputing. Obviously in this verse the word has a bad meaning. Doubting does not seem to fit; rather *orgē,* wrath, suggests wrangling. That Paul should deplore wrath in prayer causes no surprise; but we wonder how much wrath and wrangling characterized the prayers of the congregation at Ephesus. If the word could be interpreted to mean *doubting,* it would clearly be applicable elsewhere. Even so, the term *wrath* or *anger* remains. Doubtless prayers are made in churches today by people whose hands are not holy; but can anyone remember a prayer made in wrath or anger? Perhaps Paul does not mean a prayer the words of which express anger, but rather a prayer which, though no anger is manifested in it, a man makes while he is angry at someone he does not even allude to.

*Compare *Genesis* 18:22; 24:48; *Exodus* 9:29; 17:11; *Numbers* 14:5; 16:4; 22:13; *Deuteronomy* 9:18, 25, 26; *1 Samuel* 1:26; *1 Kings* 8:22, and many verses in the *Psalms* and later books.

2:9, 10

So also [I desire] women to make themselves attractive in decent dress with modesty and good sense, not with braids and gold or pearls or expensive clothing; but, what is fitting for women who profess godliness, by good works.

Some expositors stress the word "Likewise" and insert the verb *to pray* from verse eight, thus regarding the phrase as directions how women should pray in church: Men should pray without wrath, and likewise women should pray in modest apparel. One objection to this interpretation is that it suggests that whereas men are tempted to pray in wrath, women have no temptation to wrath but only to ostentation. In addition to this objection based on the sense of the passage, Meyer makes a grammatical objection: "The infinitive *kosmein* is against the construction." That is to say, a second infinitive cannot be fitted in.

In the Minutes of the 154th General Synod of the Reformed Presbyterian Church, Evangelical Synod this very verse is discussed. On page 76 the infinitive *kosmein* is noted, and one might have expected the committee to accept Meyer's remark. But by the next page the infinitive is forgotten, and the *Report* stresses the word "Likewise" as needing a succeeding verb. In effect the *Report* argues that "Likewise" would have no meaning unless the following verb were "to pray." They seem to miss the obvious interpretation that Paul *wishes* men to do one thing and likewise wishes that women do something else. Meyer is quite right; the infinitive *kosmein* prohibits the inserting of any other infinitive. Paul desires the women to make themselves attractive without ostentation; he does not desire them to pray. There is no grammatical way to make this verse an instruction on how women should pray. Now, it may be said that the verse does not prohibit women to pray in church. The main point here is that it does not authorize women to pray in church. It is verse 11 that contains the prohibition.

There is no grammatical way to make this verse an instruction on how women should pray.

Many American coeds, even Christian girls, are puzzled that Paul should prohibit braiding the hair. Surely braids are not immodest. Now, though Paul's injunctions are not culturally conditioned, the meaning of Greek words is. Braiding the hair, in the Roman Empire, was a much different thing from what we call braids. The wealthy women braided their hair by using it to hold costly emeralds, pearls, and gold ornaments. It was a display of wealth. It was done to impress. And this is no less obnoxious in public worship today than it was then.

Meyer cannot be so confidently followed in his interpretation of the last part of the verse. As punctuated above, the verse says that instead of adorning themselves with extravagant decoration, the women who profess godliness should adorn themselves with good works. This seems to make good sense. I doubt that Paul meant to prohibit all jewelry; he certainly prohibits ostentation. But his main point is that women should be attractive because of their spiritual activities. However, Meyer disagrees. He wishes to connect *good works* with *professing godliness.* Rather than an intimation of how women can properly be attractive, he reads it: Women who profess godliness by means of their good works should not wear expensive clothing and jewelry. Grammatically the neuter relative *ho* suggests that "what is fitting for godly women" is a parenthesis; then "but . . . by good works" contrasts with external extravagance.

Thus understood, the verse need not be dismissed as "a culturally conditioned" mistake by Paul. Styles of women's clothing, and of men's clothing too, have changed from age to age; but in any age Christians, women and men alike, should be unpretentious. Nor does this encourage sloppy dress. In order to be a good Christian it is not necessary to wear tattered blue jeans nor to eat peas with a knife.

2:11, 12

Let a woman learn quietly in all subjection. I do not permit a woman to teach, nor to have authority over a man, but to be quiet.

In any age Christians, women and men alike, should be unpretentious.

A woman is not to preach or pray in public.

Paul's divinely inspired teaching was not culturally conditioned, but too much contemporary exegesis is.

The question as to whether the previous verse was giving directions for women praying in church is somewhat clarified here. If women are not to pray publicly at all in the worship service, then those directions were not directions as to how women should pray. I have translated verse 11 as weakly as possible, so as not to run the risk of exaggeration. However, the word *silently* is just as good a translation as *quietly*. The repetition of *quiet* at the end of verse twelve makes it fairly obvious that a woman is not to preach or pray in public. Good Christians will not modify the Scriptural commands to satisfy abortionists and women's lib. Paul's divinely inspired teaching was not culturally conditioned, but too much contemporary exegesis is.

Those who understand the previous verses as relating to public worship consistently apply these two verses in the same way. Indeed, there is a degree more probability in this case than in the former, for *teaching* seems to envisage regular church services. Nevertheless, the reason given in the following verses permits an application to the home and elsewhere if there be such places. This does not mean that mothers should not teach their children, either in the home or in Sunday School, for the word *man* refers to adult men. Note particularly that Timothy seems to have been taught by his mother and grandmother. See further the comment on *Titus* 2:3, 4, 5.

The words *man* and *woman* are often properly translated *husband* and *wife*. This does not seem proper here. Since the instruction seems to be for the church service, *man* and *woman* is the better translation here. Similarly, the exercise of authority indicates ecclesiastical government. No doubt the husband has authority at home, and he may also explain the sermon to his wife. This has a bearing on contemporary attempts to induct women into the offices of deacon, elder, and pastor. Where this is done it is destructive, not only of the church, but of the home too, for a woman deacon or elder would be superior to her husband, and this conflicts with the following explanation.

Before we consider the next two verses, one may note a somewhat parallel passage in *1 Corinthians* 11:3-16 and 14:34. The first of these begins by stating that Christ is the head of every man, and the man or husband is the head of the woman. As with the next verse in *Timothy*, so in *Corinthians* too, Paul bases his argument on the order of creation. In the second of these passages Paul, as in Timothy, requires women to remain silent in the church, "for they are not permitted to speak . . . for it is improper for a woman to speak in church." Clearly many churches today have no regard for biblical teaching; and it is not strange that the churches with women pastors and elders also try to accept and even ordain homosexuals.

In the Reformed Presbyterian Church, Evangelical Synod those who favor "women's rights" and wish to ordain women as deacons for an entering wedge inserted some extra words into this verse, at least in their thinking if not in published translations. They understand it to mean: I do not permit a woman to teach, that is, to be an elder or pastor, nor to have this sort of authority over a man; but she may have a deacon's authority over a man. Of course this insertion is gratuitous. Nor does it make good sense, for it would make the two phrases tautological: A woman must not teach nor may she have authority to teach. If one may insert words, it is more plausible to say, I do not permit a woman to teach nor to have any authority over a man. Surely the word *any* is in accord with the repeated term *quiet.*

Paul bases his argument on the order of creation.

2:13, 14

For Adam was formed first, then Eve; and Adam was not deceived, but his wife, deceived, fell into transgression.

Naturally, Paul takes the *Genesis* account of man's creation as a recital of actual events. Evolutionists presumably believe that females preceded males. In any event those who reject the Bible have vastly different notions relative to the relations between the sexes in the home, in the church, and in politics. They have little regard for life-long marriage or the sanctity of infant life. Homosexuals and other heathen advocate that all federal and state laws be based on what can be "rationally" proved, and not on any religious grounds. But if this assumption were consistently and logically followed, there would be no criminal law at all. Secularism, based on empirical observation, cannot justify any normative propositions whatever. Observation at best can collect statistics on murder and adultery, and thus describe what happened. But empiricism can never decide what ought and what ought not to happen.

Paul takes the Genesis account of man's creation as a recital of actual events. Evolutionists presumably believe that females preceded males.

Secularism, based on empirical observation, cannot justify any normative propositions whatever.

This is a basic logical flaw in modern behaviorism. Behaviorists aim to control men as men now control machines. Empirical psychology will determine what the best conduct is. Penal laws, marriage laws, all laws will be made to conform to behavioristic conclusions. In effect, this means that the populace will be forced to submit to the prejudices of the behaviorists. One author says they will decide whether monogamy, polygamy, or no family at all, shall be enforced by the government. Crime will be abolished, for all punishment is bad. If some people do things we now call bad, it is society, not the criminal, who should be changed. If the change in soci-

Behaviorists aim to control men as men now control machines.

ety does not alter the criminal's behavior, and he remains a psychopath, we cure him by execution. Of course, execution is not punishment; it is simply social readjustment.

One remembers that the federal government refused to admit Utah to statehood until the Mormons abandoned polygamy. But the Mormons were more moral than behaviorists now are. They were more intelligent too, for behaviorists think that statistics determine what is good and what is bad.

Some Christians are almost, but not quite, as bad as the behaviorists. This minority—I hope it is a minority—thinks that the Biblical laws obligate only Christians. For them God is not King of kings and Lord of lords. He is King only of his worshipers. This implies that there is no law against murder, adultery, or theft that obligates all people. Nothing in the Bible supports this peculiar view. Paul here lays down some rules for human relations, and he bases them on the Mosaic account of creation. If God is not the Creator, as Moses said he was, Paul reflects only his own absurd opinions. Otherwise God's laws obligate all human beings.

Some Christians are almost, but not quite, as bad as the behaviorists.

Adam knew very well that he had to choose between Eve and God.

Adam was indeed the more guilty, but he was also the more intelligent.

In addition to these implications from the verses, there is something that lies nearer the surface, even if it is less certain than the doctrine of creation. Adam was created first, then Eve. This is clear enough. But what does it mean when it says that Adam was not deceived, but Eve was?

That Eve was deceived needs no explanation. She believed Satan's lie. Does this make her more culpable, or less? I think less. Adam was guilty of a greater sin. He was not deceived. He knew very well that he had to choose between Eve and God. Had he refused to eat the fruit, he would have lost Eve forever. He would have remained perfectly righteous, and Eve would remain in Satan's kingdom. But Eve was so beautiful, and Adam was so lonely. So he deliberately chose Eve rather than God. Milton in his *Paradise Lost* (Book Nine) gives substantially the same explanation; but in some details the spat between Adam and Eve after the fall is not consistent with the Scriptural material. In any case, Adam was by far the more culpable. But if men are more culpable than women, why should not woman be the head of the house? The answer is that woman was deceived. Adam was indeed the more guilty, but he was also the more intelligent. Furthermore, they are now both sinners, and so far forth on the same relative level they previously occupied. Sin did not alter the fact that Adam was created first, that Eve was his helper, and that therefore the man is the head of the house and the office-holder in the church. If he had not chosen Eve instead of God, there would have been neither home nor church. At least so we may surmise.

2:15

She shall be saved through childbirth, if they remain in faith and love and holiness with prudence (good sense).

This verse is exceedingly difficult to understand. Does *she* refer to Eve alone, to all regenerate women, or to all women? Does *saved* mean saved from death in childbirth, or does it mean everlasting spiritual salvation? Is childbirth the cause and means of salvation, or, if not, what?

Commentators, embarrassed by supernaturalism yet retaining still some respect for the Scriptures, will probably say that in spite of the birth pangs with which God cursed Eve, all women (with few exceptions) will survive, not by means of, but through childbirth. Concisely: Giving birth is not fatal. But can we believe that Paul had nothing more in mind than health and physiology?

There is another much more wonderful—and therefore more suspicious—interpretation. Unfortunately, many contemporary exegetes pay it scant attention. Barrett makes only a simple allusion and concludes that Paul is talking not so much about Eve as about women in general, and that therefore he thinks women's sphere is in the home and not in public life. Guthrie, after referring to Chrysostom's desperate attempt to avoid an absurdity, adds, "Another equally improbable suggestion is that the words should read as in the RV, 'she shall be saved by means of child-bearing' (i.e. the Messiah)."

Since modern expositors are so brief, it seems only fair to quote one of the best defenders of the Messianic interpretation. Cowles writes,

> There is no apparent reason for any other than the usual sense of the word "saved"—i.e. saved unto everlasting life—not in the sense—borne through a dangerous crisis in the mother's life. . . . Moreover, this condition of their being saved—"if they persevere in their Christian life"—is good for the usual sense of "saved" but is not true and therefore not admissible in reference to the perilous crisis referred to.
>
> Yet again, Paul did not say "*in* child-bearing," but because of—by means of *(dia,* not *en*). And further, the noun rendered "child-bearing" has the article and therefore refers not to all births of children but to one birth in particular—*the* one which would readily occur to the reader of Gen. 3, from which the apostle is drawing his facts—viz. the birth of *that* seed of the woman who "should bruise the serpent's head." Thus we have this admirable meaning: But (notwithstanding her very great sin in the fall) she shall be saved (with the salvation of the gospel) by means of that wonderful human birth (the child Jesus) the promised "seed of the woman." This promise shall be good, not to all women, but to all who continue in faith, love, and holiness.

One of Cowles' strong points is that the preposition *dia* with the genitive denotes agency, *by means of. Acts* 15:27 refers to a report by word of mouth. *John* 1:3 says, All things were made by him. No one can deny that *dia* with the genitive indicates agency, sometimes. Unfortunately for Cowles' argument, it can also mean *during*. *Acts* 1:3 says that Christ appeared during a period of forty days. *Acts* 5:19 has "during the night." Compare *Acts* 16:9. Hence the present passage can mean during childbirth. Note that it does not have to mean *during;* it can mean *because of.* The problem is to decide which. Cowles' argument here is not compelling; but neither is he refuted by Greek grammar.

Cowles makes another point that is less than compelling. He said that the noun "child-bearing" has the article and therefore refers not to all childbirths, but to one in particular. This is barely possible, barely because there has been no previous hint of it. Furthermore, the article can also introduce an abstract or general noun and can, contrary to what Cowles says, refer to all childbirths in general. Can, but not must. The point remains undecided.

Cowles seems to make a better point when he says that the verb *save* usually means saved to everlasting life. Yet *Matthew* 14:30, 27:40, 42, 49 and *James* 5:15 refer to a cure from an illness. Though Cowles' Greek is not perfect at this point, Paul's reference to faith, love, and holiness carries a soteriological connotation.

Yet even this reference tells against Cowles' interpretation, for the subject is plural, all women, and not Eve alone, at least all Christian women. This is not the only difficulty. If the salvation be Gospel salvation, should not Paul have said both men and women will be saved by the birth of a particular child? But he refers only to women. This fits in much better with the pain and danger of childbirth than with entrance into Heaven.

The preponderance of evidence—the change to the plural, the reference to continuing in faith, the absence of any reference to the salvation of men—militates against the Messianic view. Nor can we be satisfied that Paul has simply physical survival in mind. After all, it was perfectly clear through some thousands of years that childbirth was not fatal. And this was true of all women, not just of women of the covenant. Above it was noted that hesitant liberals sometimes misrepresent Paul in order to preserve his reputation. Sometimes vigorous opponents of Christianity acknowledge the meaning clearly, though they do not believe it. Here Conzelmann, who reduces the pastorals to the level of forgeries, nonetheless understands some of the content. Not that he is without noticeable bias. There is no basis for supposing that *2 Corinthians* 11:3 refers to sexual seduction; nor the verb *exapatetheisā* (the woman was deceived) here in 2:14. Briefly it is this:

The preponderance of evidence—the change to the plural, the reference to continuing in faith, the absence of any reference to the salvation of men—militates against the Messianic view. Nor can we be satisfied that Paul has simply physical survival in mind.

> The words do not refer to Eve, nor to all women, but only to Christian women. . . . If we compare Titus 2:4 we cannot exclude the possibility that the author here also has the education of children in mind.

It is not completely unnatural that after Paul had mentioned men, then women, the idea of mothers' instructing their children should have passed through his mind. This goes well with the last words of the verse: "if they remain in faith . . . with prudence."

Alford, who of course, lived before the time of Conzelmann, mentions and rejects this interpretation, as well as Cowles'. Stressing the spiritual rather than the physical nature of the word *saved,* and bringing in *1 Corinthians* 3:13-15, Alford notes that the pain of giving birth is part of God's curse. It is not merely physical but spiritual: It is a curse. It is not a means to salvation. Then Alford concludes,

Alford notes that the pain of giving birth is part of God's curse. It is not merely physical but spiritual: It is a curse. It is not a means to salvation.

> What then is here promised her? Not only exemption from that curse in its worst and heaviest effects; not merely that she shall safely bear children: but the Apostle uses the word *sōthēsetai* purposely in its higher meaning. . . . Just as that man should be saved, as passing through fire which is his trial, his hindrance in his way, in spite of which he escapes, so shall she be saved through, as passing through, her childbearing, which is her trial, her curse, her (not means of salvation, but) hindrance in the way of it.

This is a much better interpretation, exhibiting great intelligence, possibly correct, but is it completely satisfactory?

Chapter Three

3:1

Trustworthy (credible, faithful) is the saying: If anyone desires [to be] a bishop (overseer), he desires a good work.

Church government is as much a matter of doctrine as the Trinity and the atonement.

This is the second of the "faithful sayings." Some doubt its appropriateness on the ground that it has no soteriological importance. Nevertheless, it has great importance for ecclesiastical organization, and especially in the first two centuries when Christian leaders were highly visible targets for persecution. This consideration also removes the objection that the saying encourages unworthy ambition. Another doubt quotes a popular adage, whose origin is not clear, "The office should seek the man, not the man the office." What then does the text really mean?

Two different verbs are here both translated *desire*. The first is *oregetai;* the second is *epithumei*. Some commentators think that the first envisages a stronger desire than the second; others say the reverse. Probably we should conclude merely that Paul did not want to use the same word twice in so short a sentence.

There has also been some difference of opinion as to whether the faithful saying is found in the preceding verse (2:15) or in 3:1b. One argument is that all faithful sayings must, just must, refer to salvation, and since 2:15 contains the word (understood as Cowles understands it), 2:15 must be the faithful saying. Now, aside from the fact that 2:15 cannot refer to the salvation of men, but only women, there is the further observation that it isn't much of a "saying." In a rapidly expanding church it is at least possible that people would begin to say, It is good to desire to be a bishop. Besides, most of the epistle has to do with ecclesiastical organization, so that the idea of a bishopric, though of much less importance than salvation, is not inappropriate to the situation. Then, too, although the phrase, "This is a faithful saying," can introduce a new subject, attaching the phrase to the preceding would make a very abrupt break at 3:1b.

Just above, the word *bishopric* occurred. Perhaps the intention was to disturb some anti-establishmentarian activists. Paul, and Jesus himself, attached importance to organizing churches. They both laid down some rules. Church government is as much a matter of doctrine as the Trinity and the atonement. Doctrine is teaching; and here Paul teaches how to organize a church.

Bishopric, however, is a poor word because of its present episcopal and papal connotation. Even Anglicans admit that Paul is not referring to a diocesan bishop, but to an officer in a local church. If there were any diocesan bishop, it would be Timothy himself; but here Paul instructs how to choose overseers. We may well suppose that these men are what one now, and what the New Testament elsewhere, calls elders. If this were not what is meant, the omission of any reference to elders would be extremely peculiar. The work of an elder is a good work.

Bishopric, however, is a poor word because of its present episcopal and papal connotation.

This last sentence removes the objection about sinful ambition. The verse tacitly praises the man who seeks the office; but explicitly it is the office itself that is called good.

3:2, 3

It is necessary that a bishop be irreproachable, husband of one wife, temperate, prudent, respectable, hospitable, didactic, no wino, no brawler, but gentle, peaceful, not greedy for money.

Because the office is so good, the aspirant must satisfy certain requirements. Most of these qualifications require no exegesis. There is no plainer language. It may surprise us that none of these standards is peculiarly Christian. They could describe a competent bank teller. Just perhaps the reason is the very low morality of most converts from paganism. What was true in Corinth was most probably true in Ephesus, also. Hence Timothy, and the congregation after Timothy departed, required this elementary instruction. If this be so, then various suppositions fall, which base themselves on the principle that these qualifications apply to all Christians and not to elders only. They do apply to all; but for the well-being of the congregation they should be more strictly enforced upon the officers.

Some such discussion has occurred with reference to the phrase "husband of one wife." Obviously it prohibits polygamy. But does it forbid a widowed elder to marry again? Whether it forbids a congregation to elect a bachelor is a problem for the next verse. Alford, and the Greek Orthodox Church, insist that a widowed bishop shall never marry a second time. Although Alford recognizes that many Jews still practiced polygamy, he believes that Paul would not have explicitly restricted the bishops in something all communicant members were obliged to avoid. This clearly is a false premise, for the verse also mentions drunkenness and greed. In spite of this Alford concludes that Paul must have meant a second marriage, not polygamy. This is an invalid argument, even though the Greek church came to accept it.

There are opposing reasons. One is that bishops are men and they face the same temptations other men face. Paul therefore could very well warn them because in their position they should be particularly careful to resist temptation. Another and more conclusive reason is that Paul, in this epistle, advises young widows to marry a second time. Would not widowers have the same privilege? Other epistles also explicitly allow a second marriage. The intended sense must be the plain and simple prohibition of extra-marital relationships, including polygamy. If not everything is said in this verse, there are other passages where a husband's obligations to his wife are clearly spelled out.

Many elders today, as everyone knows, are not apt to teach.

The deliberate attack on New Testament regulations shows that some denominations are apostate. They no longer are Christian churches.

The bishop must be a married man "having children."

Another qualification for the elders is more particularly Christian than moral in general. They must be "didactic." The usual translation is "apt to teach." Many elders today, as everyone knows, are not apt to teach. Perhaps they were the best candidates the congregation could produce. Much worse—a deliberate perversion of Christian principles—is the legislation in some denominations requiring the election of a proportion of teenagers. Proportional representation, infringing on majority rule, is bad enough in any government; but the deliberate attack on New Testament regulations shows that some denominations are apostate. They no longer are Christian churches.

3:4, 5

ruling his own house well, having children in subjection, with all respectfulness (holiness); if someone does not know how to rule his own house, how can he take care of the church of God?

These two verses expand the qualifications for the office of bishop, elder, or overseer. He must be a married man "having children." When the children show him respect, the congregation can judge him to be a competent official. Once again we see the anti-biblical posture of churches like the United Presbyterian Church. Teenagers do not meet the biblical standards. Even if these were not qualifications required by Scripture, one would think it only common sense to elect men whose competency has already been tested.

3:6

Not a neophyte, lest, conceited, he fall into judgment of the devil.

The word *neophyte* no doubt means a recent convert, rather than a teenager. All teenagers are immature, but not all neophytes are teenagers. The reason for avoiding rapid promotion in the church is the danger of conceit. The man begins to be proud of himself. This leads to disaster. It may be a disaster for the church. But the verse speaks only of the disaster to the man, and calls it the condemnation of the devil. The words could of course mean that the devil judges or punishes him. But this does not seem quite right. Would not the devil rather commend him and increase his conceit? Taking devil as an objective genitive, the words can also mean a fall into the same or a similar sort of condemnation that the devil has received. The devil does not judge; the devil is judged.

This is surely the correct interpretation, but some commentators have expanded it beyond the limit of what can be strictly proved. The devil is supposed to have sinned by reason of conceit or pride. Therefore the neophyte, elected bishop, falls into precisely the same sin by which the devil originally fell, and thus also into the same judgment. This would be a good interpretation, if only it could be proved from Scripture, instead of from Milton, that the devil's first sin was pride.*

The only activity we can be sure of, since it is the only activity mentioned in the preceding verses, is teaching.

3:7

It is necessary also that he have a good reputation among outsiders, in order that he may not fall into disgrace and [the] snare of the devil.

Teaching is the only function specifically mentioned in this chapter.

The first half of this verse is an additional qualification for the office of bishop. Its wisdom cannot be mistaken. The second half somewhat repeats the preceding, though this does not mean that the objective genitive there prevents a subjective genitive here. Instead of the judgment of the devil, we have the snare of the devil. The devil may not judge, but he certainly lays snares.

Here we may interrupt the exegesis for a paragraph or two and try to determine as best we can what sort of official activity a "bishop" engages in. The only activity we can be sure of, since it is the only activity mentioned in the preceding verses, is teaching. All the other qualifications fit nearly any office whatever. Hence we may immediately conclude that the bishop was, in modern Presbyterian terminology, a teaching elder.

That *overseer* was a title used in the pagan world is of no importance to us. As a title it can be used in connection with all sorts of trades, jobs, businesses. We want to know what it meant in the Christian church. *The Shepherd of Hermas (Sim.* 9, 27, 2), a devotional book written before A.D. 150, leads some scholars to think that the overseer was a deacon, a financial officer, who took care of the poor. The inference, however, is poor because the text says merely that "Bishops [*episkopi*] and hospitable men . . . received the servants of God into their houses gladly . . . and the bishops ever ceaselessly sheltered the destitute and the widows."

But this need mean no more than when a pastor finds someone destitute he does what he can and then calls the deacons to continue the work. It surely does not imply that the bishop or pastor spent all his time administering a relief program. Conzelmann agrees with this, but adds, "Teaching cannot be presupposed as a *special* function of the bishop." On the contrary, teaching is the only function spe-

* Patrick Fairbairn *(An Exposition of Ezekiel,* Sovereign Grace Publishers, 1960, 310-316) rejects the Satanic interpretation of *Ezekiel* 28:11-19. Cowles takes the reference to Eden as a sarcastic description of what Tyre thought of itself.

cifically mentioned in this chapter. The assumption that the bishop is the pastor of a particular congregation, whose title today is teaching elder or presbyter, will help rather than hinder the exegesis of later sections in the pastorals.

3:8, 9

Deacons likewise, dignified (or, serious; translated respectful in verse 4) not double-tongued, not given to much wine, not greedy of gain, having the mystery of the faith in a pure conscience.

The secrets of faith are the faith itself. They are the doctrines God has revealed.

This verse refers to deacons in the technical, ecclesiastical sense, not in the common usage of any kind of servant. This meaning enforces the point that the "overseers" were presbyters; both because the meaning is technical and because otherwise there would be no reference to pastors. How could Paul have deleted the pastors and inserted nondescript overseers? Again the qualifications for deacons, like those for elders, relate more to general morality than to official duties. But again also, there is one official specification: The man must hold the faith in a pure conscience. The *New English Bible*, whose translations are often poor, and it is poor here too, nonetheless gives a good interpretation: "They must be men who combine a clear conscience with a firm hold on the deep truths of our faith."

One might suppose that deacons, occupied with taking care of the poor, would not need great theological training, and the supposition seems to be correct; but one must not suppose that they needed none. Theology is needed for all church officers, and for all the laity as well. Whether Meyer wishes to belittle theology or not, is not clear; but he seems to contradict himself in two consecutive sentences. "*Pistis* is not the doctrine of faith, but subjective faith. *Musterion* is the subject matter of faith, i.e. the divine truth." Now it seems to me that the subjective element is in the participle "holding." The deacon is to hold the mystery, the secret of faith. *Secret* or *mystery* means something that a man can obtain only by revelation. The secrets of faith are the faith itself. They are the doctrines God has revealed. That faith here is objective and not subjective is supported by the fact that it has the article: not simply faith, but "the faith." If any one must find some subjectivity in the verse, the words "a pure conscience" will suffice. Nor does it injure this objective interpretation of faith to refer to chapter one where something was said about heterodoxy.

3:10

Let these also be evaluated first and then let them serve, if they are above reproach.

The word *also* indicates that the deacons as well as the leaders must be tested, proved, evaluated before they can begin to serve. Just how they are to be scrutinized is left unsaid. The process will no doubt vary from person to person and place to place. If the man has been a member of the congregation for a long time, his character will be well known and no further investigation may be needed. *Acts* 6:3, though so early in the history of the church, seems to imply that those who voted in the election already knew the character of the candidates. The text, however, allows for some additional evaluation.

3:11

W__ . . . similarly [should be] honorable, not slanderers, temperate, faithful in everything.

It is the first word, and somewhat the second, that causes difficulty here. The particular qualities listed hardly need explanation. The word translated *honorable* occurred in 3:4 as *respectable.* It could be translated *grave* or *honest.* One has to choose the English word with the most appropriate connotation for the context. Any of these English words seems satisfactory.

If some women were deacons, further qualifications would be unnecessary.

But the first word of the verse cannot be translated without begging some important questions. Does it mean *women or wives?* As was said before, *gunē*, here the plural *gunaikas,* in classical and Hellenistic Greek, can mean either a woman, a female, in the generic sense, or it can mean a *wife.* This is strange to people who speak English; but German reproduces the ambiguity exactly. The substantial question now becomes: Does Paul refer to the wives of deacons or to female deacons?

Incidentally, there is no feminine form for the Greek word *deacon.* It is always masculine; and if there had been "deaconesses," they would have been called *deacons.* In the women's liberation movement of today, when women are ordained as ministers, no one calls them ministeresses or pastoresses. If the Roman Church should ever elect a woman as pope, would they call her *il papa?*

Some commentators, especially contemporary commentators, argue that Paul refers to women deacons. They use, among others, two overlapping arguments. The word *likewise,* they say, indicates a third class of ecclesiastical persons. Not a third office, but a third class of persons. Since, too, the passage states the qualifications of elected officials, elders and deacons, the *likewise* introduces qualifications for this third group of officials. Then, too, since the text does not say *their* women (wives), it cannot mean *wives,* but must mean female deacons.

These overlapping arguments are flawed. They fail to note that if some women were deacons, further qualifications would be unnecessary. One does not state the qualifications of a United States Senator and then add something additional for red-haired senators, western senators, or women senators. Then, too, the word *likewise* does not imply a class of offices. One can just as easily say, "Deacons should have certain qualifications, and their wives likewise."

The word *their* is missing; but first it is not too unusual for Greek to omit an article or demonstrative pronoun. Here there is a possible reason for the omission. Had *their* been in the text, most readers would refer it to the wives of the deacons. But before going on with other qualifications for deacons, qualifications that women cannot meet, Paul inserts a note with respect to the wives of both deacons and elders. At any rate, the grammatical omission is far from justifying women deacons. Note also that if extra words are to be inserted into the text, the word *their* changes the meaning of the text far less than the insertion of the word *deacons*. Those who favor the ordination of women mutilate the text to a much greater degree than those who translate *gunaikas* as wives. Indeed, this is not a mutilation at all.

Phoebe was Paul's helper, not his superior officer.

A third argument holds that Phoebe, in *Romans* 16: 1, is called a deacon. This is a point on which the feminists place great stress. But it is a worthless argument. The word *diakonos* usually does not mean *deacon*. It is just the ordinary Greek word for *servant*. If the pope claims to be the servant of the servants of God, it does not follow that every servant is a pope. Nor is every French *garçon* a waiter.

The feminists try to bolster up Phoebe by noting that Paul also calls her a *prostatis:* "Receive her in the Lord . . . for she herself has also been *a prostatis* of many and of myself as well" (*Romans* 16:2). The masculine form is *prostatēs*. The meaning is: *defender, guardian, protector*. Liddell and Scott give *front-rank man, leader, chief, ruler,* or *president*. One advocate of the ordination of women argues that in modern terms, we should address her as Madame President. The conclusive refutation of this type of argument is that Paul called Phoebe "my *prostatis*": "for she was a *prostatis* of many and of me." Clearly Phoebe was Paul's helper, not his superior officer.*

These refutations should be sufficient as answers to proposals for the ordination of women. On the positive side, one may add that none of the apostles was a woman, nor were any of the original deacons. And conclusively (in conjunction with other epistles) 2:12 excludes women from all church offices.

It should also be kept in mind that a *deaconess* is not a female deacon. The Reformed Church in America and the Presbyterian Church in the United States of America (now, UPCUSA) cooperated for many years in supporting a deaconess school on Pine Street in Philadelphia. These young ladies became paid assistants to pastors and were never ordained.

To conclude, Calvin says, "He here refers to the wives of both bishops and deacons."

3:12

Let the deacons be the husbands of one wife, governing their children and their own household well.

* See the *Appendix* for the controversy in the Reformed Presbyterian Church, Evangelical Synod.

This verse confirms the meaning of the preceding verse. The deacon must be a husband, therefore a man, with one wife (woman), and children. Since one of the qualifications is to govern his household well, the deacon cannot be a woman because Paul forbids women to govern their husbands. If Paul had approved of female deacons, he could not, after speaking of female deacons, insist in the very next verse, that they should be husbands. The liberal translation just ruins the progress of thought in the passage.

3:13

For those who served [have served?] well as deacons gain for themselves a good grade and great confidence in faith in Christ Jesus.

Although the participle *diakonēsantes* does not have to mean "serving as deacons," and can mean simply *serving,* thus applying to anyone, the context here, contrary to Hendriksen (135), requires the idea of serving as deacons.

After the congregation has elected a board of deacons, some perform better than others. These achieve a better grade-point average. This advanced standing does not refer to any reward in Heaven. Alford argues that the participle *served* is aorist, not perfect *(have served),* and hence points to a time in the future when one can look back and see the deacon's service as one single whole, "at the great day" (328). "The *diakonēsantes,* as above stated, is used with reference to their finished course at that day" (329). It is also true that Alford makes some subsidiary room for a reference to the present time. But note that the text has no reference to that great judgment day. The words "gain . . . great confidence" clearly refer to this life. Just what "confidence in faith" means is hard to determine. It can hardly mean that the good deacon is now more confident of his own ability to handle his task. He may indeed be more confident in his ability, and even rightly so; but this is hardly "confidence in faith." Perhaps the phrase means that he has fewer doubts as to the truth of the Gospel.

The deacon must be a husband, therefore a man, with one wife (woman), and children.

Contemporary critics who reduce Paul's instructions to culturally conditioned prejudices have no rightful place in the house of God.

3:14, 15

These things I write to you, hoping to come to you quickly; but if I delay, that you may know how to conduct [yourself] in the house of God, which is the church of [the] living God, pillar and seat of the truth.

Again Paul states the purpose of his letter: He wants Timothy to know how to conduct himself in church affairs, and how church affairs should be conducted. The church is the house of God, and God gives it direction. Contemporary critics who reduce Paul's instructions to culturally conditioned prejudices have no rightful place in the house of God.

The word *edraiōma* is very rare. It is related to *edra,* a seat, both in the usual sense of a chair, and as a *seat* of government. It can refer to a temple, the seat of the gods. The adjective means *sedentary, steady, steadfast,* or *firmly appointed. Edraiōma* can well be translated *stay* or *support.*

Were this word translated *foundation,* so that the church would be the foundation of the truth, the connotation would be seriously in error. The church does not invent the truth; the truth produces the church. There is not first a fellowship of kindred spirits, who then articulate their common beliefs, and change them with changing conditions; no, there is first a body of doctrine and those who believe the doctrine are thus brought into fellowship with each other. Their fellowship or *koinonia* is the fact that they hold the doctrine in *common.*

The church is the pillar and seat, the mainstay, the bulwark, the support of the truth. In less metaphorical language this means that the church proclaims, defends, and propagates the Gospel. Its task is to declare all of God's revealed truth. In these days when the neo-orthodox exclude truth from religion, when they and others reduce religion to the status of emotion, when even secular scientists reject the idea of fixed truth and adopt relativism (I do not mean Einstein's theory of relativity), and when the fundamentalists, though asserting absolute truth, assert very little of it, a Christian who is honest with himself ought to reconsider the New Testament's constant emphasis on truth; for whenever intellectualism is rejected, Christian truth cannot be retained. If the church is not the bulwark of the truth, there is no church.

Were this word translated foundation, so that the church would be the foundation of the truth, the connotation would be seriously in error.

There is first a body of doctrine and those who believe the doctrine are thus brought into fellowship with each other.

The church is the pillar and seat, the mainstay, the bulwark, the support of the truth.

Whenever intellectualism is rejected, Christian truth cannot be retained.

3:16a

And confessedly, great is the mystery of godliness

The word *confessedly,* by common confession (*New American Standard*), suggests that the following lines might have been recited in some congregations much as we recite the *Apostles' Creed.* But this is only a supposition. That these lines were part of a hymn that they sang is unfounded speculation. The *New English Bible* has the intolerable translation "beyond all question." Even the *King James,* which is not nearly so bad a translation as modern editors try to make it out to be, has the inaccurate phrase "without controversy." The word *eusebeia,* translated as *piety* in 2:2, becomes *religion* in the *New English Bible.* The *King James* and the *New American Standard* make it *godliness.* The word will later occur in 4:7, 8; 6:3, 5, 6, 11; and in other epistles. *Religion* is the poorest translation.

The mystery of godliness is of course the truth that was mentioned at the end of the previous verse.

3:16b

Who appeared in the flesh, was justified by the Spirit, was seen by angels, was preached among the nations, was believed by the world, was received up into glory.

The first word of the phrase is "who." Some manuscripts have the word "God." In the manuscripts the two words, especially when *God* is abbreviated, look very much alike. The modern critical texts are presumably correct in deciding for the relative pronoun. Alford defends it with both enthusiasm and in detail. However, the change in the sense is much less than some interpreters think. These seem to say that *who* refers to Christ, while *God* would not. But *who* cannot refer to Christ in any grammatical sense because the previous mention of Christ Jesus is too far back. *Who* must refer to God, mentioned twice in the previous verse. The sense, however, is the same, for if *God* was manifested in the flesh, this still refers to Jesus. It must, because only Jesus, not the Father, came in the flesh. Since *who* as a relative refers to God, once again God is Jesus for the same reason. It is not the word *God* versus the word *who* that determines the sense; it is the phrase, "was manifested in the flesh." Both texts identify Jesus with God. Incidentally, *who* cannot refer to mystery because *mustērion* is neuter, and *who* is masculine.

It is not the word God versus the word who that determines the sense; it is the phrase, "was manifested in the flesh." Both texts identify Jesus with God.

The phrase "appeared in the flesh" immediately suggests the incarnation. Alford, however, identifies that appearance with Christ's baptism; and he holds that the succeeding clauses follow the temporal or historical order of Christ's life as a whole. Though one may grant that the ascension was the final event of Christ's life on Earth, a strictly chronological order for these phrases is not too clear.

The next phrase is, "was justified by the Spirit." To preserve historical chronology Alford refers this justification to Christ's victory over Satan's temptations in the desert. But even so, Alford admits that Christ's sinlessness throughout all his life justified him. Or, one may say that Christ's resurrection was the justification of his claim to Deity. One remembers *Romans* 1:4 "who was declared with power to be the Son of God by the resurrection from the dead, according to the Spirit of holiness." This verse in *Romans* also suggests the idea that the Spirit can justify, whereas we usually think of justification as being an act of the Father.

Another commentator combines good and bad when he writes, "He was vindicated when God raised him up. . . . This was done 'in the spirit.' . . . it was the Spirit of God, not the flesh itself, which was capable of effecting resurrection." Though it is indeed true that Christ's claims were vindicated, this interpretation unfortunately requires a lower case letter and a capital: spirit and Spirit. Nor is the idea of resurrection completely correct, for although the Spirit may have raised Jesus' body to resurrection life, the phrase itself speaks of *justification* in the spirit or by the Spirit, not *resurrection*.

Cowles has another point of view: "justified (sustained) in his claim to be the eternal Son of God by his manifestation of [sic] spirit; i.e. in and through his higher spiritual nature." To avoid this odd interpretation and to avoid other difficulties, someone has suggested a different punctuation, with this result: He who was manifested was justified in the body [by the resurrection?], appeared in the spirit to angels, and so on. Since the chief objection to this is merely stylistic, in that it destroys the neat parallelism, we would regard it as excellent unless we can find as good an interpretation while preserving the parallelism.

From the standpoint of intelligibility it is better to deny the parallelism; but if one feels the "poetic and lyrical" character of the words, in spite of the impossibility of scansion, one must still by some means produce the indicated sense.

If we keep the parallelism, the next phrase is "was seen of angels." The objection that angels cannot see because they are incorporeal spirits is not compelling. God is incorporeal; he has no eyeballs or retinas; yet "You, God, see me" (*Genesis* 16:13). The language is metaphorical, here referring to divine omniscience. Even the phrases, "see with the eyes and hear with the ears" do not refer to sensations. The phrase in question occurs in *1 John* 1:1, 3,* where it reproduces language from the Old Testament: *Deuteronomy* 29:4; *Isaiah* 6:10, 11:3, 44:18; *Jeremiah* 5:21; *Ezekiel* 12:38, 40:4. *Matthew* 13:14-16 uses the same phrases. *1 Peter* 1:12 speaks of angels "bending over to look into" some Gospel truths. *Colossians* 2:15 also has something similar. There is therefore no difficulty in thinking that Christ could be "seen" by angels, especially if we use the punctuation which gives "appeared in the spirit to angels."

Even the phrases, "see with the eyes and hear with the ears" do not refer to sensations. The phrase in question occurs in 1 John 1:1, 3, where it reproduces language from the Old Testament.

A German commentator, De Wette, wants "seen by angels" to form a contrast with the unexpressed descent of Christ into Hell. Now, first, contrasts must have at least some textual connection. There is none here. Second, the idea of a descent into Hell is, I assert, a misunderstanding of what Peter says.†

Nor does this seeing have to refer to, can hardly refer to, the ascension. *Luke* 10:18 is the puzzling verse that says, I beheld, or I was watching, Satan fall from Heaven like lightning. Presumably this was the effect of the preaching of the seventy. Sometimes Satan is supposed to have fallen when Christ died on the cross, or at least when he rose. Hence "seen by angels" surely does not have to refer to the ascension. A further reason is that the sixth line of the confession indicates the ascension, and if the sixth line is chronologically after the third, the third cannot be the ascension. Unfortunately, lines four and five conflict with the chronology.

After all these difficulties in the first three lines, we are relieved to find practically no difficulty in the last three: (4) Christ was preached among the nations; (5) he was believed on in the world; (6) he was received into glory. I cannot accept the attempt to preserve the chronology by referring the sixth line to some future exaltation of Christ. After all, the verb is aorist, not future. Nor should one try to support the future sense by translating *en* as *throughout* the world on to Christ's return. *Preached* itself is aorist; and *en* cannot be dragooned into *throughout* future centuries. The Greek preposition *en* has several meanings. Possibly in Helladic (before 1000 B.C.) Greek it may have always designated spatial inclusion. Even today

* Compare my commentary on *First John* (The Trinity Foundation, 1992 [1980]).

† Compare my *New Heavens, New Earth*, (The Trinity Foundation, 1993 [1980]), 125ff.

some Baptists, in an effort to defend immersion as the sole method of baptism, insist that *en* is always local. But this is not true even of Hellenic (1000-300 B.C.) Greek. One might doggedly maintain that *in war* is a local usage. But to be engaged *in philosophy* (Plato, *Phaedrus,* 59a; *Republic,* 489b) is hardly a localization. "In friendship," "in fear," "in wrath," "in silence" are not local. Nor are to see *by* one's eyes, *by* prayers, *by* words, *by* night, *during* the time, *during* the archonship, *in* three months—all found in classical Greek. In Koiné or Hellenistic Greek (300 B.C.-), the New Testament has numerous examples of *en* designating the means or agent, to be translated as *by.* These linguistic details explain why there can be a parallelism of phrase in Greek where there can be none in an English translation. "In the flesh" can be taken as *local,* though *state* is a better grammatical analysis; but then where this phrase is taken to imply that "in the spirit" and "in the nations" and "in the world" must be local, the argument is invalid. Since the Spirit, the Holy Spirit, is not a locality, *en pneumati* cannot be the local *in.* The parallelism exists solely in the word as a word. Though it may not be the best of puns, yet if we say "the fast horse was tied fast," we smile because the same four-letter word is used. Better than a pun, we may say, "the members of this congregation show their faith in thought, word, and deed." Yet here, though the word *in* is used only once, the phrase attaches two or even three meanings to the one word. So much for the tedious details of linguistics.

Since the Spirit, the Holy Spirit, is not a locality, en pneumati cannot be the local in.

Chapter Four

4:1

The Spirit says explicitly that in later times some will apostatize from the faith, entertaining errant spirits and devils' doctrines.

True evangelical ministers, and of course those who claim to be evangelical and are not, hardly ever mention demons and infrequently oppose false doctrine.

The word *explicitly* is *rhētōs: in words.* This has some bearing on verbal revelation. *Acts* 1:16 says, "The Holy Ghost by the mouth of David spake concerning Judas." The Holy Ghost governs the words his messengers use. He speaks in words through them. The revelation is verbal.

When, then, did the Spirit speak the warning Paul here refers to? Was it part of his own previous writings? Was it said by Jesus himself? Were there several prophecies? It is not necessary to restrict the reference to one. *2 Peter* 2:1, which could easily have been written before *1 Timothy*, says, "There will also be false teachers among you, who will secretly introduce destructive heresies." (Compare *1 John* 2:18 and 4:1-3.) Even if Jesus did not explicitly refer to the church in Ephesus, *Mark* 13:22 predicts a series of false teachers. Paul himself, earlier, by the inspiration of the Spirit, gave similar warnings. He had previously called the elders of Ephesus to Miletus and warned them against savage wolves (*Acts* 20:29). Another better known passage is *2 Thessalonians* 2:1-12. These all justify the term *rhētōs* (*expressly*). Now *2 Thessalonians* may refer to a time subsequent to the twentieth century, our own century; but the other passages include all time since Paul. In the present passage, *1 Timothy* 4:1, he rather clearly speaks of something that will shortly take place in Ephesus; in fact, something already begun. *Later* times is not restricted to the *last* times.

Worthy of a short note is the mention of errant spirits and teaching of demons. These are the sources of the human apostasy. Such ideas are unpopular in our era. The behaviorists in their atheism deny not only the existence of God, but, consistently, human souls or spirits as well, not to mention demons and devils. True evangelical ministers, and of course those who claim to be evangelical and are not, hardly ever mention demons and infrequently oppose false doctrine. Biblical language, such as Paul uses here, hardly ever adorns a Protestant pulpit.

The human teachers whom Paul here warns us against are false teachers because they have *apostatized. Depart from, fall away, desert* are good enough translations, but the actual Greek word is *apostatized.* Apostatized from the faith. That is to say, they had rejected Biblical theology and substituted contrary beliefs or doctrines. The text uses the word *doctrines* or *teachings.* Once again we must note the recurring objectivity of Paul. Quite likely these false teachers were guilty of a certain amount of immoral conduct. Paul often condemns sin and disobedience to the law. But that is not the point here. Quite certainly these false teachers subjectively believed this or that. But Paul places the emphasis on the object of their belief. They have drifted away from Christian doctrines and now accept the theological systems of devils. Faith in the sense of the psychological activity of believing has no value in itself. Its merit or demerit lies in the object, the truths or falsehoods, the propositions believed.

Faith in the sense of the psychological activity of believing has no value in itself.

Paul's concern for truth and his opposition to error are sadly lacking today. The public derides "heresy hunters." In fact, *heretic* is almost a term of honor. It indicates freedom of thought and expression, intellectual independence, modernity as opposed to the witch-burning Dark Ages. Did not Calvin have Servetus burned because of his discovery of the circulation of the blood?*

Paul's concern for truth and his opposition to error are sadly lacking today. The public derides "heresy hunters."

4:2

Speaking lies in hypocrisy, seared [with branding iron, cauterized] in their own consciences,

There is somewhat of a puzzle in this verse. Offhand, one would think that it is the "some who have apostatized and who interest themselves in demonic teachings" who speak lies in hypocrisy with their consciences branded. But the nearer antecedent of the adjective *(pseudologōn)* is *daimoniōn.* This identifies the demons as the liars. But if these who have apostatized have seared consciences, how can they be hypocrites? A hypocrite is one who disguises his beliefs. He says one thing while believing something incompatible. Do teachers of demonic doctrines secretly believe the incompatible Gospel truth?

The question concerning the grammatical antecedent has a plausible answer. The demons so completely indwell the apostates that Paul can treat the two as one. They are both liars, for they both preach the same falsehood. The matter of hypocrisy is more difficult to explain, and commentators generally ignore it. There is, how-

The demons so completely indwell the apostates that Paul can treat the two as one.

* No, he did not. Calvin himself, when charged with Servetus' death, appealed to the judges themselves to testify that he opposed the execution. Nor did he mention beheading instead of fire, as some try to evade his clear statements. As for the facetious reference to physiology, I suppose that Servetus did not discover the circulation of the blood, but on the word of his defenders, was about to, and would have done so, had not the court interrupted his studies.

ever, a possible explanation, but the reader of the present commentary must himself assume the obligation of evaluating it. The Greek verb *kekaustēriasmenōn* frequently, perhaps usually, means *branded.* In the Roman Empire slaves and criminals were branded as our western cowboys used to brand their animals. Hence, one can suppose that the apostates were branded, without supposing that they were completely convinced of the demonic teachings. They still secretly half-believed some parts of the Gospel. This made them inconsistent heretics. Far be it from me, the present author, to insist on this interpretation, for it is hard to believe that Julian the Apostate and others did not wholeheartedly believe their anti-Christian doctrines.

There is another possible supposition. It is exemplified today, and may also be hinted at in New Testament times. *2 Peter* 2:3, 14 describe the false teachers as greedy. In *1 Thessalonians* 2:5 Paul denies that he is greedy. It is possible, then, for the false teachers had other faults too, that they were hypocrites: They had selected some demonic falsehoods, not so much because they were convinced of their truth, but because they thought such preaching would bring in good contributions from people with itching ears.

In Corinth, licentiousness was rampant, and no one advocated celibacy. In Colosse, asceticism found considerable favor.

Abstinence from foods must not be based on allegedly divine dietary laws.

4:3

forbidding marriage, abstaining from foods which God created to be received with thanksgiving by those who believe and know the truth,

This describes the doctrines of the heretics. Consider now three churches: the Corinthian, the Ephesian, and the Colossian. Their characteristics and Paul's troubles in each were different. In Corinth, licentiousness was rampant, and no one advocated celibacy. In Colosse, asceticism found considerable favor. One may then surmise that the Ephesian church included both of these extremes. If asceticism, in the Corinthian culture of our twentieth century, seems to be a most unlikely life-style, one must remember the early Christian anchorites, Simon Stylites, early monasticism, and of course the Jewish Essenes. Some of the gnostics too advocated celibacy. And, of course, all the Jews acknowledged the food laws. Therefore, even in Ephesus there was cause for Paul's opposition to asceticism.

One may also note that the middle phrase in the verse can refer to the custom of saying grace before meals. We are to receive our food with thanksgiving.

Presumably thanksgiving comes naturally to those who believe and know the truth. Refraining from pork and oysters is the result of ignorance. Following the even stricter Talmudic rules is deeper ignorance. This does not mean that one must eat pork and oysters to be a good Christian. If one suspects the possibility of trichinosis, it is safer not to eat. That a convinced vegetarian can be a good Christian is doubtful. In any case, abstinence from foods must not be based on allegedly divine dietary laws. Believers, that is to say, those who know the truth, receive whatever foods they enjoy with thanksgiving.

4:4, 5

Because every creation of God is good, and nothing rejected if received with thanksgiving, for it is sanctified by the Word of God and prayer.

Grammatically, these verses are part of the sentence beginning at verse one. Complicated sentences are characteristic of Paul. Also, the two verses partly repeat and partly carry forward the thought of the preceding. The idea of thanksgiving is repetition. While we today are not so bothered about food laws, perhaps we need, surely some need, to be impressed with the appropriateness of saying grace before meals. I have known some Christians, at least moderately devout, who omit it.

Although God at creation viewed the whole world, mountains, oceans, and fields, and pronounced his creation good, the context here requires us to say that everything God created as food is good as food. We neither eat granite nor drink sea water.

An added thought, not immediately clear, is "for it is sanctified by the Word of God and prayer." One interpretation is that we should also read a section of Scripture before meals. One or two commentators suggest that when the father of the family says grace, he should include some Scriptural phrases in his prayer. Is it not better to understand the passage as saying that God's Word, Scripture, revelation, sanctify all foods for eating, and that the grace sanctifies the food served at a particular meal?

The epistle constantly emphasizes teaching and doctrine.

4:6, 7

By teaching these things to the brethren you will be a good deacon of Christ Jesus, being nourished by the words of the faith and of the good teaching which you have followed. But reject worldly old-wives' mythologies. Train yourself for piety.

The epistle constantly emphasizes teaching and doctrine. Timothy must teach what he has learned—the words or doctrines of the faith. These doctrines are good teaching. They nourish a person. As Christ himself said, "The words that I have spoken to you are Spirit and are life" (*John* 6:63). Timothy not only had been nourished by these doctrines, but he is also now being nourished by them. One remembers and adds to earlier lessons. If Timothy in turn teaches his theology to the Ephesians he will be a good minister. The Greek word is *diakonos.* Clearly Timothy was not a deacon in the official sense of the word: As a servant, he was officially a minister, a teaching elder.

Verse 7 is the appropriate contrast with verse 6. It can be translated in several ways without much changing the sense. The word *profane* could be substituted for *worldly,* but the connotation does not seem right. Similarly, *myths* or *mythologies* could be made *fables,* except that *fable* suggests the type of literature Aesop wrote. *Superstitions* might be a good word. The last phrase of the verse begins the contrast with verse 8.

4:8

For bodily gymnastics is useful for little, but piety is useful for everything, having a promise of life both now and hereafter.

Some commentators have interpreted "bodily gymnastics" to mean the asceticisms of verse 3. But verse 3 is now quite a ways back. The convincing objection, however, is that Paul would never have admitted that asceticism is profitable even a little. Rather, Paul used the word "*Gymnastic* yourself to piety," either without considering what he would say next, or he deliberately chose the word to prepare for the coming contrast.

Many semi-educated ministers berate "the Greeks" for believing that the body is evil and that only the mind is important.

Why, then, do not professedly evangelical ministers decry American sports instead of the Greek philosophers?

These "evangelical" ministers think it safer to berate the ancient Greeks rather than present-day evils.

Many semi-educated ministers berate "the Greeks" for believing that the body is evil and that only the mind is important. They insist that the body is the temple of the Holy Ghost and that man is a unity, not a duality of body and soul. This view misrepresents both "the Greeks" and Christianity too. "The Greeks" divide into three groups: (1) the general populace; (2) Plato; and (3) the other philosophers. Plato in one place said "the body is a tomb." Now, Plato was of course a pagan. He lived four centuries before Christ and seems never to have heard of the Jews. Many of his ideas, particularly his communism, are anathema to Christians; though we ought to grant him some respect for initiating the heliocentric theory of the solar system. But as for the Platonic-Pythagorean view that the body is a tomb, we must remember (1) no other school of Greek philosophy agreed, and hence we should not accuse "the Greeks" on this score; and (2) Calvin, not Plato, but Calvin calls the body "a prison house" (*Institutes* 1, xv, 2).

The other Greek philosophers, rather than being defenders of the immortality of the soul, tended rather toward some form of materialism. In spite of the great differences between them, both the Epicureans and the Stoics were materialists. Hence the attribution of a Platonic doctrine to "the Greeks" is poor scholarship. In fact, it is mystifying that the theologians in question show so much animosity toward Plato and never or hardly ever attack Aristotle. Now, third, the general Greek populace, those who above all may properly be called "the Greeks," were as little interested in philosophy and as much interested in sports as sports-loving Americans are. With diminishing gasoline supplies in 1979, fifty to a hundred thousand people drove to a single stadium to see a baseball or football game. Counting smaller contests there are at least a hundred football games on an autumn Saturday afternoon. More likely two hundred. The newspapers fill at least a third of their pages with sports. Why, then, do not professedly evangelical ministers decry American sports instead of the Greek philosophers? I mentioned Saturday afternoons. What about Sabbath desecration? Apparently these "evangelical" ministers think it safer to berate the ancient Greeks rather than present-day evils.

The apostle said, "Bodily gymnastics is useful for little." The *New*

American Standard translates it, "Bodily discipline is only of little profit." The *New English Bible* also mistranslates it: "The training of the body does bring limited benefit." I challenge any Greek scholar to prove that my translation is wrong. At least Alford agrees: "for but little in reference only to a small department of man's being: not as in James, 'for a short time,' as the contrast *pros panta* shows." Yet some commentators want it to say, Bodily exercise profits for a little while. It is true that *oligon* can refer to a short time (*James* 4:14). It can refer to a little of anything. Here in *1 Timothy* 4:8 it cannot refer to time, for, as Alford said, it is balanced by the word *panta:* "Bodily exercise is profitable for little, but piety is profitable for all things." This includes time, as the next phrase shows, but the *panta* covers the qualities of the profitableness, not simply a bare duration.

Even aside from the drugs they take to pep them up, and the medication used to desex the women contestants and turn them into masculine freaks, the athletes have chosen the wrong values and lead wasted lives.

I willingly acknowledge that Greek grammar allows (but does not require) the translation, "exercise profits a little." The English indefinite article assigns some small profit to gymnastics. Dr. Knight (*The Faithful Sayings,* 67-68) defends this view. "*Pros oligon* means 'for a little' and not 'for little.' " He urges that the contrast between "little" and "all things" requires this interpretation. It seems to me, however, that if "little versus all" is a good contrast, "nothing versus all" is a sharper contrast. Then, the second part of Dr. Knight's argument is one I wish to use for my own view. It is the Pauline reference to sport in *1 Corinthians* 9:25. In that passage Paul contrasts the athletic laurel crown, which withers in a few days, with the incorruptible crown that Christians are to receive. Referring to the Olympic athletes Dr. Knight insists, "But they do receive a crown." This is really an incredible argument. It makes much better sense to suppose that Paul is contrasting the stupidity of the athletes in training so strenuously for a prize worth nothing and the wisdom of Christians whose values are sound. Today, of course, they do not give the Olympians a few laurel leaves. They give (apparently) gold medals at a present price of some $400 an ounce. Even so, the gold is not of sufficient worth to justify months and years of training. Even aside from the drugs they take to pep them up, and the medication used to desex the women contestants and turn them into masculine freaks, the athletes have chosen the wrong values and lead wasted lives. Godliness or piety, on the other hand, is profitable in relation to every aspect of life, both now and forever.

But wait a minute; perhaps that is not just the way it should be said. Does the text mean that godliness conveys various favors both in this earthly life and in the life to come as well? This would indeed make a good contrast, for surely athletics conveys no heavenly favor. Yet Dr. Knight (73-76) has a better interpretation. He notes that in *2 Timothy* 1:1 the thing promised is life, not some various blessings that are given during one's life. The question naturally follows: Is the promise here the promise of life now and hereafter, or is it simply various blessings that come now and hereafter? The text itself is slightly ambiguous. Or perhaps we do not understand the connotations of Greek well enough. In English it says, "of life the now and the coming." If the word *life* had been repeated—the present life and the future life—the idea of different times would have been evident. But with only one occurrence, it could mean "the life that now is and continues into the future."

Dr. Knight puts the question very clearly: "Is it a promise *for* this life and that which is to come, or is it a promise *of* the life which now is and that which is to come?"(74) He might have said, the life which now is and continues after death. He goes to some little trouble to support his view. For example, though *Romans* 15:8 speaks of promises of blessings in history, the word *promises* is plural; whereas the singular, *promise,* with the genitive, usually denotes the content of the promise. Among other verses Dr. Knight cites *2 Timothy* 1:1, where *life* in the phrase "promise of life" is the content of the promise.

Dr. Knight goes on, as anyone even slightly acquainted with the New Testament would anticipate, to show that the word *life* here means the life everlasting that Christ brings to us. It does not mean just ordinary living on this Earth, for the worst sinners continue to live in this sense. Nor does it mean simply a life after death, for unfortunately sinners also have an existence after death. Piety or godliness, therefore, is useful in every respect, because it contains the promise of a regenerate life both now and hereafter.

4:9

Faithful is the proposition and worthy of all acceptation.

No doubt some readers judge that my diatribe against sports is overdone. Yet if the faithful proposition of verse 9 is the preceding, not the following, verse, some emphasis against sports is legitimate. Many commentators hesitate between accepting the one or the other as the proper reference. Two reasons favor or even require verse 9 to refer to verse 8. First, verse 10 does not sound at all like a "saying." Second, verse 10 is given as a reason for something else. Thus it is natural to take verse 10 as an explanation of the importance of verse 8. Some think this second reason is weak because the faithful saying itself in *2 Timothy* 2:11 is introduced by "for." If, then, one faithful saying can be so introduced, why cannot *1 Timothy* 4:10 be the faithful saying? The weakening, however, is miniscule because *2 Timothy* 2:11-12 is not an explanation of anything in the text, either before or after; whereas *1 Timothy* 4:10 not only has "for," but also "to this purpose." It must be an explanation. At any rate, the first reason alone is conclusive. *1 Timothy* 4:10 is simply not a "saying," though either all or at least the last part of 4:8 can be.

4:10

For to this [end] we labor and suffer reproach because we have hoped in the living God, who is the savior of all men, especially believers.

Instead of "suffer reproach" modern critical editions have "agonize." In his *Textual Commentary* Bruce Metzger acknowledges that the decision is difficult. He thinks *agonize* has the better textual support and also is better suited to the context. *Agonize* could be suspected of being a slight hint of athletics and the Olympic games, whereas nothing in the preceding few verses suggests that Paul suffered reproach. But from this the reading *agonize* can gain only the slimmest support. Nor can it be confidently maintained that it has better textual support. Meyer confidently argues for "suffer reproach." While an editor must print something—he can't leave holes in his text—the decision is a toss-up.

Paul labors and agonizes because he hopes in the living God. The dominant subjectivism among contemporary evangelicals receives support from the undeniable fact that believing and hoping are subjective mental acts. But an intelligent Christian must recognize the objective emphasis in the New Testament. No matter how lively, how sincere, or how emotional a hope may be, its value and efficacy depend on the object of that hope. Here Paul has put his hope in the living God. I suppose hope was not a prominent part of pagan Greek religion; but had it been, it would have been misplaced. Subjective hoping that Zeus would help was vain, for there was no Zeus. It is the object hoped on that counts.

No matter how lively, how sincere, or how emotional a hope may be, its value and efficacy depend on the object of that hope.

One might think that Paul used the phrase "the living God" to distinguish Jehovah from Zeus or Artemis. This would indeed fit the situation. But more probably he is reproducing the language of the Old Testament, which often refers to God as the living God. See *1 Samuel* 17:26, 36; *2 Kings* 19:4, 16; *Psalm* 42:2, 84:2; *Isaiah* 37:4, 17; *Jeremiah* 10:10, and elsewhere.

If universalism were true, the word especially would make no sense. All men would equally arrive in Heaven.

Paul then adds that God is the savior of all men, especially of believers. The present commentary has already given lengthy consideration to universalism. One point can be added here. If universalism were true, the word *especially* would make no sense. All men would equally arrive in Heaven. It is patent that *especially* indicates two kinds of salvation. This may seem strange to devout evangelicals in the twentieth century, but it was not so puzzling in Paul's day. In the Old Testament God is a savior, not only in the sense of everlasting heavenly salvation, but also of rescue from famine, from peril, from defeat and death in battle. In *Judges* 6:14 God through Gideon saves the Israelites from the hand of the Midianites. *2 Samuel* 3:18 says that "By the hand of my servant David I will save my people Israel out of the hand of the Philistines, and out of the hand of all their enemies." In the New Testament, *Acts* 27:20, 31 describe salvation from shipwreck.

There are other ways to distinguish between a salvation applicable to all sorts of men and a salvation restricted to the elect. The distinction might mean that God is the only possible Savior: No man can have any other. Or, overlapping this, God has provided a salvation suitable to all men. Or the meaning could be restricted to natural means for preserving life to three score years and ten. I do not think these suggestions very plausible. But it is plausible and certain that God is savior in two different senses, the second being the salvation he provides for believers. If anyone think that the two words "especially of believers" is somewhat weak as a reply to universalism, they were too strong for one commentator who said they were "by no means a graceful addition." Meyer takes the opposite view: "By 'especially of believers' it is indicated that the will of God unto salvation is realized only in the case of believers. 'Especially' does not stand here unsuitably. . . ."

Timothy was no teenager. The Scriptural references to Timothy show that Timothy could hardly be younger than thirty-five; he might have been forty.

4:11

Issue these orders and teach.

Or one might translate it, Command and teach these things. It takes a brave minister these days to issue orders or command. Some ministers nonetheless are brash and command—but command other things. Paul tells Timothy to command and teach these things—the things Paul has been saying. And if it still seems too brash, the verb *teach* softens it some. Teaching must be a patient process. A drill sergeant can command and expect immediate execution; but a professor often wonders how his students can be so slow. The situation is worse when the teacher is younger than his pupils.

4:12

Let no one despise thy youth, but be an example for believers in word, in conduct, in love, in faith, in purity.

Modern readers are almost sure to misunderstand the first phrase of this verse. One denomination requires local congregations to elect a certain number of teenagers as elders. This of course restricts the liberties of majority voting. It is the theory of proportional representation that so weakened France before World War II. If the denomination or denominations which demand the election of teenagers were interested in obeying the Scripture—which they are not—they still could not appeal to this verse. Timothy was no teenager. The Scriptural references to Timothy show that Timothy could hardly be younger than thirty-five; he might have been forty. One possible reason for Paul's advice is that Paul may have realized his life was in danger, and Timothy would be one on whom the future of Christianity would depend. I totally reject the suppositions of C. K. Barrett (and others) that this verse "cannot fail to suggest, though it does not prove, that we have here the work of a pseudonymous writer, consciously but not quite successfully reconstructing the relations between Paul and his young follower."

The position of young ministers, particularly in their first pastorate, is difficult. Just out of seminary, about twenty-five years of age, they must administer a congregation that contains at least one or two conceited, touchy, inconsiderate members, and even some evil ones. Inexperience results in innocent but thoughtless remarks. Minor misunderstandings become major. Some young men, instead of being too timid, are too brash. I have seen young ministers destroy congregations, and I have seen congregations destroy young ministers. Should seminary graduates be restricted to the level of assistant pastor until age thirty-five?

The second part of the verse tells Timothy to be an example to believers, especially in five respects. The first, *logō,* may mean ordinary conversation, that is, in speech, or it may mean in the Word of God, that is, doctrine. Most commentators prefer the former, perhaps because it is the more inclusive. Similarly, the last item mentioned, purity, should not be restricted to sexual chastity but should be understood to cover all forms of conduct. *Conduct* and *love* hardly need comment; and, if *word* above means speech in general, *faith* can be taken as doctrine, thus receiving special emphasis.

Some young men, instead of being too timid, are too brash. I have seen young ministers destroy congregations, and I have seen congregations destroy young ministers. Should seminary graduates be restricted to the level of assistant pastor until age thirty-five?

4:13

Until I come, attend to reading, exhortation, and teaching.

The reading referred to is undoubtedly the public reading of the Scriptures from the pulpit. This may have been a more important admonition then when not everybody could read. Even now, when nearly everybody can read (except modern high school graduates), most people do not read the Scriptures at home. Many fundamentalist churches read only a few verses from the pulpit. The Anglicans and Episcopalians, required to follow the *Prayer Book*, read many Scriptural passages in every service. This is excellent, if only the sermons conformed to the reading. Once I attended a Navajo service on the reservation. Probably the minister read some Scripture, though of course I didn't understand a single word. But at one point the minister sat down on the platform with his feet hanging over, and all the people began to babble out loud. This lasted about five minutes. The American missionary later explained to me that that was the memorization period. In spite of the indecorous babble American churches might well imitate the Navajos, unless they have a better memorization program.

The other two points are exhortation and teaching. Peter (*Acts* 2:40) and the others spent some time in exhortation. It is indispensable. But even the best of procedures can be overdone. Even teaching: Since we are no longer Puritans, two-hour sermons would put us to sleep. Imagine—Paul preached from early evening to midnight. In the liberal churches there is little if any exhortation. As a contrast, on the UHF-TV some Georgia evangelists bellow exhortations in a high-pitched voice until one would think their throats would crack. They do very little teaching. Each pastor who wants to take Paul as an example must decide wisely the proportion of time appropriate for these two indispensable activities.

4:14

Do not be careless of the [divine] gift which was given to you in consequence of prophecy with the laying on of the hands of the presbytery.

"Charisma" in the New Testament does not carry the connotations recently attached to the word in colloquial American speech. Of course, it is not secular; nor must it be something exceptional. Any divine gift can be called a charisma. God gave Timothy the gifts of teaching and of administration. These may be called natural endowments; they are nonetheless divine gifts.

"Charisma" in the New Testament does not carry the connotations recently attached to the word in colloquial American speech.

But there was another gift to Timothy that came in consequence of prophecy. Something similar was mentioned in 1:18. Do these two references refer to the same prophecy and the same time? Hendriksen suggests that bystanders in Lystra (*Acts* 16:2) prophesied to Paul about taking Timothy as his understudy. Possibly. But the two passages probably refer to different times. The prior reference gives no hint as to the time and place. The present reference dates it at Timothy's ordination. This argument, of course, is not conclusive. We may note, however, that 1:18 speaks of prophecies in the plural. Here, although the spelling is identical, the word is very likely genitive singular. *Dia* with the accusative plural would strongly suggest the (here impossible) meaning of *through* in space. Also a single prophecy would have been more likely at an ordination than many prophecies.

At any rate, however we sort out the prophecies, presbytery at the ordination ceremony conferred on Timothy, as a gift, the authority to preach the Gospel. Grammarians insist that this authority was not conferred *by means of* the laying on of hands, but *along with* the laying on of hands. Even so, this hardly permits a presbytery to omit the ceremony. Clearly presbytery conveys the gift. Therefore the action of presbytery is not a mere recognition by the presbytery of gifts the candidate has already received. It is a gift that presbytery confers.

4:15

Attend to these things, be in them, that your advancement may be evident to all.

The middle phrase here has been very literally translated. The verb is indeed the verb *to be*. The *New American Standard* reads, "Be absorbed in them." The *King James* has it, "give thyself wholly to them." The *Revised Standard Version* gives, "Practice these duties, devote yourself to them, so that all may see your progress." Some sentences do not respond to literal translation. Yet, so far as is wise, literal translation is preferable.

The intent of this verse is to enforce the preceding instructions. As such, every minister, whether a young forty or an old eighty, does well to examine his practices on the basis of these verses. It is interesting to note that Paul does not say, "Obey these instructions in order that your congregation may make advances in the Christian life." He says, "Follow these instructions so that your congregation may see your advancement." C. K. Barrett's liberal bias questions whether the pseudo-Paul's advice is appropriate to forty-year old Timothy.

4:16

Pay attention to yourself and to the teaching; persevere in them; for in so doing you will save both yourself and those who hear you.

Far be it from this commentator to suggest that evangelical pastors fail to pay attention to their moral behavior. As a group they excel in watching themselves. Of course we all sin. A few, unfortunately, but only a few are guilty of great scandal. There was one minister who engaged in the contemporary popular activity of pastoral counseling. A woman came and cried on his shoulder, with the result that he divorced his faithful wife and married the other woman. At least he didn't murder the woman's husband as David did. But these deplorable instances are really very rare. I do not believe that the legal profession, the medical profession, or college faculties maintain so good an average.

The fundamentalist churches, which have the reputation of believing the Bible from cover to cover, do not preach very much of it.

But when it comes to paying attention to the teaching and persevering in the doctrine, the contemporary evangelical church is less exemplary. The liberals of course accuse the Bible of many errors; but the fundamentalist churches, which have the reputation of believing the Bible from cover to cover, do not preach very much of it. Paul wrote these pastoral epistles to instruct ministers how to live and serve. It would be well if all pastors seriously compared their performance with Paul's injunctions.

Chapter Five

5:1, 2

Do not rebuke an old man, but entreat him as a father, and young men as brothers, elderly women as mothers, and young women as sisters in all purity.

Paul here confines his attentions to the sincere believers

However important, indeed indispensable, doctrine may be, pastors must attend to other matters as well. Paul here instructs Timothy how to treat the members of his congregation. He first mentions old men. The word is *presbuterō*. In the contemporary drive to ordain women as deacons (and as pastors in some churches) the ordinary word *servant (diakonos)* is forced to mean *deacon* in its official sense. But if *presbyter* can mean simply an old man, all the more can and does the word *deacon* mean a servant. That *presbyter* in this verse means an old man is clear from the context. Since he speaks of young men, elderly women, and girls, all in the plural, it is necessary to take the singular "an elderly man" as general, and not as a reference to a presbyter or official elder. It remains strange, however, why Paul first used the singular and then turned to the plural.

There is also the question whether the phrase "in all purity" refers to the young women only, or to all the classes mentioned. Since we saw in 4:12 that *agneia* is not restricted to a narrow sexual meaning, the phrase can properly refer to all. Donald Guthrie comes to the opposite conclusion.

One may also be puzzled by the command not to rebuke an older man, when one remembers other directives to rebuke, reprove, refute the heretics and heterodox. Now, it happens that the verb here does not appear anywhere else in the New Testament.* Yet it is not likely that the puzzle can be solved by supposing some slight difference in meaning among the verbs. I suggest that Paul here confines his attentions to the sincere believers. Indeed, if "do not rebuke" applies, not only to older men, but to the other classes as well, as the

* I do not understand why the Arndt and Gingrich *Lexicon* cites *Matthew* 12:15 and *Luke* 24:43.

syntax surely requires, there would be, without this interpretation, an impossibly stupid contradiction in Paul's instructions.

5:3, 4

Honor widows who are really widows. But if a widow has children or descendants, let them first learn to show piety in their own home and give a recompense to their progenitors, for this is acceptable before God.

Verses 3 to 16 make it almost indubitable that one of the pressing problems in the first century church was the care of widows. Some of the churches were not quite so poverty-stricken as the church in Jerusalem; the church at Ephesus may have been one such; but evidently the widows were numerous enough to pose a problem. The verb "honor" also means *compensate;* and the noun *timē* can mean a price or compensation. The phrase "widows who are really widows" sounds strange. A widow is a widow is a widow, is she not? But Paul's intention is clear. He means a widow who is destitute; one who has no children or grandchildren to take care of her. Since the Christians were generally poor, and even today a congregation's or denomination's spiritual attainments are inversely proportional to its wealth, the support of too many indigents would be a crushing burden. Clever and not so clever cheaters sponge on the welfare handouts, as most American citizens know. A small congregation has better knowledge of its members' needs. Hence widows who have children must get their support from them.

Since the Christians were generally poor, and even today a congregation's or denomination's spiritual attainments are inversely proportional to its wealth, the support of too many indigents would be a crushing burden.

At first sight this might seem to contradict another of Paul's injunctions. In *2 Corinthians* 12:14 Paul says, "Children are not responsible to save up for their parents, but parents for their children." This is a good Christian principle that Marxists do not like. *The Communist Manifesto* wants to disinherit children and confiscate their parents' savings. The American federal and state governments push in this direction as much as politics permits them. Our immoral Social Security system impoverishes the younger workers to get money for buying the votes of the elderly. Equalization of poverty seems to be the aim. Share the misery. Christianity requires the parents to save up for their children. But now in *1 Timothy* 5:4, Paul instructs the children to support their widowed mother. This really does not contradict *2 Corinthians* 12:14. Much as parents may want to, they may find it impossible to do so. Besides careless expenditures on the part of the parents, besides incompetency in business, the parents may be victims of fraud, of natural disasters, and of governmental-induced inflation. Military defeat also produces rampant inflation, as the Germans and the world discovered in the 1920's. In such cases, the children have an obligation to care for their parents. Indeed they have an obligation, a lesser obligation, to alleviate the sufferings of non-relatives who are destitute, though charity, and piety, begin at home. This alleviation should be channeled through the church to those who are "really" widows.

If anyone does not provide for his own, and especially for those of his household, he has denied the faith and is worse than an unbeliever.

5:5

The real and solitary widow has hoped on God and continues in supplications and prayers night and day.

Such is the literal translation; but I suspect the meaning is that a "real" widow is one who hopes in God and prays night and day. It should be obvious that pagan widows, however solitary and destitute they may be, do not hope in God and pray. Unfortunately there may have been, even in the Christian church, solitary widows who did not trust in God. Recently brought under Christian influences, they may have found support elsewhere, as the next verse suggests.

5:6

But she who is frisky [lives luxuriously, or, voluptuously] is dead.

"Frisky": like lambs. Guthrie mentions "immoral living as a means of support." Moffatt translates it "plunges into dissipation." Barrett confidently asserts, "It is not licentiousness, but luxurious living that is meant." This last would be hard to prove. If the luxurious widow had inherited a good estate from her husband, she would not qualify for support at all. If she had been left penniless, and so seemed to qualify on that count, her luxury must have come from other men. Obviously the church will not support such a woman.

5:7

Insist on these things also, that they may be blameless.

These prescriptions are formal obligations laid upon the church; but who are "blameless"? It may mean the widows. If the pastor faithfully instructs his congregation regarding the treatment of widows, a woman recently widowed might be deterred from seeking outside support. This interpretation makes good sense and appeals to most commentators. But the following verse suggests that these prescriptions are to be obeyed in order that the church may be blameless. Alford objects on the ground that verse 8 has the weak adversative *but (de)*. This is a weak reason. In reply one may note that each instance of the word *widow* in verses 4, 5, and 6, is singular; but in verse 7 *blameless* is plural, and can be masculine. As a two declension adjective, it can be either masculine or feminine. Hence it can mean the members of the congregation.

5:8

If anyone does not provide for his own, and especially for those of his household, he has denied the faith and is worse than an unbeliever.

The general sense of the verse needs no explanation; but one may wonder why, after "his own," Paul says, "especially those of his household." Are not those of one's household *especially* one's own? It seems that Paul here distinguishes between one's relatives—aunts, cousins—and one's parents.

There is a possibility that Paul has Essene influence in mind. The Essenes lived in authoritarian communistic communities. Everything and everyone was regulated. We in America have seen similar stifling societies. Some, but not all, Essenes insisted on celibacy. Being communistic, without private property, and favoring a monkish asceticism, they may have made themselves incapable of providing for their own parents. Such people are worse than unbelievers.

5:9, 10

Let her be enrolled as a widow if she is not less than sixty years old, the wife of one man, attested by good works, and if she has raised children, if she has been hospitable, if she has washed the saints' feet, if she has aided those in tribulation, if she has engaged in every good work.

In the history of exegesis two distinctly different views of verse 9 have competed. Schleiermacher, the father of modernism, took *widows* to mean deaconesses, an order of a later century, and thereby concluded that first century Paul could not have been the author of this epistle. These widows would have to promise, in order to enter upon their office, never to marry again. Baur, more radical than even Schleiermacher, thought some of these deaconesses were not widows, though as ascetic virgins they bore the name. This may fit the Romish practices of a later century, but it does not fit the text. The text requires these women to have been the wife of one man.

In any case, this view carries with it the idea that the widows were employed by the church and paid for doing some useful work. Once again the text furnishes no support whatever for this assumption. Being placed on a roll can mean and most plausibly does mean that the woman named satisfies the requirements for financial assistance. Note in this regard that good works, raising children, hospitality, and other Christian services are not tasks yet to be performed, but qualifications that must have been met in earlier years.

The second view is that the church, never too wealthy, should enroll for widow's compensation only those who met the listed qualifications.

A condensation of Alford's remarks will prove useful. He asks, What is the purpose of this list? It is not, he says, a list of those who are to receive relief from the church, for the limitation to women over sixty is too harsh. Many widows might be destitute at a far earlier age. Similarly, relief should not be denied to widows who had a second husband, especially since Paul himself urges young widows to marry again.

Alford has a point here; yet if the church was very poor, and indeed this was the case, the number of enrollees would have had to be restricted. Widows under sixty could still attract a husband.

Alford continues to the effect that the qualifications enjoined in

The Essenes lived in authoritarian communistic communities.

Being communistic, without private property, and favoring a monkish asceticism, they may have made themselves incapable of providing for their own parents. Such people are worse than unbelievers.

Good works, raising children, hospitality, and other Christian services are not tasks yet to be performed, but qualifications that must have been met in earlier years.

verse 10 presuppose some degree of competence, and very poor widows lacking executive ability would be excluded no matter how destitute.

I would reply that the good works of verse 10 do not require a degree in Business Administration.

Alford, however, does not look upon the list as a list of deaconesses. His reasons are (1) sixty is too old for bearing the strain of this work. And he notes that the Council of Chalcedon fixed the age of deaconess at forty. (2) Not only widows, but virgins also were deaconesses. (3) These widows were bound not to marry again, but deaconesses could. But this leaves him with an order of vague and dubious duties. He suggests that they are female presbyters, ordained, but having no authority over the male presbyters. He refers to such an order having been abolished by the Council of Laodicea. But if Alford's meaning had been Paul's, the Council should not have abolished the order.

The idea of an office or monastic order is totally absent.

We do not decide the question by noting second-century customs. We judge second-century customs by the first-century text. The second century was no model either in theology or conduct.

In my opinion, none of these arguments is sufficient to dispose of the interpretation that Paul simply intended a list of destitute widows who needed relief very badly.

There is a minor puzzle related to the qualification of having raised children. If any widow has no one to depend on, it is surely the widow who unfortunately had not borne children. Why should such be excluded?

In considering the arguments pro and con, the preceding context is some help. One may note that chapter 5 begins with instructions concerning the treatment to be accorded to various groups of people: old men, young men, older women and young women. None of this has any reference to ecclesiastical offices. Then verse 3 takes up the matter of support for destitute widows. References to children, grandchildren, parents concern family affairs, not deacons or elders. Verses 5 and 6 speak of good widows and not so good. Verse 8 indicates the responsibility of the head of the family. The idea of an office or monastic order is totally absent. The relation between verse 12 and verse 14 may also puzzle us, but even these two verses support the conclusion, support it unmistakably, that Paul is concerned about the support of widows, not about an order of nuns.

In favor of an order of nuns several commentators cite Tertullian and others who testify to the existence of such an order in the second century. This begs the question. We do not decide the question by noting second-century customs. We judge second-century customs by the first-century text. The second century was no model either in theology or conduct. Justin was a martyr, but his soteriology would have barred him even from membership in a fundamentalist church, not to mention a Reformed church. A study of the Ante-Nicene Fathers is useful and instructive; but their views are not normative.

Another difficulty is the phrase "wife of one man." In 3:2, "Husband of one wife" can be understood as a prohibition of polygamy (see above). Here in 5:9 it must mean, wife of only one husband. The woman is a widow; at the moment she is not the wife of any man; thus the phrase must be a prohibition of a previous second marriage. However peculiar this may seem when compared with other passages, there seems to be no other way to interpret this phrase in this place. Presumably the widow who had had a second husband was likely to be less destitute than the widow who had married only once.

5:11, 12

Reject younger widows, for when they behave wantonly before Christ, they want to get married, condemned because they set aside their first faith.

It is not a Christian grace to poke one's nose into other people's business.

Those exegetes who think that the enrolled widows were salaried deacons assume (1) that these widows promised not to marry again; and (2) that younger widows were likely to break their initiating vow. We have seen, however, that the text assigns neither duties nor salaries to these women. It is plausible, since the church was short of funds, that younger widows, who could more easily find a second husband, should not burden the list. Yet this explanation does not fit the phrases "behave wantonly," "condemned," and "set aside their first faith." These strong phrases cause the difficulty. Since the very next verse recommends that young widows should marry again, these words that seem so strong to us must be softened somehow. We may suppose, without assuming an order of female deacons, that elderly widows would consent not to marry again. Perhaps they made an explicit promise, perhaps it was only implied. Younger widows were likely to break this promise. Breaking a promise is a cause for condemnation. The phrase "first faith" or "earlier agreement" could refer to this implied condition. Breaking such a faith or promise could be called "behaving wantonly before Christ," even though the modern connotation seems too strong. It is simply these connotations, and not the actual circumstances, that make interpretation difficult.

5:13

At the same time also they learn to be idle, going around [from house to] houses, and not only idle but also gossips and busybodies, saying things they should not.

Paul continues his unflattering opinion of young widows. They neglect their housework, and possibly their children if they have any youngsters. But what is worse, in their idleness they visit around and gossip. It is not a Christian grace to poke one's nose into other people's business. Balzac wrote a novel in which the inquisitiveness of one person led to the death of thirteen others. Of course Balzac exaggerates to produce fiction, but less dramatic tragedies are painful enough. It is nice to think of a congregation as one big happy family. But it is not a family, and one should not intrude on another. Married women with children have less time for meddling; and Paul has a good remedy for widows on the loose: Get married!

5:14, 15

Accordingly, I want young [widows] to marry, to bear children, to keep house, to give no occasion to the enemy for reviling; for already some have turned back after Satan.

These two verses must control the interpretation of 5:11, 12 with their seemingly harsh phrases. Paul is not opposed to marriage. Calvin, with his knowledge of the French court (and presumably of Henry VIII also) and their imitators among the lower classes, speaks very plainly. He opposes licentiousness and he also opposes the often hypocritical and surely unbiblical Romish exaltation of celibacy.

It is nice to think of a congregation as one big happy family. But it is not a family, and one should not intrude on another.

The late twentieth century exhibits an unrestrained licentiousness and a deluge of pornography, while at the same time the Roman pope reinforces the celibacy of the nuns and clergy.

After quoting the phrase, "I desire therefore that the younger widows marry," Calvin begins: "The supercilious laugh at this instruction of Paul's. 'As if,' they say, 'there were any need to encourage any further a desire that is already too strong: for who does not know that nearly all widows have a spontaneous desire to marry.' Fanatics would estimate this teaching about marriage as quite unbecoming for an apostle of Christ. But when all is considered, men of sound judgment will agree that what Paul teaches is completely salutary and necessary. On the one hand, widowhood provides many with a greater opportunity for licentiousness and, on the other, there are always coming forward hypocritical deceivers who think that sanctification consists of celibacy, as if it were angelical perfection, and who either totally condemn marriage or pour scorn upon it as if it savored of pollution of the flesh."

It is wryly interesting to note that the late twentieth century exhibits an unrestrained licentiousness and a deluge of pornography, while at the same time the Roman pope reinforces the celibacy of the nuns and clergy. How contemporary Paul is!

Young widows can easily provoke slander against the church, and they may do so unwittingly. How much more those who deliberately turn back after Satan. The "enemy" in the previous phrase is less probably Satan than it is a secularist or pagan who hates Christianity. Or, perhaps, Paul may not distinguish between the two.

5:16

If any faithful [woman] has widows, let her help them, and let not the church be burdened, so that it may help real widows.

The first part of this verse sounds strange. What can it mean to speak about a woman who has widows? Meyer answers that in any home, if a widow is to receive care, the wife, her daughter, is the one to do the caring. There are indeed many manuscripts that read, "if any man or woman has widows." Even so, the husband does not need to be mentioned, since the wife does the caring. Still it is strange that a married couple should "have widows." Erasmus wanted it to say, "if any mother has a widowed daughter." This makes perfectly good sense in itself, but the text gives it no support. Another interpreter suggests that a wealthy wife may have received a widow or two into her home. In fact my mother, far from wealthy, cared for a widow, and at another time a maiden lady, while they waited for admission to a Home for the Aged.

The main thought of the verse, however, is perfectly clear. The church itself is far from wealthy, and its funds must be conserved to support widows who have nowhere else to turn.

At the present time, not only in Communist nations, but also in the U.S.A., the governments harass the activities of the church. As a Director of a Home for the Aged I know some of the absurd restrictions. Attending board meetings, my wife and I were assigned a small room. It was very nicely furnished, and perfectly comfortable for a night or two. Of course, it was too small for two healthy adults, if they had to live in it. But the state prohibited its use for even one person confined to bed because it was a foot too narrow. Yet the private bathroom had a door wide enough for a wheel chair and the ample shower space had handles on the walls that a paralytic could hold on to. This Home was built and is supported by the gifts from three, or at least two, denominations. The project was initiated chiefly for widows in those denominations. Yet the state tries to force us to take anti-Christian "guests" and frowns upon our religious activities. I believe the state would be happy to confiscate the entire establishment.

At the present time, not only in Communist nations, but also in the U.S.A., the governments harass the activities of the church.

Christianity is not egalitarian. A man is not paid on the basis of the time he works, but on the quality of the result.

5:17, 18

The elders who rule well are worthy of double pay, especially those who labor in word and teaching; for the Scripture says, "You shall not muzzle the ox while he is threshing," and "The workman is entitled to his wages."

Paul now reverts to elders. Some suggest that here he contrasts *elder* with *widow,* and hence means any elderly man. This is clearly not the case. Paul speaks of men who rule. Hence the persons envisaged are officials of the church. This becomes even clearer in a moment when their activity is described.

Now, among any body of officials some operate more efficiently than others. They all receive their pay; but the more efficient workers should receive double pay. The idea that good elders should receive double the amount given to widows is jejune. The paragraph on widows is finished. Paul now discusses elders.

One may note that Christianity is not egalitarian. A man is not paid on the basis of the time he works, but on the quality of the result. The Levelers in England were wrong; and the Communists are worse wrong. Christianity does not advocate a classless society or the equalization of wealth. Paul does insist, however, that elders be paid. A rejection of socialism does not justify keeping ministers at a starvation level.

In addition to the distinction between elders who do their work well and those who do not do so well, there is the further distinction between those who rule and those who labor in word and teaching. This probably does not, at least it need not, refer solely to preaching the Word. Good preaching requires previous study. A minister ought to spend at least three hours a day studying. Ideally this should be in addition to his sermon preparation. A young minister might require more time on his sermons. But if he constantly studies, he will amass a great amount of material, with the result that sermon preparation requires less time. At least it should require less time finding the material; there still remains the very important task of arranging it logically. As a college professor, I think I shocked some younger colleagues by remarking that any professor who has to prepare for his classes is incompetent. I remember all too well my early inadequacies when I had to prepare for every lecture. But now I could give a five-hour lecture on Plato, Descartes, or Kant right off. Of course, sermons cannot be repeated year after year; though their ideas must be repeated, repeated, and repeated.

Good preaching requires previous study. A minister ought to spend at least three hours a day studying.

Paul enforces his insistence that the elders must be paid by citing *Deuteronomy* 25:4. If an animal earns his food, how much more a teacher of the Word! Paul used the same quotation in *1 Corinthians* 9:9. The second quotation comes, with the change of *food* to *pay,* and the omission of *for*, from *Matthew* 10:10. *Luke* 10:7 has the word *pay,* as Paul has, but also *for*, as in *Matthew* and not in *1 Timothy*. By coupling the words of Matthew and Luke with those of Moses, Paul evidently recognizes the Gospels as Scripture. Note that the liberals no longer dare to date *Luke* in the 80's, and so deny that Paul could have quoted him. With the present early dating of all the Gospels, even John, we can have Paul quoting these two.

By coupling the words of Matthew and Luke with those of Moses, Paul evidently recognizes the Gospels as Scripture.

5:19

Do not receive an accusation against an elder unless on [the word of] two or three witnesses.

Here again Paul makes use of *Deuteronomy* (17:6). The principle is restated in *Matthew* 18:16. This principle applies to all men, but Paul emphasizes it in the case of elders because they are especial targets of malicious enemies. Calvin says, "None are more exposed to slanders and insults than godly teachers." Even the honest heathen have to admit the wisdom of this procedure, and Calvin repeats Plato to the effect that the multitudes are malicious and envy those above them. Of course, some elders sin grievously. Witness last century's case of the husband of Hanna Smith, author of the theologically unsound piety in *The Christian's Secret of a Happy Life.* It was handled discreetly in a very Christian way, and Mr. Smith, so I believe, never appeared in Christian conferences again.

Yet one may note that Paul does not say, Condemn him on the word of two or three witnesses. He says, Receive the accusations, initiate the trial. Then the witnesses must be cross-examined, as Matthew implies, so that "every word may be confirmed." This again comes from *Deuteronomy* (19:15).

5:20

Publicly rebuke those who [continue in] sin, in order that the others may be afraid.

While an elder should receive the benefit of any doubt, and not be condemned until the testimony of two or three witnesses has been confirmed, yet once established that he has sinned, Timothy must rebuke him publicly. The present participle *(amartanontas)* most probably means "continue to sin," rather than "has sinned" just once, which sense ought to be aorist. Some sins are indeed single acts; but others are repeated and constant. Calvin notes, as was remarked just above, that guilty elders must be rebuked. They must be publicly condemned. This principle needed emphasis in Calvin's time. He writes,

Guilty elders must be rebuked. They must be publicly condemned.

> And certainly we can see with how many different privileges the Papacy protects its clergy, so that even if they live the most scandalous lives, they are yet immune from every accusation.

We can see with how many different privileges the Papacy protects its clergy, so that even if they live the most scandalous lives, they are yet immune from every accusation.

To condemn a bishop, Calvin notes, required seventy-two witnesses, none of whom could be a layman or even an ecclesiastic of inferior rank.

The purpose of publicly announcing the guilt of an elder, or at least one purpose, is that others may fear like exposure if they sin. The "others" are, in the first place, other elders; but if the communicant members see an elder so punished, they will understand that they too may be subjected to the same procedure.

5:21

I adjure you before God and Christ Jesus and the elect angels, that you guard these things without prejudice, doing nothing by inclination (by partiality).

This solemn charge refers directly, I believe, to the accusations against and trials of elders. Paul says that this is extremely important. No knowledge of Greek will help anyone decide whether "these things" also refer to verses 17 and 18. Ministers are worthy of remuneration, but this adjuration seems too solemn for that purpose.

The adjuration includes the elect angels. The angels are mentioned probably because angels surround the throne of God. This does not warrant an implication of the final judgment. It is an oath, similar to that placed upon Christ by Pontius Pilate. Hendriksen and Bengel disagree; but I favor Meyer.

Note that these angels are elect angels. Not only does this distinguish them from the fallen angels, it indicates that they maintained their righteous state because God had chosen them. Election is a doctrine that applies to angels as well as to human beings.

The specification of impartiality needs no explanation. One may, however, consider how difficult it is to remain impartial, unless one is a legally trained judge. Others need this admonition.

5:22

Do not lay hands on any one hastily, nor share in other men's sins. Keep yourself pure.

Election is a doctrine that applies to angels as well as to human beings.

Directions for the administration of the church continue. The verse deals with the matter of ordination. Some interpreters suggest a laying on of hands that grants communicant members forgiveness of sins. Nothing in the context supports such an idea; nor is there good evidence that such a rite was practiced in New Testament times.

As for sharing in the sins of other people, there have also been differences of opinion. Those who hold that absolution rather than ordination is in view think that the absolving priest shares in the sins of the ostensibly penitent person, if he acts too hastily and makes no effort to distinguish true penitence from false. Of course, liberal commentators who, like Conzelmann, consider the epistle to be a forgery, can take this view, and on their basis it is a reasonable explanation. But no one who accepts the Pauline authorship and no one who confines himself to New Testament teaching, can take that view.

The next suggestion relative to sharing the sins of other people is that those who hastily ordain someone who later is discovered to be unworthy, shares in the sins of the unworthy elder. This is Hendriksen's position: "ordination without preceding thorough investigation would render Timothy coresponsible for the wrongs which such elders might subsequently commit"(185). Guthrie seems to agree, though his wording is a little vague. In fact he agrees that since an absolving presbyter can hardly be held responsible for the sins of so many penitents, the verse must refer to ordination. Ordinations are less numerous than absolutions, and hence the ordainer is more responsible. Meyer also agrees. Of course, "ordination without preceding thorough investigation" is bad. It may justly be condemned. Yet Calvin has an alternate explanation, which on the whole seems preferable:

> There are those who out of a desire for novelty [or because of nepotism] would seek to ordain some person who is hardly known at all, just because he has given one or two not unsatisfactory performances. . . . The bishop who assents to an illicit act of ordination brings on himself the same guilt as its impetuous instigators. . . . It often happens that even when our

own judgment is sound, we allow ourselves to be carried away by the folly and stupidity of others.

5:23

Don't drink water any longer, but use a little wine for your stomach and your frequent weaknesses.

Possibly there is a sharp break between the preceding verse and this one. We have no reason to assume that Paul could not change the subject abruptly. One who wishes to minimize the break might say that Paul intended to guard against a misinterpretation of the previous instruction: "Keep yourself pure." This instruction could be taken to favor asceticism; and as Timothy seems to have been somewhat inclined in that direction, Paul wishes to correct that misapprehension.

It often happens that even when our own judgment is sound, we allow ourselves to be carried away by the folly and stupidity of others.

It is certainly clear that Timothy was not in good health. And no doubt the water in Ephesus then was as bad as the water in Mexico today. Commentators agree more completely on the meaning of this verse than on many others. Here are a few disconnected phrases from Calvin:

> Timothy should form the habit of drinking a little wine for his health's sake. He does not forbid him to use water at all. . . . Why does he not simply advise him to drink wine? He seems by speaking of "a little" wine to be guarding against intemperance and [more particularly] to obviate the slanders of wicked men. . . . It is clear that Timothy was so frugal and austere in his way of life that he did not even take proper care of his health. . . . How few there are today who need to be forbidden water. . . . We should be temperate in eating and drinking, every one of us should take care of his health . . . excessive abstinence is blameworthy when it brings on or promotes disease.

There is little possibility in the U.S.A. today that water will promote disease. But if pollution goes too far we may have to drink a little wine for our stomach's sake. Since I don't like the taste at all, I shall choose fruit juices.

5:24, 25

The sins of some men are quite plain, preceding them to judgment; in other cases they also follow. Likewise also good works are evident, and those that are otherwise cannot be hid.

Though the wording of these two verses is completely general, one must suppose a particular reference to the process of ordination. Some men are so obviously unfit, publicly scandalous, that their sins are known before any investigation begins. Others have hidden sins that can be brought to light only after they have come before the court, presbytery, or session. The judgment is not God's future judgment: It is the church's present decision. God's future judgment is of no help in electing elders now.

The sins of some men are quite plain, preceding them to judgment; in other cases they also follow. Likewise also good works are evident, and those that are otherwise cannot be hid.

There is one peculiar word in this verse: "also." "In some cases they also follow." This sounds as if some men's sins both precede and follow their examination before the church court. While this is no doubt the factual truth, for even a publicly scandalous man has some sins other people do not know about, this truth does not fit the context. In particular it destroys the parallelism with the next verse.

Verse 25 states that in this respect good works are similar to sins. In some cases they are evident and well known. "Those that are otherwise"—not otherwise than good, but otherwise than evident and well known—will eventually come to light.

Although the parallelism of verse 25 determines the sense of the preceding, a person who knows some Greek will want a better explanation of the *kai.* This conjunction has numerous uses. One is its use to indicate something unusual, or if not unusual, at least something to be noted. Hence, a paraphrase might be: In other cases their sins indeed follow them; or, in other cases their sins of course follow them. The idea is that after Paul notes the more extreme and unusual case, he prevents us from overlooking what is the usual situation. This makes good sense because he is advocating caution.

Chapter Six

6:1

Let those who are slaves under a yoke consider their own masters as worthy of all honor in order that the name of God and his doctrine be not blasphemed.

Studying commentaries is interesting. With respect to the word "own" *(idios),* one says it should be understood in a weak sense, hardly necessary at all; but another says it is emphatic because it stresses the personal relation. Since slaves could hardly be expected to show honor to other masters than their own, the emphatic sense seems a little awkward. Another difference is that one takes these slaves to be elders in the church, while another applies it to the communicant members as well. Interesting differences of opinion! Did I say interesting? I meant insignificant.

If the slave increased his efficiency, reliability, and faithfulness, his owner would soon be better disposed toward the strange religion.

Many commentaries insert a paragraph here on the condition of slaves in the Roman Empire. They had few or even no rights. Galley slaves died from exhaustion, or, chained to their benches, drowned in battle collisions. There were also talented teachers whose masters treated them well and with respect. Epictetus was one. Remember that Aristotle defended slavery: Greeks were naturally free; barbarians were naturally slaves. Three hundred years later, Roman citizens were free, and if a Greek was not a Roman citizen, he was just out of luck. But enough of sociological data. Many Christians were slaves, and this became a church problem. The heathen master, even if not a brute, would not be predisposed to favor a new religion. He would, rather, be suspicious of a Christian slave. To counter this very natural response, to protect as much as possible the slaves' safety, and above all to inspire a good opinion of God's name and the strange new theology, Paul instructs his converts to honor their masters. This was eminently good advice. If the slave increased his efficiency, reliability, and faithfulness, his owner would soon be better disposed toward the strange religion. It would not be necessary, indeed it would be counterproductive, for a Roman Sparta to massacre its revolting helots. This policy worked well with many private owners. Even Caesar's household had Christian slaves; perhaps some Roman nobles became Christians. But the policy did not work with the emperors themselves: despicable Nero, Marcus Aurelius (161-180), a philosopher-emperor of whom better things might have been expected, and cruel Diocletian (284-305), the last and probably the worst of all, who wanted to be worshipped as a god.

What the speed reader is apt to miss in this verse is the repetition of the importance of doctrine. Doctrine and the name of God, that is, God himself and his truth, must not be blasphemed. Today liberals, humanists, behaviorists, and the neo-orthodox attack doctrine; but what is worse, those who think of themselves as devout evangelicals, strongly insisting on the inerrancy of Scripture, ignore doctrine. They favor pastoral counseling, they prate about four spiritual laws, sing gospel dance tunes, testify to their happiness, even read some of the Bible, but they read it without trying to understand it. If they tried, would they be satisfied with churches whose creed, whose belief, was expressed in five short articles? Nor is the major blame to be placed on the congregation, most of whom know no Greek; the major blame lies on ministers who know no Greek and not much theology. They do not speak evil of God's word: They simply do not speak of it. A friend of mine, who did his best to preach the whole counsel of God, had a conversation with a very popular preacher and author. Said the popular idol to my friend, I believe the same doctrines you do. Said my friend, I am delighted, I wouldn't have known it, if you hadn't told me. Now, back to the Roman slaves.

Doctrine and the name of God, that is, God himself and his truth, must not be blasphemed.

Those who think of themselves as devout evangelicals, strongly insisting on the inerrancy of Scripture, ignore doctrine. They favor pastoral counseling, they prate about four spiritual laws, sing gospel dance tunes, testify to their happiness.

The major blame lies on ministers who know no Greek and not much theology.

6:2

Those who have believing masters should not despise them because they are brethren; but rather let them serve [well] because those who profit by the service are believers and beloved. Teach and preach these things.

The English translation is ambiguous. The word *because,* when it follows a negative verb, can express two different thoughts. One is paraphrased thus: Don't despise Christian masters because they are brethren; despise them for some other reason. One might say today, Don't buy stock in that company because I advise you to: Read the financial report and make your own decision. This is not what the verse means. It means, Don't despise a Christian master for any reason; remember he is a Christian. Note the progress of Paul's admonition. First, he speaks of pagan masters. Not only were most masters pagan, but Paul adds the descriptive phrase "under a yoke." By and large pagan masters were hard, if not always cruel. Naturally slaves resented them. Paul gives them good advice. But now some masters are believers. Paul omits the phrase "under a yoke." A Christian master might be strict, he might be thoughtless, but he would not be cruel, and some would be beneficent. Nevertheless the Christian slave would likely argue: If my master is really a believer, he would free me—why should I be a slave at all? Hence, the sense of the ambiguous translation is, Don't despise Christian masters. The reason is that they are believers, they are beloved—God loves them—and therefore the profit of slavery in this case goes to a Christian.

I think this is the correct interpretation of the verse; but several commentators think otherwise. Guthrie mentions both interpretations, but does not decide between them. Meyer gives the paraphrase: "Serve your masters all the more, that they, devoting themselves to kindness toward you, are believers and beloved of God." Hendriksen agrees and stresses the prefix *anti,* with the result that the masters *reciprocate, give back* again to the slave an equal profit, if not in money, at least in kindness. The translation would be: Those who have believing masters are not to despise them just because they are Christian, but rather serve them, because they (the slaves!) who receive back the profit (from their masters) are believers and beloved of God. The major public versions (*King James, New American Standard, Revised Standard Version, New English Bible, and the New International Version*) allow themselves a slight ambiguity or show clearly that they reject this latter interpretation.

The heterodox and heretical, in order to destroy the Gospel, clothe themselves in a perverse misinterpretation of love.

The verse ends with Paul's instruction to Timothy to "Teach and preach these things." But since the versification is neither apostolic nor logical, this last phrase may refer to what comes next.

6:3, 4, 5

If anyone teaches otherwise and does not agree with healthy reasonings, those of our Lord Jesus Christ, and with the teaching that is according to piety, he is conceited, knowing nothing, but is sick with searchings and semantic disputes, from which arise envy, strife, blasphemy, evil conjectures, irritations of men who have corrupted their minds and who have been robbed of the truth, who think that piety is a means of gain.

As suggested above, it is rather silly to suppose that the last sentence in verse 2, followed by these three verses, refers only to slavery. This exhortation, indeed this divine commandment, applies to all Paul's instructions. The verses contain strong language: conceited, ignorant, sick, semantic disputes. Do we hear such language in our pulpits today? We do not. Is this because all teachers in the visible churches are obedient to Paul's injunctions? The reason is, I believe, that the heterodox and heretical, in order to destroy the Gospel, clothe themselves in a perverse misinterpretation of love. Paul spoke a great deal about love—not only in *1 Corinthians* 13, but here and there throughout his epistles. What the liberals and even many conservatives fail to realize is that love requires the protection of the sheep from the wolves and the unmasking of conceited, ignorant, blasphemous false teachers.

One may note the contrast between healthy reasonings and sick, corrupted minds, though there are so many terms in these lines that very likely this was not an intended literary contrast. More likely an intended contrast is that between *healthy reasonings* and *semantic disputes (logomachias).* Anyone who thinks that Paul disparaged reasoning lacks all appreciation of the epistles. Is not Romans full of reasoning? And here Paul appeals to the words, sermons, arguments of "our Lord Jesus Christ" himself. Did not Christ argue at length with the Pharisees? He accused them, not only of hypocrisy, but also of not understanding the Old Testament.

Love requires the protection of the sheep from the wolves and the unmasking of conceited, ignorant, blasphemous false teachers.

Anyone who thinks that Paul disparaged reasoning lacks all appreciation of the epistles.

We cannot control circumstances, but we can control our reaction to them.

Paul probably did not have the Pharisees chiefly in mind. By the time he wrote this letter there were many Gentiles in the church. But since we know little in detail about them, the Pharisees remain a good example of what Paul is denouncing. They were indeed conceited, ignorant of the truth though well informed on rabbinical minutiae. Their conjectures, particularly about Jesus, were evil; and emphatically their minds had been robbed of the truth. The phrase "who have corrupted their minds" leads on to being "robbed of the truth"; but the participle itself, *diephiarmenōn,* bears the literal sense of deterioration, or the decay of the body after death. As used metaphorically here, it means these men have rendered themselves incapable of logical thinking. Then, too, they thought that their fallacious piety was a means of gain, if not monetary gain, gain in public repute.

Overarching all is the concept of truth, not the everchanging "truth" of relativism, not the logical-positivist "truth" of sensory verification, not even the absolute "truth" of Hegelianism, but the absolute, unchanging truth of Biblical revelation. This is why Scripture should be studied; and if commentaries help, praise be to God.

6:6

Piety, with self-sufficiency, is [indeed] great gain.

As Calvin said, "In an elegant manner and with an ironical turn he quickly throws back at his opponents the same words with the opposite meaning." This gain which piety brings is not first of all our reward in Heaven. The gain comes in this life. It is described by a term from Stoic philosophy: *autarcheias,* self-sufficiency, in modern versions translated *contentment.* It means to be immune from earthly or external distractions. As the Stoics said, we cannot control circumstances, but we can control our reaction to them. In Philippians 4:11 Paul said, "for I have learned to be self-sufficient in all circumstances." Of course, this does not mean independence from God. *2 Corinthians* 3:5 says, "not that we are sufficient of ourselves . . . but our sufficiency is from God." It is true that here the word is *ikanotēs,* not *autarcheia;* but the meaning is the same.

6:7

For we have brought nothing into the world (and it is evident) that we cannot take anything out.

The parenthesis here indicates a textual difficulty. If *dēlon* is in the text, it will read "it is evident that." If *dēlon* is omitted, the verse will read ". . . nothing into this world because we cannot take anything out." The original *Aleph, A, G,* and some lesser manuscripts omit the *dēlon;* a third hand correction of *Aleph*, a third hand correction of *D*, a few other uncials and a long list of cursives have it. Metzger's *Textual Commentary* favors the omission on the ground that the inclusion makes better sense! Indeed, the omission makes no sense at all.

Metzger's Textual Commentary favors the omission on the ground that the inclusion makes better sense! Indeed, the omission makes no sense at all.

The main difficulty lies in connecting this verse with the preceding. How can "we have brought nothing into the world" be the reason for "piety with self-sufficiency is great gain"? Would not piety have been great gain even if we had brought something into the world? The truth of each statement is not to be contested, but their relationship is puzzling. Unfortunately, all the commentators I have read ignore the difficulty. Surely Hendriksen does not solve the problem, if indeed he has it in mind at all, when he says, "Earthly possessions do not pertain to the 'self,' which is clear from the fact that nothing did we bring into the world" (98). No doubt this is true: Money is not the self or soul. But this throws no light on the logical problem. Commentators are loathe to admit ignorance, but frankly I do not know how to connect the two propositions.

How can we avoid such absurd inferences? They are absurd, for Abraham and Job were extremely wealthy.

6:8

But having food and clothing, we shall be content with them.

The term *clothing* or *covering* includes *shelter* also. Whichever English word we use, it fails to include both explicitly.

The verse sounds as if all Christians are, or should be, content to live in abject poverty without any money to pay for fire insurance. Far from having a car and buying gasoline at $1.50 a gallon, they cannot even own a horse or a bicycle. Other New Testament verses can be interpreted to mean that if anyone has possessions he should sell them all and give to the poor—so that the poor will have more than just food and clothing and lose their self-sufficiency.

How can we avoid such absurd inferences? They are absurd, for Abraham and Job were extremely wealthy. Jesus told the rich young ruler to sell all he had; but he did not so tell Nicodemus, who must have been at least fairly well off. One attempt to avoid absurdity has been to take the future tense as imperative. This can sometimes be done in Greek and it would solve the present problem, for it would then mean, "if you find yourself impoverished, nevertheless be content." But usually, perhaps always, the future verb as an imperative occurs in the second person. Sometimes too a future can be used as a hortatory subjunctive. Both these attempts are measures of desperation. They strain the Greek too much.

Nevertheless, the actual meaning of the verse must be somewhat as indicated. In addition to the historical examples of Abraham and Job, there is also the injunction, as we have seen and as is clearly inconsistent with the absurd inferences, that parents should build up an estate for their children. Paul does indeed come down hard on avarice and greed, here and in the next three verses; but their wording opens a door of escape from the difficulty.

6:9

But those who wish to be rich fall into temptation and a snare and many irrational and harmful desires, which drown men in destruction and perdition.

The wish or desire to be rich is evil, rather than the wealth itself.

The first hint of the solution is in the words "wish to be rich." Hendriksen notes the "beautiful alliteration. The constantly recurring letter p strikes the eye . . . as if we were to say, 'Those who desire to be opulent precipitate themselves into evil promptings and perilous pitfalls and into numerous precarious passions.' " The Greek has nine p's, plus four b's. From this—the hint, not the alliteration—we may surmise that the wish or desire to be rich is evil, rather than the wealth itself. Many, possibly most, who inherit great wealth are not tempted to commit embezzlement. A man of moderate means may be. The butler of a Philadelphia magnate, who had risen from very moderate circumstances to great wealth, described him as willing to trample over his grandmother's body to make a gain. The last several presidents, and vice presidents, of the Teamsters Union are even better, or, should I say, worse examples. They have gone to their own place.

6:10

For the love of money is a root of all [sorts of] evils, and desiring this [money] some [church members] have wandered away from the faith and have pierced themselves with many griefs.

Here we get the full explanation of the otherwise strange language of verse 8 and the strong language of verse 9. What is condemned is a love of money. Greed is evil and it results in all sorts of evil. Most commentators note that "desiring this" or "which, desiring" verbally refers to the single word "love-of-money"; but logically it refers to money, since now the notion of *desiring* occurs as a separate word. Hence, some poor people and some wealthy people fall under Paul's condemnation; but other poor people and other wealthy people do not.

6:11

But you, O man of God, flee from these things. Pursue righteousness, piety, faith, love, perseverance, and meekness.

Here begins a general concluding exhortation, no doubt relating to all the contents of the preceding chapters, though in verse 17 closely tied in with the notion of money and greed. Since Timothy himself had no desire for unrighteousness, hatred, or pride, we must understand this to include Timothy's obedient application of this exhortation to the church members, and so on down to the present. Of the six Christian virtues listed here, only one is ambiguous. I agree with Meyer that *faith* is "not faithfulness or conscientiousness, but faith." This is consistent with the words in the previous verse, "wandered away from the faith."

6:12

Fight the good fight of the faith; grasp eternal life, to which you were called and confessed the good confession before many witnesses.

Meekness or gentleness does not preclude fighting the fight of the faith.

Such effectual calling is obvious in spectacular conversions, such as Paul's, but is just as real and necessary for those who learn the Gospel from their mothers and grandmothers.

Meekness or gentleness does not preclude fighting the fight of the faith. Paul has already condemned the false teachers. Meyer's American editor is quite mistaken when he says that "*pistis* does not here or indeed in any place in the Pastoral Epistles, as, also, it does not elsewhere in Paul's writings, mean the system of faith, the doctrine believed by Christians. It always refers to subjective faith" (200). How can anyone be so obtuse!

We note, but do not now emphasize, the fact that God called Timothy out of his state of original unrighteousness into his present state of grace. Such effectual calling is obvious in spectacular conversions, such as Paul's, but is just as real and necessary for those who learn the Gospel from their mothers and grandmothers.

Exegetes have given three possible interpretations of the "confession before many witnesses." One is his confession of faith when he was received as a communicant member. The "many witnesses" were, then, the congregation. This confession and this reception into membership may have occurred along with his baptism. The second possibility is his confession at his ordination. The many witnesses would then be the presbytery plus any who attended the service. But more likely is Calvin's opinion that Timothy's confession, like his fight, was his life-long ministry. This would fully justify the reference to "many witnesses." Calvin's view includes the other two; and while *confession* suggests *words,* and therefore *vows*, and therefore baptism or ordination, preaching is also verbal confession. It seems difficult to exclude Timothy's ministerial career and confine the meaning to either set of vows.

6:13, 14

I urge you, before the God who gives life to all things, and Christ Jesus who testified a good confession before Pontius Pilate, that you yourself keep the commandment stainless and irreproachable until the appearing of our Lord Jesus Christ

The critical editions bracket the first "you," because the following "yourself" makes it unnecessary. But a resumptive *yourself* is no impossibility.

The adjuration by the name of God and Christ Jesus shows how emphatic Paul wanted to be. Those today who pay little attention to the Scriptural directions on ecclesiastical matters should pause and consider. God is described by a verb that can mean either *give life* or *maintain life.* In *Luke* 17:33, and *Acts* 7:19 negatively, it means "maintain life." Although in this verse the word refers to physical life, the previous reference to eternal life might incline one to translate it "give life" rather than "maintain life." For that matter it could be understood as combining both meanings.

Paul may very well have meant, "You keep the commandment unblemished and unbroken."

Paul and the Gospels, too, teach a delayed return: an event quite later than the first century.

Timothy is to keep the commandment stainless. We are apt to say "stainlessly." What is logically attached to Timothy, the text stylistically attaches to the commandment. But this is not necessarily the case. Paul may very well have meant, "You keep the commandment unblemished and unbroken." The term *anepilēmton* ordinarily means *irreproachable* and refers to conduct; *aspilon* (stainless, unblemished) refers both to persons and to things or animals. There seems also to be one instance, from a Jewish source, of *anepilēmton* referring to a vow. Hence, the reader is free to decide which is more probable here. I incline to the personal interpretation, because (1) Timothy cannot preserve the commandment itself unbroken, since many people break it; and (2) it is Timothy, not the commandment, who keeps the return of Christ in mind.

That is to say, this preservation of oneself blameless and irreproachable is to continue until Christ returns. Whether this phraseology suggests an imminent or a delayed return can hardly be determined. There are New Testament passages that seem to predict an imminent return. Liberals conclude that Paul was first mistaken and then changed his teaching to a distant return. The explanation is otherwise. Paul and the Gospels, too, teach a delayed return: an event quite later than the first century. But the significance of the event psychologically cancels the literal time so as to seem quite near. This is not a New Testament invention. *Isaiah* 13:6 pictures the destruction of Babylon as vividly present, although chronologically it was three centuries future. In his second epistle, chapter 3, Peter meets the same objection of his contemporaries. The liberals simply do not understand eschatological language.

6:15

[the appearance] which the blessed and only Potentate, the King of kings and Lord of lords will display in his own times

Some commentators, relying on imagination rather than on evidence, suggest that Paul here quotes a hymn—as if Paul could not by his own intelligence praise God in these terms. We today might well quote Paul; it is fitting to address our prayers to God in these words.

Potentate is a better translation than *sovereign,* for *dunastēs* has *power* as its root meaning. The *New English Bible*'s translation is ridiculous: "God who in eternal felicity alone holds sway."

Once again Paul makes no attempt to say when Christ will return: God will display, make visible, or cause Christ to appear in his, God's, own times.

Modern European and American civilization since 1870 has not much been bothered by kings and potentates. The dynasties or powers lost power. Calvin in his day and with his education saw the emperor and the kings in the light of ancient times. He had studied Roman history in high school. Therefore, he can write naturally that "These titles of honor are used to exalt God's kingly power so that we may not be dazzled by the brilliancy of the princes of this world. . . . We see in Cicero's *Pro Flacco* what heights of insolence he reaches. . . ."

The New English Bible's translation is ridiculous.

But since World War II democracy—better, limited government—has been replaced by *Demokratische Republiken*, tyrants, and terrorists. They violate human rights, confiscate private property, engage in mass murder, and take ambassadors as hostages. We live in a frightful time. So then, like Calvin, we must fix in mind that God is the only Power, the Ruler of those who rule, and in his own times will bring upon them sudden destruction. In the meantime we may hope that liberal churchmen and violent agitators will fail to overthrow our tottering government. But our surer hope is in the return of our Lord.

6:16

who alone has immortality, dwelling in light unapproachable, whom no man has seen or can see: to him be honor and strength for ever, Amen.

Here are more phrases that we can and should use in prayer. I have sat in prayer meetings, particularly in two groups; items of petition were listed on a blackboard—every one of which was a legitimate matter for prayer—and a dozen or more persons prayed. But there were no ascriptions of praise. Since their procedure displeased me, I usually did not pray. In one meeting, out of a score of prayers, only one elderly lady asked God for forgiveness. In both groups no one used an ascription beyond "Our Father," or "O Lord." The prayers were 100 percent petitions—every one legitimate, but the prayers showed little appreciation of the Lord's glorious majesty. An ejaculatory prayer, made suddenly in time of danger, does not need to imitate Solomon's prayer of dedication; but from a combined group of fifty people over a period of two years one expects something less abrupt.

The phrase "who alone has immortality" does not deny that we shall live forever. Yet, strictly, we are not immortal—in two respects: (1) we do die, our souls may in a sense be immortal, but our body dies; then (2) our immortality depends on God's decision, grace, and power; we are not immortal in our own right, but only by God's providence. God alone is essentially and self-dependently immortal.

God alone is essentially and self-dependently immortal.

Yet it is wrong to make too great a contrast between righteousness and truth. Overt acts of righteousness are in accord with true moral propositions.

Before one commits an overt sin, he must sin intellectually first. It is his thinking that determines his action.

We cannot approach omniscience because omniscience is not the result of a learning process.

God dwells in light unapproachable. It is unfortunate that many commentators, of whom Hendriksen is one example, can write literarily devout paragraphs without in the least explaining the meaning. *Light* is a metaphor; Paul is not speaking about the sun. If we look at the sun, we are blinded. But Augustine quotes *Psalm* 36:9, "In thy light shall we see light." Of course this verse does not tell us exactly what *light* means. *Psalm* 43:3 says, "Send out thy light and thy truth, let them lead me." Anyone who wishes may object, but it seems to me that here *light* and *truth* are synonymous. The Old Testament mentions light with some frequency; in the New Testament the word occurs about seventy times. For example: *Matthew* 4:16, quoting *Isaiah*, says that those who sat in darkness saw a great light. What was this light and darkness? *Luke* 2:32 similarly speaks of a light to lighten the Gentiles. *John* 1:9 says Christ was the true light. Compare *John* 8:12, 9:5, and 12:46. Then there is *2 Corinthians* 4:4, "the light of the glorious Gospel of Christ," which is contrasted with the blinded minds of unbelievers. The reader himself may now look up the other sixty-five or so references, some of which signify plain, ordinary, literal light. But *light* as a metaphor evidently means truth. Granted, it also means righteousness. Yet it is wrong to make too great a contrast between righteousness and truth. Overt acts of righteousness are in accord with true moral propositions. Nor are overt acts the only form of righteous conduct. Thinking incorrectly is a sin too. Before one commits an overt sin, he must sin intellectually first. It is his thinking that determines his action.

God then dwells in unapproachable truth and righteousness. These two divine attributes are unapproachable. Are they? Do we not, as sincere Christians, die more and more unto sin, and live more and more unto righteousness? Isn't that approaching God? Did not Paul say, "Be imitators of me, as I am of Christ Jesus"? And if we modestly refrain from boasting, did not Paul approach, no more than approach, but nevertheless approach perfection?

These questions can be answered and the meaning of the verse clarified by taking a little thought. Let us also add the phrase, "whom no man has seen or can see." Calvin is certainly right when he says, "I take this to refer not only to our bodily eyes, but also to the mind's faculty of discernment." The light and the seeing are both metaphorical and are to be explained in a single manner.

First, it is true that by studying Scripture we come to know more and more of God's truth, and by his grace to practice his precepts more consistently. But this approaches neither God's omniscience nor his righteousness. Though we learn more and more, though we make progress in understanding God's truth—why otherwise would he have given us a revelation?—we cannot approach omniscience because omniscience is not the result of a learning process.

God never learned anything. His knowledge is an eternal knowledge. To be sure, we grasp or participate in God's mind to a degree. In his light we see light; we do not sit in total darkness. The truth that God justifies by means of faith is a proposition that both God and we know. If our minds and God's mind did not have some univocal content, we would know nothing at all. If he has all truth, we cannot know any truth except the truth God knows. But this does not mean we are twenty-five percent omniscient. The matter of righteousness is similar, but with a difference also. If we were once thieves, and have now repented and steal no longer, we have increased in righteousness. But neither the eighth commandment nor any other applies to God. God cannot steal for the simple reason that he owns everything. Obviously he cannot obey the fifth commandment. God is righteous in the sense that he determines the laws of righteousness; we are righteous in proportion to our obedience to those laws. But in the case of righteousness it is even clearer than in the case of knowledge that we do not approach God's perfections,

To whom be honor and strength forever.

If our minds and God's mind did not have some univocal content, we would know nothing at all. If he has all truth, we cannot know any truth except the truth God knows.

But neither the eighth commandment nor any other applies to God. God cannot steal for the simple reason that he owns everything.

God is righteous in the sense that he determines the laws of righteousness.

God supplies us with all things richly for our enjoyment.

6:17

To those who are rich in the present world give orders not to be haughty nor to hope on uncertain wealth, but on God who supplies us all things richly for enjoyment,

This certainly sounds like an anti-climax. The Holy Spirit indeed inspired the apostle's words; but it is clear that he made use of the authors' literary abilities or disabilities as they had been educated. God, for some reason, did not want all the New Testament written in the style of *Hebrews*.

The return to the subject of wealth may indicate that there were more wealthy Christians in the Ephesian church than in other churches. It was a wealthy city. More converts here than elsewhere needed these instructions.

The last phrase of the verse further alleviates the supposed harshness of the earlier language. God supplies us with all things richly for our enjoyment. Riches are uncertain. Many wealthy men became poverty stricken overnight in 1929. Virtually everybody became poverty stricken in Germany a few years earlier. But so long as God gives us wealth, he intends us to enjoy it.

Let us not think that all wealthy people are haughty and overbearing. For thirty years I knew a Jewish gentleman who probably was in the highest one percent of wealthy persons in the United States. He drove a Chevrolet; his clothes were not much better than mine; he attended to his professional duties faithfully; and he was snooty with no one. On the other hand a young millionaire I knew, who had inherited much less money than my Jewish friend owned, was snooty to nearly everybody.

Then there was Marie Antoinette, who said, Let them eat cake. I don't think she was snooty, at least in that statement. She simply did not realize the deep poverty of the French peasants. Her fault was not haughtiness but reprehensible ignorance.

People differ in an infinite variety of ways, but presumably wealthy people in general need to be reminded of the other ninety percent. And especially from a Christian perspective they should not put their trust in uncertain riches, but in God.

6:18, 19

to do good, to be rich in fine works, to be generous and to share, treasuring up for themselves a good foundation for the future, that they may grasp hold of real life.

Timothy was to guard the truth that had been entrusted to him.

Schleiermacher and Bultmann are not to be ignored. Their false religions have permeated American seminaries and because insufficiently contested have ruined Protestantism by and large.

These two verses hardly need any explanation at all. The most that can be mentioned is that all the New Testament recommends good works and obedience to the commandments, as here, but none of the New Testament makes good works the basis of effectual calling, regeneration, or entrance into the eternal glory.

6:20, 21

O Timothy, guard your trust, turning away from irreligious empty talk and counter-propositions of knowledge falsely so-called, which some, professing, have departed from the faith. Grace be with you.

If verses 17-19 seem anti-climactic, these two form a fitting conclusion. Paul returns to his main concern with truth. Timothy was to guard the truth that had been entrusted to him. It was a sacred trust to be preserved entire. He must turn away from sophistry and the counter-propositions of other religions. Liddell and Scott give "counter-proposition" as one meaning of *antithesis*. This is better than "oppositions of science," and, at present, *knowledge* is a better translation than *science*. The latter word has taken on a restricted meaning in modern times.

There are two mistakes to be avoided in understanding this verse. Hendriksen insists that Timothy "must not waste time on the inanities of these false teachers." Now it is possible that the empty talk of some false teachers is so inane that it is best to ignore them. And there may have been some such in Ephesus. But it is disastrous to ignore all false teaching. Peter insists on a vigorous apologetics. Schleiermacher and Bultmann are not to be ignored. Their false religions have permeated American seminaries and because insufficiently contested have ruined Protestantism by and large. They must be exposed.

There is a second, and, if possible, a worse mistake. Strange though it seems, for Paul explicitly says, "Knowledge falsely so-called," chapel speakers in Christian colleges, and some faculty members too, warn the students against knowledge in general. To know too much (as if any student could), to earn too high a grade point average, is denounced as unspiritual. Ignorance and intellectual confusion seem to be the criteria of sanctification.

This viewpoint is bolstered by a reference to *Colossians* 2:8, "Beware lest any man spoil you through philosophy." A better translation is, "Beware lest any man spoil you through his philosophy." The remainder of the verse connects this philosophy with "vain deceit after the traditions of men . . . and not after Christ."

But if anyone ignores this added description and prohibits all study of philosophy, he would also have to recommend ignorance and stupidity on the basis of *1 Timothy* 6:20. Such talk is in reality blasphemy—a depreciation of God; for God is a God of wisdom and knowledge (properly so-called); he is a God of order and not confusion. He has created us, distinct from the non-rational animals, as rational human beings, in his image. Those who think and profess otherwise have departed from the faith. Grace, the grace of the God of truth, be with you, my college students.

Ignorance and intellectual confusion seem to be the criteria of sanctification.

Such talk is in reality blasphemy—a depreciation of God; for God is a God of wisdom and knowledge.

Second Timothy

Chapter One

1:1, 2

Paul, an apostle of Christ Jesus by the will of God according to the promise of life which is in Christ Jesus, to Timothy, beloved son: Grace, mercy, and peace from God [the] Father and Christ Jesus our Lord.

When Paul says that he is an apostle by the will of God, he does not mean simply that God commanded him to preach the Gospel. Paul has in mind the eternal decree by which God in eternity predestinated him to this position. It is the *will* of God, not just a *precept.* Though the phrase "will of God" sometimes refers to a precept, it would preclude the common confusion if we agree to denote the eternal decree as God's *will*, and distinguish his commands as *precepts.* This accords with *Romans* 9:19: No one has ever resisted his will, but we all violate his precepts.

Though the phrase "will of God" sometimes refers to a precept, it would preclude the common confusion if we agree to denote the eternal decree as God's will, and distinguish his commands as precepts.

The phrase "according to the promise of life" occasions some discussion. What was according to what? Was the will of God according to the promise, or was Paul an apostle according to the promise? The former would be peculiar, since clearly it is the promise that is in accord with the will of God. But then it is also queer to say that Paul became an apostle according to the promise. The promise is the promise of life in Christ, not God's promise to someone that he would choose Paul as an apostle. Another interpretation stretches the Greek and makes it "Paul was an apostle by the will of God for the purpose of preaching God's promise of life through Jesus." The sense is good, but the Greek is not. The more usual sense of *kata* can be retained without saying Paul became an apostle according to some promise or other; but rather by saying that Paul's apostleship, which of course was by the will of God, was according to the promise of life, for this promise involved the appointment of apostles to preach it. Let us put it this way: "the promise of life is the fundamental thing in conformity with which all offices in the church and all commissions to preachers and messengers are given of God" (Meyer's American editor).

Conzelmann and Dibelius do not accept this epistle as genuine, though they think it is a better imitation of Paul than the first epistle. Says Conzelmann,

> This complex of ideas in 2 Tim. presents a problem. The advocate of authenticity will resolve it by reference to the historical situation of Paul. But then he must leave unresolved the even greater problem of such an early date for the Pastoral Epistles' concept of Christian citizenship. If the inauthenticity of the epistles is assumed, the situation of the readers must be reconstructed (98).

Paul, as a Roman citizen himself, could hardly have avoided thinking about "Christian citizenship."

Conzelmann's argument seems to be that during Paul's lifetime no one could have had the concept of Christian citizenship that these epistles describe. Therefore, the epistles must have been written in the second century. The reply to this argument is so easy that there is no need to appeal to divinely revealed information. Date these epistles as early as you wish, it does no honor to Paul's undisputed intelligence to suppose that he could not have foreseen persecution. He had already been persecuted, and in Ephesus, too. Paul, as a Roman citizen himself, could hardly have avoided thinking about "Christian citizenship." Conzelmann only demonstrates how ingenious a person must be if he wishes to deny Pauline authorship.

The two words "beloved son" refute the exaggerated notions of Timothy's timidity, vacillation, or estrangement from Paul. Timothy had been selected by prophecy, therefore by God, and he would prove as faithful as Paul himself. Alford very mistakenly says, "Certainly there is throughout this epistle an altered tone with regard to Timotheus—more of mere love, and less of confidence, than in the former." This may not be so bad as Conzelmann's supposition above, but love neither indicates lack of confidence, nor does confidence preclude encouragement.

1:3, 4

I thank God, whom I worship from my ancestors in a pure conscience, as I unceasingly remember you in my prayers night and day, longing to see you, remembering your tears, that I may be filled with joy,

In verse three I have translated the verb *latreuō* as *worship*. The verb also occurs in *Romans* 1:9. Several points of similarity invite comparison between these two passages. Both thank God, though the words for *thank* are not the same. Both use the same word for *unceasingly* or *unceasing*. *Romans* has *always*, and *2 Timothy* has *night and day*. In both Paul longs to see the persons or person addressed. Of course there are also differences between the two passages. A minor one, which most readers miss, is the word *ōs,* which in Romans means *how* and here means *as.* Both small and major differences are important, for if *2 Timothy* had been a forgery, the writer would have imitated Romans more closely. The similarities show the same mind at work; the differences show the freedom of that same mind.

However, to return to the translation of *latreuō* as *worship.* Admittedly *latreuō* regularly means *serve,* and even serve as a slave. Liddell and Scott note that in religious contexts it refers to celebrating the required rites. Since Paul mentions his ancestors, Jews of course, and therefore has in mind the temple *services,* the term *worship* preserves at least one aspect of what Paul has in mind. His forebears offered the required sacrifices and obeyed the Mosaic law.

Timothy had something Paul did not have: He had a Christian, an early Jewish-Christian, mother and grandmother. Timothy was a third-generation Christian.

However much Paul honored his own ancestors, he seems here to have an additional reason for mentioning them. Timothy too had similar ancestors, at least his mother and grandmother, about to be mentioned in verse 5. Though this draws attention to a similarity between Paul and Timothy, there is a difference also: Unlike Paul's ancestors, Lois and Eunice were Christians, Jewish Christians indeed, but Christians nonetheless. They served God through Jesus Christ.

Since there is no punctuation in the Greek text, a speed reader may come up with the remarkable statement, "remembering your tears in order that I may be happy." Tischendorf actually punctuates it so. But obviously "remembering your tears" is parenthetical, and the main clause is "longing to see you that I may be filled with joy."

Timothy's tears may have been those shed in Acts 20:37, or those of a later parting after Paul's first imprisonment in Rome. That men would cry, especially in public, seems not to have been unusual in those days. On some occasions the Jews hired professional mourners. Today it is in poor taste for men to cry. It is not in bad taste to be happy at a reunion.

1:5

being reminded of your unhypocritical faith, which at first dwelt in your grandmother Lois and your mother Eunice, and I am persuaded that also [it dwells] in you.

Whereas Paul pointed to his long ancestry of devout Jews—they also served God with a clear conscience—he compliments Timothy only as far as two generations. Two reasons sufficiently explain this. First, Timothy's father was an unbelieving Gentile. Timothy therefore did not have the covenant ancestry that Paul had. Then second, Timothy had something Paul did not have: He had a Christian, an early Jewish-Christian, mother and grandmother. Timothy was a third-generation Christian.

The words "being reminded" could be translated "having been reminded," the participle of the aorist. Because of this, several commentators suppose that a message or messengers had come from Timothy to Paul. Some of these commentators are adamant that Paul could not, or at least did not, remember spontaneously. The choice between a message having come and Paul's having a spontaneous recollection is rather insignificant; yet one would like to understand the construction of Paul's complicated sentence. The question is, What does "having remembered" attach to? Should we say, I give thanks to God . . . having remembered your sincere faith? This makes good sense, even though the participle comes four full lines after the antecedent. It also has the grammatical advantage of attaching the participle to the main verb. This does not mean, as one exegete objected, "I give thanks to God for my recollection." No, it means, My recollection stimulates me to thank God for your faith. This is a good interpretation. Another possibility is: Desiring to see you because I now remember your faith. This is neither grammatically nor logically impossible, but the sense is weaker. The poorest sense would be, Remembering your tears because I remember your faith. Nor is "filled with joy" a good antecedent. Paul is not filled with joy as he remembers Timothy's faith: He longs to see Timothy in order to be filled with joy. The first interpretation is so good that Meyer wishes to substitute the present participle, *lambanōn,* which he says Tischendorf adopted, for the aorist *labōn;* but my (seventh) edition of Tischendorf has *labōn.* In any case I do not see that the aorist prohibits the preferred interpretation.

The word rekindle need not be taken as evidence that Timothy was about to demit the ministry through timidity. It simply cannot mean that he had already done so.

None of this supports the idea of Timothy as timid and weak. The entire paragraph expresses, not only affection, but commendation. The decisive words are, "your unhypocritical faith [as in your mother and grandmother] . . . I am persuaded that also [it dwells] in you." This ends the complicated sentence that began with verse 3, or does it?

1:6

For which reason I remind you to rekindle the gift of God which is in you through the laying on of my hands,

It is an editor's choice to make "for which reason" continue the long sentence, or translate the three words as *Therefore* and make it a new sentence.

The word *rekindle* need not be taken as evidence that Timothy was about to demit the ministry through timidity. It simply cannot mean that he had already done so. The verb *rekindle* in its literal meaning denotes starting a fire where the previous fire had gone out. But this was not true of Timothy. We must take the verb in a weaker sense, remembering that all fires need additional fuel from time to time. One could paraphrase it: Keep your fires blazing up. What needed to be rekindled was a gift from God, a gift Timothy had received at his ordination.

High Anglicans use this verse to support the episcopal or papal theory of ordination, since only Paul's hands are mentioned. But we must remember that it was not Paul alone who ordained Timothy. It was the presbytery (*1 Timothy* 4:14). Once again we note that ordination is not a recognition of gifts previously received, but the bestowing of an additional gift not previously possessed. This gift or *charisma* is the authority to preach the Gospel. Too many sincerely evangelical pastors overreact against the Romish theory of ordination and view the laying on of hands as trivial. Then there are the charismatics, who are obsessed with the gift of tongues, and are willing to compromise with Romanists, if only they are charismatic. The only cure for these aberrations is a study and acceptance of the Biblical teaching. Though ordination is not a sacrament, it is nonetheless a holy ordinance. In one sense it is more sacramentarian than baptism, for the water of baptism is the sign and seal of an inward grace, but the gift of ordination is actually conferred by the act of presbytery. In neither case is the legitimacy of the act *ex opere operato;* for both the act of baptism and the act of ordination, that is, "going through the motions," can be performed by apostates on apostates. In a different connection this point will be further supported in verse 9.

To defend Timothy against exaggerations of his timidity is not to assert that Timothy never needed encouragement. Paul himself had times of depression.

1:7

for God did not give us a spirit of fear, but of power and love and prudence.

This verse gives a reason for the preceding. Timothy must stir up the gift because God did not give us a spirit of fear. Interpreters have discussed whether or not the *spirit* in this verse is the Holy Spirit or the characteristic of the human mind. The discussion also includes the word *us;* does it refer to all us Christians, or to us ministers? The context, with the ordination of Timothy and the encouragement given to him being the main ideas, rather requires "us ministers." That God does indeed give various endowments to laymen is irrelevant. Similarly, while the Holy Spirit can be called the Spirit of power—he is powerful—and the Spirit of love—he is loving—we hesitate to say that the Holy Spirit is prudent. Not that prudence says too much, but that it says too little. Hence it seems better to say that the Holy Spirit gives his ministers a disposition or spirit of strength, love, and prudence. Thus Paul encourages Timothy. To defend Timothy against exaggerations of his timidity is not to assert that Timothy never needed encouragement. Paul himself had times of depression. Even Luther had. Every minister needs encouragement.

1:8, 9

Do not be ashamed of the witness of our Lord nor of me his prisoner, but suffer evil with [me] in the Gospel according to the power of God, who saved us and called [us] in [or, with] a holy calling, not according to our works, but according to his own design and grace, which he gave us in Christ Jesus before eternal times,

The word *witness* or *testimony* is *marturion.* It had already acquired the connotation of opposition, suffering, and persecution. Not much later it would come to mean *martyr,* that is, one put to death for his faith. The death was usually degrading, and in contemplating the possibility one might not only be perturbed by the physical pain, but also might well feel ashamed, dishonored, and disgraced. Or, one step further away, one might feel ashamed to associate with anyone who was in danger of this humiliation. Remember the disciples all forsook Jesus and fled (*Mark* 14:50). Paul therefore encourages Timothy not to be ashamed of *him,* as well as to be unashamed of the Gospel. Paul takes the view previously expressed by Peter when "rejoicing that they had been considered worthy to suffer shame for his name" (*Acts* 5:41).

Not everyone is worthy to suffer so. God chose those who had certain qualities of perseverance. Hence Peter could rejoice that God had chosen him to suffer.

The idea of suffering needs little explanation. In this day too, our newspapers report the systematic torture of dissidents in Communist nations. But one must note more carefully what Paul says about the God for whom we suffer. The first phrase is, "suffer with respect to the Gospel according to the power of God. . . ." What is meant here by "according to the power of God"? Does it mean that God by his power sustains us through persecution? This is not the usual meaning of the Greek preposition. Yet this is the sense adopted by the *New English Bible*: "suffering . . . in the strength that comes from God." One commentator takes it to mean, not God's power to support us through, but his assured power to receive us into Heaven at the end of the persecution. He supports this view by attaching the words to the phrases which follow. The preposition *kata* can mean *in accordance with;* and in this sense it would mean that the power of God controls the persecution.

The idea that God controls the persecution, indeed decreed the persecution and actually predestinated certain persons, that is, chose which persons should be persecuted, ties in with Peter's rejoicing. Not everyone is worthy to suffer so. God chose those who had certain qualities of perseverance. Hence Peter could rejoice that God had chosen him to suffer. Paul does not himself use the same words, but he must have had the same thought when the sword was descending on his neck.

With reference to the verb *save* in the next phrase, Barrett takes occasion to attack the epistle as a forgery:

> Though in the Pastorals words of this group *(sōzein, sōter, sōteria)* are relatively more common than in the genuine Pauline letters, they are used with less precision. In Paul salvation refers almost exclusively to a final eschatological act (cp. in the Pastorals, 2 Tim. 4:18); in the Pastorals (e.g. Tit. 3:5) it not infrequently refers to a personal event in the life of the Christian (94).

Therefore, concludes Barrett, the pastorals cannot be genuine.

That there is present in Paul's "genuine" epistles an eschatological salvation is undeniable; but one doubts the absence of a present salvation. Even in *Romans* 5:9, where the salvation is definitely future, the next verse is not clearly so, especially with the addition of verse 11. *Romans* 8:24 speaks of a future hope, but the salvation is aorist: "we were saved." *Romans* 10:9, 10 speak of a future salvation, but only future to the time when an unbeliever came to believe; and this is enforced in verse thirteen and following. *Romans* 11:14 also refers to conversion. *1 Corinthians* 1:18 is clearly a present salvation. So too is *1 Corinthians* 1:21. Of course, present salvation has an eschatological conclusion; but these two verses clearly refer to a person's acceptance of Christ in the present. *1 Corinthians* 3:15 is definitely eschatological. We do not deny that Paul often used the word *sōzein* with a future reference. We simply reject Barrett's statement that "in Paul salvation refers *almost exclusively* to a final eschatological act." Compare *1 Corinthians* 7:16 (twice); 9:22, 10:33; *2 Corinthians* 2:15; and *Ephesians* 2:5, 8.

Not only do destructive critics make such mistakes; many sincere and devout worshipers are also confused. They often say that we are saved by faith alone. This of course is false. We are justified by faith alone; but we are regenerated without any previous faith or works; we are sanctified by faith, and the result is good works; and we shall be glorified by neither. A closer study of Scripture would help us avoid confusion relative to the several distinct phases of an all-inclusive salvation.

We are justified by faith alone; but we are regenerated without any previous faith or works; we are sanctified by faith, and the result is good works; and we shall be glorified by neither.

Whether one considers the future eschatological event or the present instances of regeneration, God's power is the cause. The faith that saves is a gift of God, the immediate result of his regenerating power. Guthrie, with whom I must sometimes disagree, has an excellent page here. To quote only one sentence: "The focus on the sovereign choice of God is unmistakable." For God has not only saved us; by his eternal purpose he also called us, and this necessarily by grace.

Paul introduces the idea of grace as a contrast with works: God has "called us with a holy calling not according to our works, but according to his design and grace." Nothing in us inclines God to call us. Nothing we do is the basis of God's choice and call. As the *Westminster Confession* (IX, iii) says, "man . . . is not able, by his own strength, to convert himself, or to prepare himself thereunto." The whole matter depends on God's design and grace. Since this grace was given to us, by God's own choice, before eternal times, it is clear that we did not determine it, but it determined us. Everything was prearranged before we were born.

Nothing in us inclines God to call us. Nothing we do is the basis of God's choice and call.

1:10

being now made evident by the appearing of our Savior Christ Jesus, who both made death ineffective and brought life and incorruptibility to light by the Gospel,

The Mosaic dispensation was a dispensation of grace.

The antecedent of the participle "being made evident" is grace. The idea of God's grace being now made evident, after having been hid, occurs in several Pauline passages, for example *Ephesians* 3:4, 5; *Colossians* 1:26; and *Romans* 16:25. The word *now*, in conjunction with *John* 1:17, "The law was given by Moses, but grace and truth came by Jesus Christ," has given some people the notion that the "legalism" of the Old Testament excluded grace. A minor and a major consideration remove this misinterpretation. First, the Mosaic sacrifices were a provision of God's grace, as well as anticipations and shadows of brighter things to come. Now that the brighter things have come—the incarnation, the cross, the resurrection—some devout Christians in this age almost or even entirely forget that the Mosaic dispensation was a dispensation of grace. But, second, this verse has nothing to do with a contrast between Moses and Christ. The word *now* in verse 10 contrasts, not with Moses, but with the plan of God as it was hidden in eternity past. What was then hidden became evident in the visible appearance of Christ incarnate.

The word *epiphaneias* designates Christ's first coming. It does not refer to Christ's second coming, as Barrett and others maintain in their desire to prove that the epistle is spurious. Their argument is that *epiphaneia* and *sōter* are gnostic terms, and that therefore Christian thought is dependent on foreign religions. Barrett simply says, "It is to be noted that most of the language of vv.9 ff. belongs to contemporary Hellenistic vocabulary, which knew the formal and majestic *appearance* of divine kings who bore the title of Savior." Of course! Contemporary Hellenistic vocabulary could be used to express gnostic ideas, hermetic ideas, neo-Pythagorean ideas, and any other ideas that anyone had. English vocabulary serves Christianity, Hegelianism, logical positivism, Zen, Islam, and any philosophy or religion anyone wishes to advocate. Even Conzelmann, who surely is not biassed in favor of Christianity, is not so unrestrained; and he concludes his eight columns on the term *Savior* with this sentence: "Christians who later called Jesus 'Savior,' such as Ignatius, simply wanted to attest to his divinity" (103).

The next phrase is, "who made death ineffective." The translation "abolished death" can be misunderstood, if not by Christian readers, at least by inimical critics. Obviously death has not been abolished: People still die. Yet the context indicates that physical death is intended, not eternal death. The verb *katargeō* means: make ineffective, exhaust, invalidate, abolish, and set aside. *Make ineffective* is about the most basic meaning one can choose. The idea here is that previously given in *1 Corinthians* 15:55-57: "O death where is thy sting? The sting of death is sin . . . but thanks be to God who gives the victory through Jesus Christ our Lord." The power of death was broken, nullified, made ineffective by Christ's resurrection. Meyer very appropriately notes that the phrase is not written "with subjective reference to the power of death over the mind, or the fear of death; the discussion here is not of subjective states, but of objective power."

The converse is that Christ brought life and incorruptibility to light. In this verse Paul has in mind both physical and spiritual death. The life intended is spiritual life, as the next reference to the Gospel indicates. *Incorruptibility* looks back upon the corruptible carcass and forward to a glorified body. One should recall the powers of Christ's resurrection body, powers so incredible to non-Christians. His body, though recognizable at times, was at other times unrecognizable; he entered a room through a locked door; seemingly he traveled from Jerusalem to Galilee instantaneously; at any rate he stood visible before the disciples one moment and the next had vanished. These phenomena transcend the limits of a corruptible body. But those astounding changes do not exhaust the differences between Earth and Heaven. The more important changes are spiritual. The new life is more wonderful than bodily resurrection. When Paul concludes the verse with the words "by the Gospel," he includes all he has said both in this and in all his epistles. The Gospel brings all these things to light; and it is this Gospel

His body, though recognizable at times, was at other times unrecognizable; he entered a room through a locked door; seemingly he traveled from Jerusalem to Galilee instantaneously.

1:11

to which I myself was appointed herald, apostle, and teacher of the Gentiles.

From one point of view this verse needs no exegesis, no explanation. Of course Paul was an apostle. But from another viewpoint, a contemporary viewpoint, it very much needs a present application. Among fundamentalists the word *Gospel,* and among liberals the word *kerygma,* are used in a very restricted sense, usually left indeterminate. But Paul declared himself innocent of the blood of all men on the ground that he had preached the whole counsel of God. Liberals at one extreme have none of God's counsel left; inconsistent liberals have only fragments vaguely expressed; at the other extreme fundamentalists, at least those between the two World Wars, insisted on some extremely important and altogether indispensable parts of the Gospel, but they were far from preaching all the good news. In this last quarter of the twentieth century, the earlier fundamentalist movement seems to have disappeared. But their descendants, who claim to be evangelical, do not show much improvement. And the charismatic movement, apparently eclipsing fundamentalism, is decidedly worse. Paul preached the Gospel, all of it; and we should do likewise.

The critical text omits "of the Gentiles" *(ethnōn).* Metzger explains,

> Although the overwhelming mass of witnesses [all except six] read *ethnōn,* the Committee regarded the word as a gloss introduced by copyists from the parallel passage in I Timothy 2:7, there being no good reason for its omission if it were original here.

The fact that copyists often have no good reason for making mistakes does not deter the critics from evaluating their own subjective guesses above the overwhelming mass of witnesses.

1:12

For which cause I also suffer these things, but I am not ashamed, for I know whom I have believed, and I am persuaded that he is able to guard my deposit to that day.

The verse, which many Christians memorize and quote with great enthusiasm and less understanding, is a very difficult verse. Of course, no one finds difficulty in understanding that Paul suffered hardship and persecution. The first and lesser difficulty is in the words "whom I believe." It should not be translated "in whom I believe," though this would indeed be true. A worse translation is "whom I have trusted." One is not surprised that the incompetent *Good News for Modern Man* mistranslates it, but it is disturbing that Alford and Weymouth do so. Probably the hidden assumption behind the mistake is the theory that there is a difference between a man himself and what he thinks. If this were so, we could trust a man without believing what he says. Or possibly there is some other disjunction between trusting and believing. Arndt and Gingrich give many references to sentences in which the verb governs a dative relative, pronoun, or noun, where the translation must be *believe*. Those who deprecate doctrine do not honor God by trusting him while not believing what he says.

The fact that copyists often have no good reason for making mistakes does not deter the critics from evaluating their own subjective guesses above the overwhelming mass of witnesses.

Probably the hidden assumption behind the mistake is the theory that there is a difference between a man himself and what he thinks. If this were so, we could trust a man without believing what he says.

The second and greater difficulty in this verse centers on the words "my deposit." Does this mean that Paul deposited something with God or that God deposited something with Paul? In a most anticipatory and superficial fashion one would think that if God deposited something with Paul, Paul would be the guardian; but if Paul deposited something with God, the guardian would be God. True enough, but this only hides the difficulties. The word *my* does not settle the question. If a man deposits his pay check in a bank, he can refer to it as "my deposit." The bank officials can refer to this deposit and others as "our" deposits. Similarly, if the bank or another business firm entrusts the man in question with some property to manage, he can equally refer to it as "my trust" or "my deposit." Indeed, the present writer is a trustee, and I deposit the income of the trust. It is my deposit. The question therefore still remains. Did Paul entrust something to God, or did God entrust something to Paul?

Once more, before going into the matter thoroughly, one should note that the word *deposit,* the meaning of which is in doubt, occurred in *1 Timothy* 6:20, and will again occur two verses down in *2 Timothy* 1:14. The first instance refers to a deposit given to Timothy, not to God; and so does the second. Does *deposit* mean something else here?

On one occasion I used the material here on verses 8-12 for the

Sunday School lesson in an adult class. Verse 12 is indeed somewhat detailed and requires more attentiveness than most Sunday School lessons do. After the class a very well educated gentleman, from whom I least expected it, for his professional work was even more detailed than this commentary, complained that it all sounded like mere semantics to him. I then remembered that I had attended a prayer meeting in his home at one time. He had read ten or a dozen verses of Scripture and asked anyone who wished, to comment. Only, he said, don't try to figure out meaning; just give us your reactions. The gentleman was an elder in a Presbyterian denomination and should have had more respect for the Word of God.

As for semantics, there are occasions when disputants insist on verbal differences without intelligible distinctions. On the other hand, since English words often have several meanings, and if the communication is of any importance at all, one should try to clarify the meaning intended. With repeated technical terms this is indispensable; and in that gentleman's business he was professionally adamant about definitions. Here in this chapter there is more than a merely verbal question about using *deposit* rather than some other term. It is not silly to ask what the deposit is and where it is deposited. This is all the more true because the *King James* has "he is able to keep that which I have committed unto him against that day." Now, the *King James* translation is still one of the best, much better than many that have tried to replace it. Nevertheless, the *King James* is not inerrant, and maybe in this case millions of people are mistaken as to what Paul meant. If a good housewife, in baking, needs to distinguish between baking soda and baking powder, not to mention washing soda, it seems that once in our life we should try to understand *2 Timothy* 1:12.

Hendriksen canvassed all the possibilities, defending his own view and stating the objection to the others. Most commentators are more brief. Therefore, let us take up the points Hendriksen makes. He begins by giving his conclusion in a translation which does not meet the standards of accuracy: "For I know him in whom I have placed my trust, and am convinced that he is able to guard that which I have entrusted to him." The reader will do well to compare and contrast Hendriksen's interpretative paraphrase with what I gave above as an accurate translation. Had the Greek text said what Hendriksen reports, there would never have been a debate among exegetes as to its meaning.

Of course, Hendriksen is quite aware of the competing interpretations. He asks, "Just what is meant by *my deposit?* Is it 'that deposit which he has entrusted to me' or is it 'that deposit which I have entrusted to him'?" He defends that latter view in five arguments:

(1) God, not Paul, guards this deposit. Hence the deposit must have been placed in God's hands, not Paul's.

(2) Paul has just written, I know whom I have believed; that is to say, I know that God is dependable and will guard what I have entrusted to him.
(3) Since Paul has not yet fully received life and incorruptibility, these two remain under God's guardian care.
(4) I Peter 1:4 speaks of a treasure that God guards.
(5) Christ on the cross committed his spirit to the Father, therefore Paul must here refer to something he has likewise committed to God.

Interpreting the deposit as the Gospel message, says Barrett, "has the great advantage of giving the word deposit the same meaning in all three passages."

Certain circumstances throw varying degrees of doubt on these five arguments. The assertion of the first argument contrasts with verse 14 in which Timothy must do the guarding. But perhaps this circumstance is not decisive.

Number two is more a reassertion of Hendriksen's conclusion than it is an argument in its favor.

Argument four is entirely irrelevant. The logic of argument five clearly needs improvement. In brief, arguments one and three deserve some reply, but two, four, and five do not.

Next, Hendriksen attempts to refute the arguments his opponents use. (1) If "deposit" means the Gospel in *1 Timothy* 6:20 and *2 Timothy* 1:14, is it not likely that it means the Gospel here also? Against this Hendriksen counters that in these other verses Timothy, not God, does the guarding. This of course is true. But it is beside the point, for right now we wish to learn, not who does the guarding, but what is being guarded. It is the identity of the "deposit" that is in question. Perhaps in answer Hendriksen continues with a second of his opponents' points: (2) The term *my* in "my deposit" does not change the meaning of *deposit.* He notes that here his opponents are correct, and replies, it is not the word *my,* but the whole context that changes the meaning. Certainly Hendriksen is right on this point. The next objection is (3) that the reference to "myself and my complete salvation" does not fit in with the words "with a view to that day." Hendriksen replies that they fit in beautifully. And again Hendriksen is right. The second and third replies, however, are rather irrelevant. At most they show that some of his opponents used poor arguments. It is also possible that Hendriksen avoided some of their better arguments, so that these replies are insufficient.

Without clearly choosing sides, Barrett seems to prefer the *New English Bible*'s translation, "am confident of his power to keep safe what he has put into my charge." Interpreting the deposit as the Gospel message, says Barrett, "has the great advantage of giving the word *deposit* the same meaning in all three passages."

Meyer connects the disputed phrase with the sentence's earlier phrase, "I am not ashamed." Though Paul is in prison and might be disturbed by the thought that his preaching will finally accomplish nothing, nevertheless he is confident that God will not allow the Gospel to be silenced.

So far these remarks leave standing only Hendriksen's first argument and first reply to his opponents. They both depend on the point that it is God, and neither Timothy nor Paul, who guards the deposit. There are two flaws in this contention. First, it assumes that God can guard only what Paul deposited with him, and not what he deposited with Paul. But if God can guard his servants, as is often asserted in Scripture, he can at the same time guard what he has committed to them. Then, second, the reply contains an incomplete disjunction, "either Paul or God, but not both" is incomplete. In addition to these two possibilities, the third is very real; namely, Paul and Timothy and God all guard the deposit. God guards the deposit made to Paul. It is not necessary to say that if one of these does, the other does not. Timothy also guards it, and the next verse certainly is consistent with this interpretation.

Paul and Timothy and God all guard the deposit. God guards the deposit made to Paul.

1:13

Hold the standard of healthy (health-giving) doctrine which you heard from me, in faith and love which are in Christ Jesus.

As just intimated, here in this verse Paul makes Timothy the guardian of true doctrine, doctrine of which Timothy first heard from his mother and grandmother, but which in its fulness he had heard from Paul. The word translated *standard (upotupōsin)* needs attention. Guthrie is surely mistaken, possibly influenced by Romanism, when he says, "*Hupotupōsis* means an outline sketch such as an architect might make before getting down to the detailed plans of the building. . . . It means that the apostle claims his own teaching to be no more than a starting point." This opens the way for tradition and new revelations. But Paul himself, as already noted, claimed to preach the whole counsel of God. He omitted nothing. He preached everything that God had revealed to him. The only exception was the revelation alluded to in *2 Corinthians* 12:2-4. Paul recounts how, caught up into Paradise, he heard, not unintelligible words, but words God did not permit him to preach. Otherwise, Paul preached the whole counsel of God, and not a mere outline, an unfinished sketch, of it.

Paul himself, as already noted, claimed to preach the whole counsel of God. He omitted nothing. He preached everything that God had revealed to him.

For the word *upotupōsis* Arndt and Gingrich give *model, example, prototype,* and *standard.* The word itself can indeed mean a sketch or outline; but it cannot bear that meaning in this context. It is rather the standard to which Timothy's preaching must conform. Timothy was not an apostle, was not inerrant, and had no authority to add details of his own. That he and all preachers must apply the standard to local and temporal conditions is indubitably true; and I suspect that several readers of this commentary will agree that its author is not infallible. But like a minister in the pulpit, I try to make clear the meaning of a completely unalterable, indefeasible, indefectible (and any other adjectives that come to mind) revelation. God forbids us to subtract from it, and he also forbids us to add to it.

For comparison of views one may quote Cowles, "No emphasis should be laid upon 'form' as opposed to substance. Paul refers to the system of doctrine." Here, be it noted, Christianity is not an aggregate of disjointed truths, but a *system* of doctrine. This was always a part of Presbyterian ordination vows before some denominations became apostate and discarded the original vows. More prestigious than Cowles is Calvin who wrote,

> The apostle is telling Timothy to hold fast the doctrine he has learnt, not only in its substance but in the very form of its expression. For *upotupōsis,* the word used here, means a vivid picture, as if the object concerned were actually before one's eyes. Paul knows how prone men are to rebel and fall away from true doctrine . . . it is exceedingly harmful to corrupt doctrine even in the smallest degree.

Christianity is not an aggregate of disjointed truths, but a system of doctrine.

The reason, or one of the reasons, why Timothy should not alter the message is that orthodox doctrine gives life.

Then he refers to the Papists as examples. In addition, Meyer remarks, "*type* is to be retained. There is no reason for explaining the word by *sketch.*"

The reason, or one of the reasons, why Timothy should not alter the message is that orthodox doctrine gives life. As Jesus said in *John* 6:63, "the words [*rhematā,* not *logous*] that I have spoken to you are spirit and are life."

At this point some commentators put a period after the word *heard:* "hold the doctrines you have heard." They then begin a new sentence: "In faith and love . . . guard the deposit." Without a tedious check on the proportion of Paul's sentences that begin with such a prepositional phrase, this punctuation seems less Pauline than the usual punctuation, and at least an unnecessary change. In any case, the activity of guarding the deposit must be done in faith and love, not any sort of love, not love alone, but the sort of love that cherishes the faith. Meyer wishes to restrict "which is in Jesus Christ" to love alone, not faith. No doubt the reason is that *love* is singular and feminine; and though *faith* is also feminine, the relative article is singular.

To refer to both it would have to be plural *(tais).* This I consider pedantic.

1:14

Guard the good deposit by the Holy Spirit who dwells in us.

To support the idea that the deposit is the Gospel entrusted to Paul and to Timothy, I rejected Hendriksen's contention that God alone and neither Paul nor Timothy guarded the deposit. Here Paul tells Timothy to guard the Gospel by the indwelling Spirit. Both Timothy and God guard the deposit.

Since, furthermore, these two epistles aim to teach Timothy how to organize and govern congregations, the larger context—not just the adjoining verses, but the whole of the two epistles—recommends, and may I say, requires this interpretation.

1:15

You know this, that all in Asia, among whom are Phygelus and Hermogenes, have deserted me.

Barrett believes that this is the first verse in the epistle that comes from Paul himself. He seems to hold (10) that there are only five Pauline "fragments" in *2 Timothy* and *Titus*. If this were true, there would be little use in studying the epistle.

Since Timothy was in Ephesus, not all Asians had deserted Paul. What is meant is obviously that all the Asians who had been with Paul in Rome had now deserted him. Phygelus and Hermogenes, about whom we know nothing further, may have been named because their defection contrasted all the more with their previous greater faithfulness. Or, Paul may have named them because they not only departed physically to avoid possible imprisonment, as did others, but also doctrinally. Of course, this is all unfounded speculation.

The Romanists and a few others insist that these verses say that Onesiphoros was now dead and that therefore the epistle approves of prayers for the dead.

Paul merely says that all the Asians had left him. This was probably a harder blow to Paul than his imprisonment itself.

1:16, 17, 18

The Lord give mercy to the house of Onesiphoros because many times he refreshed me and was not ashamed of my chains, but being in Rome he eagerly sought for me and found me. The Lord give him to find mercy from the Lord in that day, and what services he rendered in Ephesus you yourself know very well.

These verses with their contrast between Onesiphoros and the previously mentioned Hermogenes are so simple and so easily understood that explanation can hardly make them clearer. Some superstitious adumbrations, however, may well be mentioned. The Romanists and a few others insist that these verses say that Onesiphoros was now dead and that therefore the epistle approves of prayers for the dead. This anti-Christian superstition depends on two points. First, no one can pray, would even think to pray, that a friend find mercy before God's judgment throne "on that day," unless the friend were already dead. Nonsense! Second, the superstitious critics have argued that since Paul mentions "the house of Onesiphoros," Onesiphoros could not have any longer been in the household: He must have been dead. Equally nonsense! If the argument were valid, then all the more would it be evident that when I pray for my two daughters and their families, their husbands must be dead. Nonsense, for the third time: Their husbands are both alive and are active in the work of the ministry.

Those Christians who are so eager to derive "practical" directions from Scriptures may well compare their practice of prayer with these verses; but it is hard to imagine a Christian so immature as not to know that he may, or even ought, to pray for God's mercy upon his friends "on that day."

Chapter Two

2:1, 2

You, accordingly, my son, be strong by the grace which is in Christ Jesus, and what you have heard from me through many witnesses, these things present to faithful men, who will be capable of teaching others also.

The verb of encouragement is better translated "Be strong" than "grow" or "become strong." While Meyer is right in insisting that it does not mean "feel strong," his appeal to *Ephesians* 6:10 fails to support his translation. I also prefer "Be strong by the grace in Christ Jesus" rather than "in the grace." The preposition *in* is too vague. The preposition *by* indicates that Christ is the agent who freely supplies strength to Timothy. Some object that if Christ supplies the strength, there is no use exhorting Timothy to be strong, for on this showing Timothy could not of himself produce any strength. Calvin answers this objection:

Paul now looks beyond his own life span and indeed beyond Timothy's. He is concerned that the church survive into future centuries.

> But someone asks, "What is the point in exhorting a man to be strong in grace, unless our free will has some part to play in co-operation with grace?" I reply that what God requires from us in his Word, he also supplies by his Spirit, so that we are strengthened in the grace that he provides. And yet exhortations are not superfluous, because God's Spirit teaches us inwardly and sees to it that they do not sound in our ears fruitlessly and in vain. Thus the man who sees that this present exhortation can be fruitful only by the secret power of the Spirit will never use this passage in support of free will.

Paul now looks beyond his own life span and indeed beyond Timothy's. He is concerned that the church survive into future centuries. Therefore, he instructs Timothy to seek out competent men who will continue the work. Not every Christian is competent. The men chosen must be capable of transmitting the Gospel to others as Paul transmitted it to Timothy.

There is a puzzle at this point. Paul transmitted the message to Timothy directly and orally when they were together. How can he here say, "what you have heard from me through many witnesses"? A frequent suggestion is that Paul gave Timothy the message in the presence of many witnesses at Timothy's ordination (so, Alford). There are two points conjoined here: the witnesses and the ordination. The text itself makes no reference to ordination. Silence, however, allows the possibility that when Paul preached the ordination sermon, the remainder of the presbytery expressed agreement and told Timothy never to forget what Paul had said. But this is just a possibility that silence allows. Hence the reference might be to several occasions when, after Paul had preached, Timothy and others discussed the sermon. In this connection a second consideration applies. The preposition *dia* with the genitive (with the accusative as well) can hardly mean *in the presence of.* Certainly Blass and Debrunner (§§ 222, 223) give it no encouragement. The meanings are: through space, through time, and by an agent. *Dia* can be used in the phrases *through* or *after* many years; or *within* three days; or *at* night; or "All things were created by him" (*John* 1:3); or "that which was spoken by the Lord *through* the prophets" (*Matthew* 1:22). This casts doubt on the interpretation "in the presence of." Indeed, apart from the wording of the text, there would be little point to Paul's reminding Timothy that there had been other worshipers in the congregation. It is required that some of these worshipers approved, attested, confirmed Paul's doctrine. The preposition *dia* means that Timothy learned something of Paul's doctrine from these other people. Nor is this situation the only possibility. The text can include some who had heard Paul when Timothy was not present, some indeed who had recently heard Paul in Rome, and had recounted to Timothy what they had heard. These communications might not only have confirmed Timothy's understanding of what he personally had heard from Paul, but might possibly have given him some additional information.

Timothy was to seek out intelligent young men who could take his place after his departure, who also could seek out intelligent young men of the following generation, and so on down through the centuries with equal faithfulness. Unfortunately it did not always work out that way.

At any rate, Timothy was to seek out intelligent young men who could take his place after his departure, who also could seek out intelligent young men of the following generation, and so on down through the centuries with equal faithfulness. Unfortunately it did not always work out that way. Paul, of course, knew that it wouldn't.

2:3, 4

Suffer evil with (me) as a good soldier of Christ Jesus. One who goes to war avoids entanglement with the affairs of [everyday] life, so as to please his enlisting officer.

It is hard to translate this verse literally and remain in conformity with modern military customs. Today a soldier hardly ever sees the enlisting officer a second time. The *New English Bible* has it, "A soldier on active service will not let himself be involved in civilian affairs; he must be wholly at his commanding officer's disposal." This gives the meaning well, but it is not a translation.

Every Christian must in some sense be a soldier of the cross. But Paul's instructions are directed first of all to Timothy and the ministers who were later to follow him. The Christian life, especially the ministerial life, is a fight, and Paul frequently uses military language. The enlisting officer is of course the Lord Jesus Christ. We must please him. I remember a young man, who entered seminary a little older than most students who choose the ministry. He was most vigorous, among his fellow students, in his repudiation of unbelieving ecclesiastical bureaucrats. But after an apparently successful first pastorate with a gratifying evangelistic endeavor, he became meek as a lamb and offered no opposition to the increasing apostasy. Whether he pleased his enlisting officer is not for me to say, but his only fight and suffering, so far as I could see, was against obesity, and he lost. The Huguenots and the Covenanters fought the devil, and suffered martydom. Not everyone is called to be a martyr; but some faithful ministers suffer from poverty imposed by unbelieving officials who shunt them into obscurity.

The Christian life, especially the ministerial life, is a fight, and Paul frequently uses military language. The enlisting officer is of course the Lord Jesus Christ.

2:5

And if anyone engages in athletics, he is not crowned unless he athletizes lawfully.

The first and last verb in this verse is a single word in Greek; hence in its second instance I have stretched the English language. The term *lawfully,* as most commentators point out, does not mean simply obeying the rules of the game while playing, such as not punching below the belt. What Paul has in mind, as it obviously fits the sense better, is the Olympic requirement of ten months' training. We are not talking about amateurs, but about professionals. The athlete, like the soldier, must sing, "What matters my wife, what matters my child; the Emperor, the Emperor is taken."

Perhaps this is putting it too strongly. Paul, who probably was a widower, never took a second wife; but he defended the right of ministers to marry. He was no Roman Catholic. And a married minister must give some consideration to his wife and child. But he must also be willing to be shot by Claverhouse and leave his wife and child to mourn. The role of a minister's wife is not a happy one. This is true also in less tragic situations.

2:6, 7

The farmer (himself) ought to be the first to partake of his produce. Think about what I say, for the Lord will give you insight in all things.

This is not only a change in metaphors, from soldier to athlete to farmer; it also seems to be a break in the thought. The previous verses stress the pain, inconvenience, and hardships of service; but here Paul has skipped ahead to the rewards. Some exegetes think the reward envisaged is the pastor's salary, as Paul defended it in *1 Corinthians* 9:10-11. Indeed, at least one commentator considers this to have been used by the unknown writer to make the epistle sound like Paul's letters. Now, while a farmer eats his produce, and a soldier receives wages, the athlete wins a crown. In spite of the more ordinary meanings, it looks very much as if Paul had also, or even chiefly, in mind the Christian soldier's heavenly crown.

The text says, "Think about what I say." It does not tell Timothy to expect additional revelations. He is to study Paul's words and deduce from them the proper conclusions.

Verse 7 refers to the beginning of the chapter at least; one may apply it to all of Paul's teaching. Serious students of the Word who also are concerned about their daily life and the lives of their fellow believers may stumble at this verse. Does God really give us insight or understanding in all matters? In view of archaeological confirmations of the truth of the Scriptures, most of us are no longer much disturbed by a few remaining criticisms; but doubts about inerrancy may arise from a verse like this, for two reasons. First, as we grow older we painfully realize how many times we have acted stupidly because of lack of understanding. And, second, if we believe that the canon is closed and that there are no longer apostolic recipients of verbal revelation, this verse makes us wonder whether the Pentecostals are right when they claim to have received additional information from God. But even the Pentecostals do not claim insight in all matters. They think—some at least have—God has revealed to them that Mr. X should marry Miss Y, whom he has never met; but they seem to lack information about buying stocks or bonds. Yet this verse says, "in all things." Even if we restrict the "all things" to the things mentioned in the six preceding verses, the difficulty, although alleviated, is not entirely dissolved, for insight into whom to ordain (verse 2) is often enough imperfect.

The particular Pentecostal difficulty concerning the apostolic authority of supposed present day revelation is, however, easily solved. The text says, "Think about what I say." It does not tell Timothy to expect additional revelations. He is to study Paul's words and deduce from them the proper conclusions. The promise does not include the stock market. But there still remains a gnawing difficulty about whom to ordain. I do not refer to the ordination of homosexuals. Such an evil is clearly forbidden in *Romans* 1:27. I refer to the ordination of seemingly devout, sincere, orthodox young men who later corrupt the faith. Paul himself, even though ordination might not have been involved, lacked insight in the cases of Phygelus and Hermogenes. The paragraph ends here, but the difficulty does not.

2:8, 9

Remember Jesus Christ, risen from the dead, of the seed of David, according to my Gospel; in which [Gospel] I suffer evil, even chains, as an evil-doer, but the Word of God is not chained.

When Paul tells Timothy to remember Jesus Christ, it is not surprising that he first mentions the resurrection. The sermons in the book of Acts all mention the resurrection. Not only is the reference to an historical event that left an empty grave, but, especially here, the fact that Christ now, in the present, enjoys a resurrection life.

Next, Paul notes Jesus' Davidic ancestry. He may have included this information here partly for the sake of the Jewish Christians in Ephesus; but more importantly, to impress Greeks as well as Jews with God's all embracing plan in universal history. Then he adds, "according to my Gospel." *Romans* 2:16 and 16:25 have the same phrase. Conzelmann pontificates that *Romans* 2:16 is "suspected of being a gloss" and *Romans* 16:25 "is not Pauline." Does not this sort of thing discredit Conzelmann's and Bultmann's claim to intelligent scholarship? Some expositors think that Paul wants to identify his Gospel with that preached by the original twelve. Much more likely his motivation was to emphasize that he received the Gospel by direct revelation without contact with the original twelve (compare *Galatians* 1:11 and following). Jerome, the translator of the *Vulgate*, and Baur, the German higher critic, make the incredible suggestion that Paul means the Gospel of Luke, Paul's companion.

The sermons in the book of Acts all mention the resurrection.

Paul envisaged the progress of the Gospel throughout all history to the day of judgment.

"In which," that is, in preaching the Gospel, Paul suffered evil, "as a criminal," perhaps with reference to Christ's suffering as a criminal. "But the Word of God is not bound." It is true that Paul had some freedom to preach while under arrest in Rome; but surely Paul's thought and these words extend further. The next verse makes this still clearer. Paul envisaged the progress of the Gospel throughout all history to the day of judgment. Hendriksen appropriately quotes the last two stanzas of *Ein' feste Burg is unser Gott,* both in Luther's German and in someone's English.

2:10

Therefore, I endure all things for the sake of the elect, in order that they also may find salvation as it is in Christ Jesus with eternal glory.

This verse surely cannot mean that Paul's suffering in prison will cause the salvation of all the elect in future ages. He knew he had to die sometime, and no doubt he suspected that he would be put to death in the not-too-distant future. But Paul's confidence that God would save those whom he had chosen enabled him to endure his present sufferings. If this interpretation seems to flounder on the purposive conjunction *in order that,* one can reply that Paul's sufferings were indeed causative to a degree, for his immediate converts would continue to preach the Gospel. He was not the only cause, but he was a most important one. Indeed, his very sufferings were causative: Consider the set-back to the Gospel that would have resulted, had Paul apostatized.

The word *also* needs a little attention. Offhand, the verse might seem to read better without it. Paul was very conscious that God had chosen him to be an apostle, but first to be a Christian. He was equally convinced that God had chosen others who would follow in later centuries. Hence Paul says, " 'these also' as well as myself God selected them as he selected me. We are all the elect." With that salvation assured by God's choice there is conjoined "eternal glory."

This first phrase of the faithful saying therefore reflects the doctrine of Christ's vicarious death. He was our legal representative and his act is legally counted as ours.

2:11, 12, 13

Faithful is the saying: For if we died with [him] we shall also live with [him], if we persevere, we shall also reign with [him]; if we deny [him], he himself will deny us; if we disbelieve, he remains faithful, for he cannot deny himself.

Several exegetes regard the first phrase of this saying, "if we died with him," as a reference to a convert's baptism. This interpretation, however, can only be a sacramentarian misunderstanding. *Romans* 6:4 is totally insufficient to support this view. Instead of misinterpreting this verse one should note that the following verses explain, at somewhat greater length, what is said here. Knight points out the close parallel:

> For if we have become united with him in the likeness of his death . . . knowing this, that our old self was crucified with him [hardly pictured by baptism] . . . if we have died with Christ, we believe that we shall also live with him.

The exegetes in question make no mention of *Galatians* 2:20, "I have been crucified with Christ"; nor of *Romans* 5:12-21 with its doctrine of the federal headship of Adam and Christ; nor of *2 Corinthians* 5:14, "if one died for all, therefore all died." This first phrase of the faithful saying therefore reflects the doctrine of Christ's vicarious death. He was our legal representative and his act is legally counted as ours.

Equally impossible is the view that the phrase refers to martyrdom. The saying states a generality that applies to all believers, and in its last half to all unbelievers. One reason for rejecting the idea of martyrdom, also noted by Knight, is that the verb *died* is aorist; if martyrdom had been meant, the verb should have been future. He also notes that perseverance through suffering should precede martyrdom, whereas the text has death first and perseverance second. Knight carefully continues to clarify the parallelism with Romans in the use of the same verb *suzēsomen,* "we shall live." The life intended is not life in Heaven, but the present Christian struggle against sin. Romans makes it clear that the future tense refers to this life after regeneration, in this world, though indeed this same life continues in glory.

The distinctness of the two parts of the one life is perhaps clearer here than in *Romans*, for here the second line is "if we persevere, we shall also reign." That Christians properly look forward to a heavenly home, and to reigning with Christ, is too often alluded to to need documentation. Once again, however, Knight shows himself to be an acute expositor:

> *Sumbasileusomen* occurs only twice in the N.T. (2 Tim. 2:12 and I Cor. 4:8). The latter passage, even though written in irony, throws further light on the concept in view. The Apostle Paul therein scores the pride and self-esteem of the Corinthian Christians. In doing so, he says that they act and think as if they are already reigning *(ebasileusate)*. . . . And they are supposedly reigning while the Apostles are still suffering. Paul speaks of them reigning "without us." . . . He then says that he would they did reign "that we also might reign with you." . . . Paul in his irony rules out any reference to a present reign. . . . This note is also evident in 2 Tim. 2:12; the reigning with Christ is a reigning together of all with Christ (121-122),

and therefore in the future.

The third line of the saying is, "if we deny him, he himself will deny us." The happiness or blessedness of the first two lines is now replaced by a more sombre hue. How sombre? We remember that Peter denied the Lord; he was forgiven. But what about Hermogenes? To answer this question, it is best to consider lines three and four together. Line four is, "if we disbelieve, he remains faithful, for he cannot deny himself." Does this mean that Christ pardons every disbeliever, or does it mean that Christ will faithfully impose the established penalty? This latter harsher interpretation gains plausibility not only from the preceding phrase, but also from *Matthew* 10:33, "Whosoever shall deny me before men, I will also deny him before my Father who is in Heaven." In respect to Peter and the fourth phrase, the translation "if we are faithless" (*New English, American Standard, Revised Standard* versions) is a source of confusion. The verb *apisteō* occurs eight times, including *Mark* 16:11, 16.* Of these eight, five must mean *disbelieve,* rather than *be unfaithful: Mark* 16:11, 16; *Luke* 24:11, 41; and *Acts* 28:24. Only a little doubt attaches to *Romans* 3:3. *Disbelieve* is highly probable. Equally probable, or even necessary, is *1 Peter* 2:7. Now, since Peter was unfaithful, though he did not disbelieve, one can hardly avoid translating *apisteo* in this verse as *disbelieve.* Barrett and Guthrie, who give little reason for their acceptance of *faithless,* must be regarded as mistaken; and Hendriksen, to prove his point, has to twist the fourth line out of shape. Alford is better: "Ellicott's note has convinced me that *apistia* seems always in the NT to imply not 'untrueness,' 'unfaithfulness,' but definitely 'unbelief.' "

Knight rejects Ellicott's lexicography and argues for the happy

* Even if the longer ending of *Mark* be spurious, it is nonetheless Greek, written by a Greek-speaking writer, and therefore bears on the meaning of the word.

interpretation. In general, the idea is that God's faithfulness regularly means his immutable determination to save his elect, and not his immutable determination to punish the non-elect. This is a very comfortable view, but we must remember that the faithful saying changed its tone from comforting to disquieting in the preceding line. Furthermore the happy interpretation would not only comfort repentant Peter, it would also guarantee salvation to the unrepentant also. Can we then assume that the unrepentant had actually been regenerated at an earlier date? The assumption is precarious. Since in this problem the milk of human kindness conflicts with sober reasoning, it might be unfortunately better to resist temptation and accept the harsher exegesis.

The happy interpretation would not only comfort repentant Peter, it would also guarantee salvation to the unrepentant also.

2:14

Remind [your people] of these things, charging [them] before God not to engage in logomachies, useful for nothing, the catastrophe of those who listen.

Logomachy, which is the Greek word in its English form, means a battle of words. It denotes attention to words without attention to their meanings. Much the same idea appeared in *1 Timothy* 1:4, 7; 6:4, 20; *2 Timothy* 2:16; and later in 3:7. Here the reader should consider again the comments above on *1 Timothy* 6:4, 20. Paul does not forbid, rather he encourages, intelligent argument; but battles about undefined terminology are useless. While today very few people engage in allegorical interpretations of genealogies, there are more than a few who bandy about such words as *evangelical, infallibility,* and even *inerrancy.* By rejecting their historic meanings and refusing to state their own definitions, if they have any, these false prophets bring catastrophe upon unsuspecting church members. When the *Westminster Confession* was written, with great care given to accurate phraseology, everybody understood what was meant by the "infallible truth and divine authority" of "Holy Scripture." Today, deceivers speak about an authority that is not infallible. I am tempted to say that what the Westminster divines have joined together, let no modern seminary put asunder.

2:15

Be zealous to present yourself, approved, to God, a workman with no need to be ashamed, correctly analyzing the word of truth.

The versions do not translate *orthomounta* as "analyze." The *New English Bible* understands *workman* as a peasant farmer, a *laboureur* in French, and has him "driving a straight furrow." This etymological meaning had faded into metaphor by Paul's time. Guthrie correctly explains:

> The idea of cutting which is inherent in the verb . . . had probably lost the meaning from which it was derived and had ac-

> quired the more general sense of right handling. It was from this sense that the derived noun came later to denote orthodoxy. In this context, however, the main idea seems to be that Timothy must be scrupulously straightforward in dealing with the *word of truth*. . . . The term *word of truth* is twice used elsewhere by Paul (Eph. 1:13 and Col. 1:5) (148).

Hendriksen also has some good phraseology:

> That the base (to cut) should lose its original, literal meaning when a prefix (straight) is added is not strange. Even *without* any affix the word "to cut" is frequently used in a nonliteral sense. Thus the Greek speaks of "*cutting* (taking) an oath," "*cutting* (diluting) a liquid." . . . He also uses the expression "cutting short" (bringing to a crisis). . . . And compare our idioms "cutting a strange figure," "cutting droll capers," "cutting a pack of cards" etc. (263).

Although the previous verse tells Timothy how to pastor his people, Paul in this verse tells Timothy how to conduct himself.

What God says is true. What God says is important. Aim to understand it "accurately."

The verb *analyze* seems to be a good translation here. Although the previous verse tells Timothy how to pastor his people, Paul in this verse tells Timothy how to conduct himself. Beyond Timothy, Paul's instructions apply to every preacher since that time. To a degree also they apply to every communicant member. Naturally, no one can work eight hours a day in the office and study the Bible eight hours a night at home. But within one's reasonable limitations, each must do his best to analyze Scripture. A rapid reading of the Bible from *Genesis* to *Revelation* gives a good survey of the book, but it is far from meeting the present requirement. One must study and analyze. Take some chapter or paragraph; read it carefully two or three times; try to express its meaning in a summary with your own words; then fit this into the larger context. Think! Compare! Meditate day and night! Remember, you are handling the word of truth. What God says is true. What God says is important. Aim to understand it "accurately" (*New American Standard*). You will no doubt make mistakes, as the present commentary exemplifies; but we shall have no need to be ashamed if we are diligent workmen.

2:16, 17

But irreligious empty conversations avoid, for they result in greater impiety, and their doctrine will spread like gangrene; of whom are Hymenaeus and Philetus,

These two verses hardly need any explanation at all. Their meaning is obvious. One minor difficulty: The *they* in "they result in greater impiety" refers to the irreligious conversations; but the *their* in "their doctrine" must refer to a group of people, among whom the two men named were prominent.

2:18

which kind of people have deviated from the truth, saying that the resurrection has already occurred, and [thus] overturn the faith of some.

Both here and in *1 Corinthians* 15:12 one notes, perhaps with some surprise, that the early church had professing members who denied the resurrection of Christ. With some surprise, because every sermon recorded in *Acts* culminates in the resurrection. That the Stoics and Epicureans, in *Acts* 17:32, refused to believe is not surprising; but at least these philosophers were honest enough not to become communicant members. They subscribed to no creed with their fingers crossed.

That the Stoics and Epicureans, in Acts 17:32, refused to believe is not surprising; but at least these philosophers were honest enough not to become communicant members. They subscribed to no creed with their fingers crossed.

In addition to the particular point at which these heretics rebelled, the general category is truth and faith. Today, too many seminaries and ministers disparage fixed, absolute truth and reduce faith to an irrational experience. Too many of them, favoring behavioristic psychology, either explicitly deny the possibility of a future life, or use such ambiguous language that no one can determine what precisely they believe. They overturn the faith of many.

Many seminaries and ministers disparage fixed, absolute truth and reduce faith to an irrational experience.

2:19

However, the foundation of God stands firm, for it has this seal: The Lord knows those who are his, and, Let everyone who names the name of the Lord apostatize from evil.

In spite of Guthrie, the *New American Standard*, and the *Revised Standard Version*, all of which make it read "the firm foundation of God stands," I prefer "the foundation of God stands firm," as given by Hendriksen, the *New English Bible* (of all things!), and the *King James*. Grammatically there is no clear choice; indeed, grammar rather favors the *New American Standard* and *Revised Standard Version*. The decision must depend on the interpretation chosen.

Hendriksen and Meyer list several possible answers to the question, What is the foundation? Hendriksen seems to have at least mentioned most of them. He dismisses the bodily resurrection and discusses (1) election from eternity; (2) Christ himself; and (3) the church. Calvin, adopting the first of these views, said Paul "reminds us of God's election which he calls figuratively a foundation, meaning by this word its firm and enduring constancy." A few lines below, Calvin makes God himself the foundation: "the elect . . . are founded on God." Hendriksen has some respect for this view: "This idea cannot be altogether discarded. Paul has just made mention of election (verse 10). . . . More especially the words, 'The Lord knows (from everlasting) who are his.' " These last words are almost decisive for election.

The second view, that Christ himself is the foundation, gains support from *1 Corthinians* 3:10-12. But Hendriksen notes that *Ephesians* 2:20 calls Christ the corner-stone. This observation has implications beyond those Hendriksen wishes to draw. In a moment we shall again see how Paul mixes his metaphors.

The third view makes the church to be the foundation. Hendriksen, Meyer, his American editor—presumably Huther—and Alford adopt this view. Meyer and his American editor say that the foundation must be something which, according to the next verse, can also be regarded as a house. A mixed metaphor. "It must be something on which the inscriptions mentioned can be conceived of as written" (244). "It is the inscription on the foundation" (236). Hendriksen gives two reasons for the same choice: (a) It "harmonizes most beautifully with the context: God's *true* church consists of those who are his." This, I hold, is irrelevant and begs the question. (b) "It is consistent with I Tim. 3:15. There too the church is called 'the foundation' or 'the support.' " He acknowledges that the term in *1 Timothy* 3:15 is not the one here. At this point the reader should return and reread the comments on the earlier verse. *Pillar* and *support* are not the equivalent of *foundation*. Then, to repeat, Paul changes and mixes metaphors. One must not assume that an analogy in one place means the same thing as the analogy in another. This applies not only to Paul, but to the Bible as a whole. For example, a lion is an analogy of the ruler of the tribe of Judah, and a lion is also an analogy of Satan who seeks whom he may devour. The tendency to take analogies as literal or consistent should be firmly resisted.

One must not assume that an analogy in one place means the same thing as the analogy in another. This applies not only to Paul, but to the Bible as a whole.

Therefore, I prefer Calvin's view, perhaps with some slight modification. Since divine election is a part of divine truth, the mention of truth in verses 15 and 18 prevents the idea of election from being irrelevant; and, as Hendriksen honestly noted, verse 10 explicitly mentions election. Then, too, if verse 19 is intended to encourage those who are disturbed by a growing apostasy, God's election is more effective than an inscription on a stone foundation. Indeed, the first "inscription" is an assertion of election. Calvin's own statement is so brief that perhaps a slight addition would not really modify his thought. The addition follows from the unity of the Godhead. Since the Trinity has but one will (not three), election is as much a decree of the Son as of the Father. Therefore, the foundation can be Christ himself as well as election, and the other Persons. At any rate, the verb "stand firm" indicates the fixed, absolute truth of the eternal decree.

Since the Trinity has but one will (not three), election is as much a decree of the Son as of the Father.

As indicated above, the first "inscription" contrasts the immutable divine knowledge of the Lord's people, individually, with the visible apostasy of false teachers who never had been elect. The inscription itself derives from *Numbers* 16:5 and following, when on that ancient occasion God made evident to his people which individuals were not his elect. The second inscription (or, more properly, seal, or perhaps not even *seal,* for the word is not plural) is intelligible enough not to need a paragraph of commentary.

2:20

In a great house there are not only gold and silver vessels, but also wooden and clay [vessels], the former for honor, the latter for dishonor.

In *Romans* 9:21 it is in the world where vessels of honor and dishonor are found. Here the great house containing these two classes of utensils is the church. Calvin remarks that one need not be surprised if God's great household contains some dishonorable items. The church session, which admits to communicant membership, can never know who is and who is not regenerate. Even Timothy (or was it Paul himself?) did not know when he admitted Hymenaeus and Philetus to the church. God works his purpose through these evil members of the visible church; he moves in a mysterious way his wonders to perform. The heresies of the two men mentioned, and the furor in the Ephesian church, undoubtedly resulted in a better understanding of the Christian faith than the membership would otherwise have achieved. We groan under the slings and arrows of misfortune, but God has willed it that way.

The church session, which admits to communicant membership, can never know who is and who is not regenerate.

2:21

Accordingly, if anyone cleanses himself from these things, he will be an instrument of honor, sanctified, useful to the Master, ready for every good work.

The word Master near the end of the verse is etymologically Despot.

Although this verse seems too simple to need explanation, expositors have suggested slightly different views. Most readers would no doubt say that the opening phrase merely exhorts Christians to avoid sin. For others this is too general and they wish to be more specific. The context allows two differing specifications. First, some say the verse is an exhortation to the church members to cleanse the church of false prophets. A slightly different view, however, seems more probable. The word *himself* in "cleanse himself" can indeed be forced to mean "cleanse himself by ridding himself of the false prophets in the church"; but no force is necessary in understanding a more personal or individual cleansing, yet not an unspecified general cleansing of any and every sin. The text says "from these." If *these* does not mean the false teachers, it can very well mean the false doctrines previously mentioned. They included wrangling over mere words, in contrast with the word of truth (verse 15); empty chatter, and a denial of a future resurrection. True, verse 19 says, "abstain from wickedness" in a very general way, but the emphasis is on the chapter's specifications.

The word *Master* near the end of the verse is etymologically *Despot*. It seems to occur ten times in the New Testament. In *Luke* 2:29, *Acts* 4:24, and *Revelation* 6:10, it means God, the Father. In *1 Timothy* 6:1, 2, it meant, as more usual in ordinary speech, the human master of the household; and it means this again in *Titus* 2:9 and *1 Peter* 2:18. In *2 Peter* 2:1, it clearly means Christ, as also in *Jude* 4.[*] Here in *2 Timothy* 2:21, it probably means God the Father,

[*] Compare my commentary on *2 Peter* [*New Heavens, New Earth*].

for, while Christ is mentioned in verses 1, 3, 8, 10, 11-13 (*him, himself*), God the Father becomes more prominent from there on. *God*, rather than *Christ*, is found in verses 9, 14, 15, and 19. This is doubtless a minor point, but still it is worth mentioning because Hendriksen here identifies *Master* with Christ.

2:22

Flee youthful lusts, pursue righteousness, faith, love, peace, with those who call upon the Lord out of a pure heart.

This verse might seem to disprove the previous interpretation of verse 21. An attempt was made there to insist on the specifications in the foregoing context. Here the language is general, modified only by the adjective *youthful.* But one can take this verse simply as an additional exhortation. However one wishes to construe it, the next verse will return to the ignorant speculations of Hymenaeus.

The translation *lust* carries, now near the end of the twentieth century, a strong connotation of sex. Nor was Timothy too old to have outgrown these strong impulses. His voluntary semi-asceticism, however, suggests that sex was not his main temptation. In fact, Paul must be using quite general language. The "youthful desires" can best be identified by their following opposites: faith, love, and peace. Nor can we say that Timothy was particularly tempted by unbelief, hatred, and enmity. Though the exhortation was directed to Timothy, it is we ourselves who need it more.

2:23

But moronic and uneducated investigations avoid, knowing that they engender [church] fights.

No doubt some readers of this commentary may think that its distinctions are often trivial. I hope they do not engender fights. Nor do I see much risk of it. Even beyond this commentary, there seems to be little in this that comes under condemnation here. Some small groups attach great importance to certain trivial details, but controversy today centers on the most basic parts of theology: the inerrant authority of Biblical truth, the virgin birth, the ever-present semi-pelagianism of Arminians and Romanists, and the reception into honor of perverts and homosexuals. One of the latter sued a congregation of the Orthodox Presbyterian Church for discharging him as organist after he had obtained his position by deceit. Sir Walter Scott in his novels pilloried the Covenanters for their rigid adherence to extremely small points of doctrine. Scott was biased; he didn't like Presbyterians; and he exaggerated. Even though they had good reason to refuse to enter William and Mary's established church, they furnished some material to Scott after 1688. But by and large, trivialities and tedious genealogies are not at present a pressing danger.

2:24, 25, 26

A servant of the Lord should not fight, but be gentle to all men, didactic, patient, in meekness instructing those who oppose [him, or, themselves]; if perhaps God may give them repentance to know the truth and [so] recover their senses from the snare of the devil, having been captured alive by him to do his will.

The admonition not to fight must be compared with Paul's previous admonition in 1 Timothy 6:12, "Fight the good fight of faith."

Repentance means a change of mind; and this is an act of divine grace. No one repents on his own initiative. Repentance is a gift of God.

The admonition not to fight must be compared with Paul's previous admonition in *1 Timothy* 6:12, "Fight the good fight of faith"; and with other admonitions and examples of contention for the faith. The present verse should be read in its context. The verb *fight* depends for its meaning on the plural noun *fights* in the preceding verse. The background is the moronic and ignorant contentions of the genealogists. Hendriksen remarks that "the servant . . . should resemble his Lord, who was meek . . . who when he was oppressed and afflicted opened not his mouth. . . ." But Hendriksen seems to forget that Christ very forcibly argued against the Pharisees. The paradox, if it seems such, derives from the difference between situations. Christ "opened not his mouth" to his persecutors during his passion. But he did answer the high priest on oath, and Pontius Pilate. These several instances, including the earlier arguments about genealogies, were frivolous. Nevertheless, Timothy had to do something. Paul not only told him to be gentle, patient, and meek, but also to be "didactic," instructing his opponents. Calvin presents the distinction as it was in his day. "Look at the theology of the Papists, what is there in it but the art of contending and disputing? Thus the more proficient in it a man is, the more unfit he will be for serving Christ." A remarkable statement from a man who contended and disputed with the Papists for most of his life! Yet he saw that Romanism engaged in many trivialities which merited no refutation.

Even though the moronic trivialities needed no refutation, the people inundated with them needed instruction. Timothy must be "didactic." He must teach. Here Paul in effect repeats our Lord's final command: "Make all nations learners . . . teaching them to keep [hold, preserve] all things whatever I have commanded you." Pastors are called *teaching* elders. How many today teach the whole counsel of God? How many teach only a few points? Do some teach nothing? Many teach falsehoods.

Timothy was to teach those opposing—opposing whom or what? No object follows the participle. There will be a similar, though different verb in *Titus* 1:9, also without an object. The context in Titus, however, makes it quite clear that the object of opposition is sound doctrine and the faithful word. The verb here in *2 Timothy*, however, as a middle voice, could be translated "oppose themselves"; that is, their trivialities injure themselves. This may even be grammatically preferable, for the middle voice does not require a following accusative. The later phrase, too, "the snare of the devil," supports this view.

Paul had a good reason for side-stepping the endless genealogies and patiently engaging in the exposition of sound doctrine. This procedure is one that God often uses before he grants a man repentance. Therefore, Timothy may hope that under his instruction, God will change the minds of these people, or some of them. Repentance means a change of mind; and this is an act of divine grace. No one repents on his own initiative. Repentance is a gift of God. If Timothy presents the truth to be known, possibly God will cause some of these people to know it.

Ordinary usage in both Greek and English, either by reason of ambiguity or more often by condensation, may easily result in misunderstandings, especially when the word in question is *knowledge.* Very likely some of Timothy's opponents already had a fair knowledge of the Gospel. Possibly some did not. Before his conversion, Paul knew the basic truths of Christianity even better than those whom he persecuted. But he then, and Timothy's opponents now, did not know that the Gospel was the truth. They knew and understood the preaching, but they did not believe it. Hence, if we expand and paraphrase the verse, we can say. "God may change their minds so that they will recognize the Gospel as truth." It is not strange, indeed it may frequently be, that those who do not accept the Gospel understand it better than those who do. Nevertheless, Timothy, not God, must present the truth to them, with the hope that God, not Timothy, will change their minds.*

The prepositional prefix *ana* in the verb *anānēpsosin* may give it the connotation of recovering their senses *again.* This would suggest that they had previously been regenerated, but had temporarily fallen into Satan's snare. However, prepositional prefixes in Hellenistic Greek had usually lost their original force. The text supplies nothing sufficiently clear to decide the question one way or the other. The ambiguity continues in the next participle, *ezōgrēmenoi,* "having been captured." Some commentators want it to mean: The genealogists recover their senses because God has now recaptured them with the result that they begin to do his will again. Others say: After having been captured by the devil so as to do the devil's will for a time, now God grants them repentance. There is also the combination: After they had been captured by the devil, God grants them repentance to do God's will. The difficulty lies in the two pronouns. Do they both refer to God, or both refer to the devil, or does the first refer to the devil and the second to God? One thing is certain: The first pronoun cannot refer to God with the second referring to the devil: being recaptured by God so as to obey the will of the devil. The present exegete prefers the second view: Perhaps God may grant repentance to those whom the devil deceived into doing evil.

* The various Scriptural usages of the verb *know* raise a problem in apologetics to which a commentary can only allude in a footnote. The common meaning is exemplified in simple sentences, such as, "I know that there is a tree on the lawn," and "I know that David was King of Israel." But sometimes, both in Hebrew and in Greek, *know* means *believe, obey, choose, have sexual intercourse.* English too uses the verb in a variety of meanings. In their opposition to the intellectual emphasis on truth, experiential, emotional, mystical, and neoorthodox apologetes have contrasted the intellectual Greek meaning with the (sometimes) sexual Hebrew meaning. This contrast is misguided because the Hebrew verb and the Greek verb are both so used. More serious than this linguistic incompetence is a flaw or a gap in the apologetics of these apologetes. It is well enough to point out the extended meanings of the verb. The verb is indeed so used. But such information is irrelevant as an argument against intellectualism and truth. The fallacy or defect is that these apologetes fail to explain *knowledge* in its basic sense. To insist on extended meanings of *knowledge* is no substitute for a basic epistemology.

Chapter Three

3:1-4

Know this, that in the last days there will come difficult times, for men will be lovers of self, lovers of money, boasters, arrogant, blasphemers, disobedient to parents, ungrateful, wicked, unloving, implacable, refusing to agree in any truce, slanderers, devils, dissolute, brutal, with no love for what is good, treacherous, reckless, conceited, lovers of pleasure rather than of God,

Calvin, surrounded by plenty of treacherous, implacable blasphemers and brutal, dissolute devils, did not look so far into the future.

This catalogue of vices supplies a sermonic base for endless illustrations and applications, but there is little need of exegesis and explanation. The most important problem for the interpreter concerns the words "in the last days." Meyer's conclusion is that this phrase "denotes a definite period, not however (as in Acts 2:17; Heb. 1:1), the present time between the appearance of Christ in the flesh and his second coming . . . but the time immediately preceding Christ's *parousia.*"

Calvin, surrounded by plenty of treacherous, implacable blasphemers and brutal, dissolute devils, did not look so far into the future. He said, "Paul warns him that the Church will be subject to grievous diseases. . . . Under *the last days* he includes the universal condition of the Christian Church. He [Paul] is not comparing his own age with ours [alone] but rather teaching what the future [future to Paul] condition of Christ's kingdom will be." Alford, without mentioning Calvin, agrees substantially with Meyer, appealing to *2 Peter* 3:3 and *Jude* 18, and concluding that "the period referred to here is . . . that immediately preceding the coming of the Lord." Guthrie does not deny the future reference, but notes also that the next few verses are in the present tense.

If Meyer's interpretation is to be viewed with caution because of his incessant attempt to find eschatology on the least provocation, Hendriksen's amillennialism may have influenced his opposing interpretation. Hendriksen writes, "the expression 'in the last days' as here used cannot be limited to the days which will immediately precede Christ's second coming. It would have been senseless to tell Timothy to avoid people who would never bother him at all!" Naturally, Hendriksen cites passages in which "the last days" clearly means "the age ushered in by Christ's appearance on earth. Accordingly Paul's words here . . . [mean] this lengthy dispensation *in which we are now living.*" Hendriksen's argument is poor insofar as "it would have been senseless to tell him to avoid people who would never bother him at all." Though addressed to Timothy, the text is not senseless, for Paul's warning was addressed not to Timothy alone, but to all Christians in later centuries. Timothy, though he did not know it, would not be bothered by whatever dangers immediately precede Christ's second advent; but those living at that later time will be. On the other hand, Hendriksen is right in saying that the expression "cannot be *limited* to a yet future age. Paul's warning, as I see it, applies throughout church history from beginning to end."

What is the relation between the list of vices and the heretics Paul denounces in these two epistles?

One problem which none of the commentaries I have read mentions or considers: What is the relation between the list of vices and the heretics Paul denounces in these two epistles? People who stupidly waste their time on allegorical adumbrations of Jewish genealogies do not seem likely to be implacable, dissolute, brutal, treacherous, or reckless, even if they are somewhat conceited and possibly lovers of pleasure and money. There are two ways of solving this paradox. One is the extreme premillennarian interpretation that limits the last days to the distant eschatological future—two thousand years or more after the apostolic age. But though the future years may be filled with worse evils than we have so far known, the text hardly supports such a rigid limitation. Therefore, one must or at least may assert a break in thought between chapters two and three, after which Paul speaks more generally than before of the church's troubles. The Roman persecutions between A.D. 90 and 315, as well as the Romish massacres of the Huguenots in the sixteenth century, were brutal and treacherous enough.

There is no consistent, logical order in the list of vices. In this respect it is similar to the list of virtues in *2 Peter* 1:5-7. It is just an additive list. Most of the words need no boring, dictionary definitions. Perhaps one should mention that *blasphēmoi* includes those who slander their fellow-men as well as those who speak evil of God.

3:5

having a form of piety [religion? godliness] but denying its power: avoid these people.

These people have a form of piety. This suggests that they are church members.

This still continues the same sentence, but it can stand separate exegesis. Three points may be brought out. First, these people have a form of piety. This suggests that they are church members. The earlier mentioned genealogists were church members; why should

These men deny that Christianity has any power or value. They hold that the Biblical doctrines are false.

One cannot suppose that the verses above refer only to the women and homes of pagan families. The picture is a sad picture of professedly Christian homes.

Nor should we suppose that the sins of these women were particularly sexual.

this list describe only those on the outside? Undoubtedly, pagan persecutions are perilous times; but internal subversion is also perilous, and perhaps more so. The duty of a pastor therefore, the duty of a synod or general assembly, is to keep the church pure. The church cannot be pure in the sense of having only sinless members, or even of expelling all hypocrites; but it can with vigilance maintain its confessional standards, though history makes even this doubtful.

Second, the phrase "denying its power" is often interpreted to mean that the evil lives of these people exhibit a powerless religion. As Hendriksen says, "These people lack spiritual dynamite. Since they are not Spirit-filled, it is not surprising that they lack power." There is both truth and error in this statement. It is true that these men lack the power of the Holy Spirit; but they all too frequently have the power of the devil to douse with cold water and extinguish a denomination's adherence to the Scriptural standards. Therefore a different and pessimistic interpretation is possible. It is that these men deny that Christianity has any power or value. They hold that the Biblical doctrines are false. It is not that their actions show no spiritual force, but that with force they positively reject the truth.

Now, third, Paul's admonition to Timothy to avoid such people, and the following verses too, show that Paul is not limiting his thought to a far distant future. He has Ephesus clearly in mind.

A very minor matter is the word *kai (and)* in the last phrase. In English it is awkward to say, "And avoid these people!" One commentator tried the grammatically possible translation, "Avoid these people *also*." But there are no other people in the text to justify the *also*. The word *and* is indeed in the text; but a translation does not quite need it.

3:6, 7

For some of these make their way into homes and captivate idle women heaped up with sins, led on by various impulses, forever learning and never able to arrive at a knowledge of truth.

Since the main subject of these epistles is church administration, one cannot suppose that the verses above refer only to the women and homes of pagan families. The picture is a sad picture of professedly Christian homes. Quite aside from any persecution from without, the internal condition of first century congregations must have been deplorable. Guthrie's (and others') interpretation of "women laden with sins in the sense of being overwhelmed in their consciences," would make the situation seem less deplorable; but there is little evidence that these women were "overwhelmed in their consciences." The fact that they took an interest in theology does not prove any great sense of guilt. Nor should we suppose that the sins of these women were particularly sexual. No doubt some were adulteresses and fornicators, but Paul distinctly says that their sins were variegated. Rather than sex, the one mentioned is a desire to dabble in false theology. These women wanted to learn, but under their instructors they could never learn the truth. Recently this was terrifyingly exemplified by the mass murders in the Jim Jones cult. But it is just as insidious in the "main-line" denominations, where little if any truth is still preached. Even the smaller denominations and independent congregations need to measure their faithfulness to truth by comparing their emphases with Paul's instructions.

Here it is well to note that the word *truth,* not to count other expressions of the same idea, occurs thirteen times in the three pastorals. It occurs twenty-five times in the *Gospel of John* and twenty times in his three short epistles. Robert Ingersoll, last century, lectured on the mistakes of Moses. The liberals reject the virgin birth of Christ and other miracles likewise. Critics attack various Scriptural assertions of cosmology, chronology, history, geography, and botany, labeling them falsehoods. The philosophical basis by which these denials are supported is excellently expressed by Helmut Thielecke. In his volume, *The Evangelical Faith,* published by the not very evangelical Eerdmans Publishing Company in 1974, he says, "Part of the intellectual honesty of adult man is that in the area of faith he will accept no truth-claim that conflicts with scientific knowledge" (66). For Thielecke, the tentative, ever-changing conclusions of science are more infallible than the unchanging truth of God.*

Rather than sex, the one mentioned is a desire to dabble in false theology.

The minds of these men have deteriorated intellectually. They can no longer think logically.

3:8

As Jannes and Jambres stood up against Moses, so also these stand against the truth, men deteriorated in mind, having flunked in the faith [exam],

In Jewish tradition Jannes and Jambres were supposedly the names of the two Egyptian magicians mentioned in *Exodus* 7. The comparison does not relate to external actions of the Old Testament and New Testament parties, but to their common rejection of the truth.

The phrase in the *King James*, "men of corrupt minds," with its connotations of immoralities, is not precisely what the text means. Of course, they were sinners and heretics. But the participle *katepharmenoi* has the same root as the verb describing the corruption of the body in death and the incorruption of the resurrection. The metaphorical idea is that the minds of these men have deteriorated intellectually. They can no longer think logically.

Because they are irrational, they have flunked the test of faith. For *adokimos* Arndt and Gingrich give "not standing the test, then, unqualified, worthless, base." These persons are unqualified with respect to the faith. Barrett, commenting on the *New English Bible*'s translation, "they have lost the power to reason and they cannot pass the tests of faith," remarks, *"adokimos* . . . conveys the sense not so much of failure in an examination as of divine reprobation." Why not both? Isn't it the professor who hands out the grades?

* That scientific "truth" is regularly retired as false, see, among much else, Percy Bridgman, *The Logic of Modern Physics* (Macmillan, 1927); Pierre Duhem, *Le Système du Monde* (Librairie Scientifique Hermann, 1913). A. R. Hall, *The Scientific Revolution* (Beacon Press, 1962); J. W. N. Sullivan, *The Limitations of Science* (Mentor 1957); G. H. Clark, *The Philosopy of Science and Belief in God.*

3:9

but they will not get very far, for their stupidity will be clear to all, as also that of those [two who opposed Moses] became.

Several commentators call attention to an apparent contradiction here. This verse says that the heretics will not get very far; but verse 13 below says that evil men will get worse and worse. Then, too, the earlier verses (2:16, 17) warn that the heresies will lead to further ungodliness and spread like gangrene. Which verses predict accurately? Will heresy "get very far," or will it not?

Bengel apparently thought that the discrepancy could be removed by supposing that the heretics themselves would get worse and worse, but that they would have less and less public effect. This would effectively remove the alleged contradiction, if indeed Bengel's interpretation were correct. Unfortunately, church history does not lend its support. Or, one could say that the genealogists will not meet with much success, as church history has shown, but that other heretics, those referred to in 2:16, 17 and elsewhere, will do great damage, as history also has made clear. This quite satisfactorily solves the paradox.

The genealogists will not meet with much success, as church history has shown, but that other heretics, those referred to in 2:16, 17 and elsewhere, will do great damage, as history also has made clear.

Another interpretation, either as an alternate or as merely additional, is possible: As Jannes and Jambres withstood Moses for a while, but were destroyed in Moses' lifetime, so the defeat of heresy will occur (not in Paul's lifetime, but) in the lifetime of the church. This comparison would be that though the durations are different, the end is the same in both cases.

3:10, 11

But you [have] followed my teaching, conduct, purpose, faith, patience, love, endurance, persecutions, sufferings, such as befell me in Antioch, in Iconium, in Lystra, what persecutions I endured; and the Lord delivered me out of them all.

These two verses and the next add some plausibility to what otherwise might seem to have been a strained analogy. I would, however, consider it an additional rather than an alternate interpretation. Let us, however, drop the matter and proceed.

Greek as an inflected language regularly drops personal pronouns as subjects of verbs. Here *you,* as a pronoun, receives the emphasis. Timothy contrasts strongly with the false teachers. He has followed Paul's teaching in conduct, purpose, endurance, and so on. Meyer (251) notes that "*parakolouthein* means 'follow' either theoretically as in Luke 1:3 ('of intellectually following after, by which the knowledge of a thing is gained . . .') or practically as in I Tim.4:6. Here it can only have the latter meaning." This statement is seriously defective. In the first place *1 Timothy* 4:6, as was previously explained, is more intellectual than practical. In the second place, the present verse specifically mentions teaching and faith. To be sure, it also mentions persecutions and endurance, but truth, doctrine, teaching are not excluded. Indeed, if it were not such awkward English, the verse should be translated: the teaching of me, the love of me. . . . the faith of me, and so on. This means the things taught, the objective faith. Subjective "faithfulness" is taken care of in the words *patience, endurance, sufferings.*

As with the list of vices at the beginning of the chapter, so here there is little logical arrangement in this list of virtues. At the most one might say that the first four are theoretical and the others are practical. To maintain such a division, the word for *conduct* (*agōgē*), which often means "way of life" (also, *carrying away, movement, tempo* in music) must be taken in its other meanings as *method of proof, style, line of argument* (compare Liddell and Scott). Most commentators do not even mention these perfectly legitimate translations.

The Lord delivered Paul, but only after he had suffered most painfully. The Lord did not prevent persecution. Nor did the Lord prevent the later execution.

The latter part of the list centers on Paul's sufferings, particularly those that occurred in Antioch, Iconium, and Lystra. Paul adds, "the Lord delivered me out of them all." In a sense this is comforting. But it blinds some overly optimistic people into expecting to live a charmed life. Yes, the Lord delivered Paul, but only after he had suffered most painfully. The Lord did not prevent persecution. Nor did the Lord prevent the later execution. Therefore, rather than promising energetic Christians freedom from tribulation, the verse seems to suggest that God will preserve his servants' lives, through tribulation, until they have accomplished the work God intended them to accomplish.

God will preserve his servants' lives, through tribulation, until they have accomplished the work God intended them to accomplish.

3:12

And all who wish to live piously in Christ Jesus will be persecuted.

This verse supports the interpretation given to the preceding phrase. Fortunately, the United States with its Puritan and Presbyterian heritage has been free of persecution. It is still free of physical persecution. But political liberalism, socialism (always anti-Christian), the emergence of women's liberation, lesbianism and homosexuality, the legal attacks made by the government on Christian schools, including jail terms for Christian parents who send their children to Christian schools, the reluctance of universities to employ outstanding Christian professors, and the activism of university students in riots, arson, and terror—all this presages the more systematic oppression that Communism inflicts on Christians.

The "main-line" apostate denominations vigorously attack Christianity, both politically and theologically.

The "main-line" apostate denominations vigorously attack Christianity, both politically and theologically. They support Marxist regimes in Africa, and, not to begin a long list of items, the Presbyterian Church (U.S.A.) recently ordained a ministerial candidate who explicitly denied the deity of Christ, after which *Monday Morning* (May 12, 1980) a pastors' periodical, published Robert B. McLaren's article defending the ordination, arguing in detail against the doctrine, and lampooning the faithful as "shamefully uninformed pastors."

3:13

Evil men and sorcerers [jugglers, cheats; NEB: charlatans] will get worse [and worse], deceiving and being deceived.

This increase in evil was somewhat explained above. Here the remark is that the words "deceiving and being deceived" indicate intellectual rather than overt activity. The pietists, who disparage intellectualism, fail to note that overt activity is controlled by intellectual belief. Before these heretics infiltrate private homes, they have already committed themselves to false doctrine. They deceive others because they themselves have already been deceived.

The pietists, who disparage intellectualism, fail to note that overt activity is controlled by intellectual belief.

The Old Testament can make us wise unto salvation through faith in Jesus Christ.

3:14, 15

You, however, remain in the things you have learned and in which you have confidence, knowing from whom [plural] you have learned them, and that from childhood you have known the sacred writings, which are able to make you wise unto salvation through faith in Christ Jesus.

Permit the present author to repeat that his method of composition begins with translation of the text. After he has written his translation, he compares it with previous translations. Sometimes he is surprised to find that he has chosen the same words as are in the *New American Standard*. "Sacred writings," instead of "Holy Scriptures," is one example. Of course, the present author changes his translation after this consultation, if he thinks the other version is superior—in meaning, not in style. I disclaim any ability to produce a lengthy version satisfactory for pulpit use.

Once again Paul uses the emphatic pronoun *you*. Though the phrases are precepts or commands, we can see clearly enough that there is also a black-white distinction between the heretics and Timothy's actual conduct. This is the force of the explicit *you*.

Although, of course, Timothy had learned much from Paul, his instruction began in childhood. This was indicated in 1:5. A few manuscripts have "from whom" in the singular, but this cannot be correct, for Paul had not been Timothy's instructor in childhood. Encouraged by his mother and grandmother, Timothy as a boy studied the Scriptures. Naturally this was the Old Testament. In them he found salvation. That Moses and David found salvation in the Old Testament does not strike us as strange; but Paul here says that the Old Testament can make us wise unto salvation through faith in Jesus Christ. Was faith in Christ revealed in the Old Testament? Yes, it was. Not so clearly as in Paul's epistles; yet more clearly than many today suppose. Let us remember that Christ, just after his resurrection, told two travelers, "O slow of heart to believe all that the prophets have spoken . . . and beginning at Moses and all the prophets, he expounded unto them in all the scriptures the things concerning himself." Note "all that the prophets have spoken," "Moses," "all the prophets," and "all the scriptures." Then read the verse in between, here omitted (*Luke* 24:25-27).

Perhaps a few readers may be interested in the grammar of the two verses. Some exegetes, including Hendriksen, after noting the main verb "remain," try to make the participle "knowing" and the phrase "that from childhood you have known" coordinate clauses giving two reasons for remaining in what he learned. But this interpretation is neither good grammar nor good sense. The *oti* clause, "that from your childhood," depends on the participle "knowing." Paul wants Timothy to know two things: his instructors and the fact that this instruction began in childhood. This is permissible grammar, even though Paul's style is not equal to that of Demosthenes.

Now to something more important than grammar: What Timothy had learned was the sacred writings, and these are the means by which we are saved. This is not to deny that Christ saves us by the blood of his cross; the idea is that only by the Scriptures could we know anything about Christ and salvation. We are saved, more exactly we are justified by faith, that is, by believing the doctrine, the teaching, the information, the good news. Faith comes by hearing and hearing by the Word of God. This idea in verse 15 leads on to the best known verse in the second epistle.

What Timothy had learned was the sacred writings, and these are the means by which we are saved.

3:16, 17

Every scripture was breathed out by God and is useful for teaching, for refutation, for correction, for instruction in righteousness, in order that the man of God may be competent, furnished for every good work.

The first two words may be properly translated "all Scripture." This is a regular and unobjectionable use of the word *pasa*. For example, *Acts* 2:36, "Let all the house of Israel know. . . ." Here *pas oikos* cannot mean *every* cottage in Palestine. And surely *Romans* 11:26 cannot possibly mean *every* Israel. In other places *every* is a good translation. The present verse can properly be translated "every scripture." One cannot understand why Barrett decides that "It would be absurd to say, 'every writing is inspired.' " Perhaps he means only that the English word *writing* can apply to Shakespeare, whereas *Scripture* means the Bible. In any case, every scripture, every verse of it, is inspired. If one wishes to minimize the distributive force of *every*, which I am far from recommending, one might say, "the whole of Scripture." *Acts* 2:36 could be read, "Let the whole house. . . ." There are thus several permissible translations; but what must be avoided at all costs is the fallacious inference embedded in the (expanded) phrase "every scripture that happens to be inspired is useful, but not the other verses which are not inspired." Therefore, the *New English Bible* is perverse: "Every inspired scripture has its use. . . ." To arrive at this mistranslation, the *New English Bible* had to disregard the *kai* (and). The Greek says, "Every scripture is inspired *and* useful." *Inspired* and *useful* are both predicate nominatives.

The term *inspired* is a poor translation. As B. B. Warfield emphatically asserted, the word is "God-breathed." The situation is not that the prophets wrote some books and God breathed I know not what into them; but, rather, and pointedly, God breathed out the words that became the books. I should like to add a comparison to Warfield's material: As the finger of God chiseled characters on two tables of stone, so God's breath put the words on some sheets of vellum. There is one difference, however, for all comparisons and analogies are defective: Moses had no part in choosing the words of the Ten Commandments, but in the Pentateuch God breathed the words onto the page through Moses' mind. Another defective comparison is: With his own lips God whistled a tune—the Ten Commandments; but he took some flutes and oboes to play the remainder of the Bible. These flutes and oboes (Moses, Isaiah, Paul) have different tonalities, but the notes, the symphony, from *Genesis* to *Revelation*, has one tune and one composer. However, since no one has ever suggested that God wrote words on vellum as he chiseled the Law on stone, we may continue with the broader problem.

As the finger of God chiseled characters on two tables of stone, so God's breath put the words on some sheets of vellum.

Those who attack the trustworthiness of the Bible ascribe to evangelicals, and fulminate against, "the dictation theory" of revelation. They hold that a stenographer's personality contributes nothing to a business letter, whereas the personal styles of the prophets and apostles are clearly different. Clearly: Who can doubt it? But the objection applies only to an imaginary straw-man, and embedded within it is the refusal to accept all Scriptures as God's word.

Had God himself written the Bible as he wrote the Ten Commandments, evangelicals would be happy enough, just as if he had sent angels to preach the Gospel. The fact, however, is that he did neither of these. Further, a message, if true, is true no matter how written. But the liberals know well enough that if men wrote the manuscripts, there is a plausible possibility of error. Apparently they think that the orthodox theologians invented the dictation theory to remove this possibility and to defend inerrancy. This is no compliment to evangelical intelligence. Dictation cannot guarantee the absence of errors. Stenographers make mistakes. If then the prophets and apostles were stenographers, "mechanically" putting words on paper, the doctrine of inerrancy would rest on a feeble foundation. But the evangelicals were never so stupid as the liberals allege. Their treatises repeatedly repudiate mechanical dictation. Dozens of instances can be found, all of which the liberals try to ignore. Hendriksen furnishes a recent example:

> The Spirit, however, did not suppress the personality of the human writer, but raised it to a higher level of activity (John 14:26). And because the individuality of the human author was not destroyed, we find in the Bible a wide variety of style and language. Inspiration, in other words, is organic, not mechanical (302).

Numerous citations of similar nature can be listed, and together they show how gross the liberal misunderstandings are. This is not to say that Hendriksen's expressions are the best. For example, the term *organic* is very vague, and the words "higher level" convey no clear idea.* Furthermore, Hendriksen and other evangelicals, and of necessity all liberals, use the term *inspiration*. Though this is the traditional term, it has caused widespread confusion. This verse in 2 Timothy does not say that the prophets were inspired; it says that the written words were breathed out by God.

So far as theology and preaching the Gospel are concerned, the difference between dictation and God's actual method is insignificant. God foreordains whatsoever comes to pass. He makes it rain by sending Aristophanes' clouds, which he had previously made. He makes the grass grow by sending the rain. So, too, he predestined Moses' style and Paul's choice of words. He predestined Moses' style by giving him an Egyptian education; he determined Paul's choice of words by educating him under Gamaliel. To try to escape God's control by refuting the dictation theory is foolish and futile. To rely on the term *inspiration* to turn attention away from the written words to the authors is deceptive. God controls everything; He certainly controls his own verbal revelation. He breathed out the *Scripture*, namely, what was written.

He predestined Moses' style and Paul's choice of words.

To try to escape God's control by refuting the dictation theory is foolish and futile.

There is another matter that needs mention in connection with B. B. Warfield. In this final quarter of the twentieth century a concerted effort, apparently led by Fuller Seminary, is being made to defend the allegation that the Bible contains falsehoods and errors. Some of the writers speak as if the doctrine of inerrancy were the invention of Warfield and the old Princeton's theologians. Such assertions derive from incompetent scholarship. From the beginning the whole Protestant movement, Lutherans and Calvinists alike, held to Biblical inerrancy. For example, Quenstedt, a major Lutheran theologian of the seventeenth century, two hundred years before Warfield, wrote,

> The canonical Holy Scriptures in the original text are the infallible truth and are free from every error; in other words, in the canonical sacred Scriptures there is found no lie, no falsity, no error, not even the least, whether in subject matter or expressions, but in all things and all the details that are handed down in them, they are most certainly true, whether they pertain to doctrines or morals, to history or chronology, to topography or nomenclature. No ignorance, no thoughtlessness, no forgetfulness, no lapse of memory can dare be ascribed to the amanuenses of the Holy Ghost in their penning of the Sacred Writings *(Systema*, I, 112).†

It would be almost impossible to write a more unambiguous, detailed, forceful assertion of inerrancy. Mueller continues by show-

* Instead of the ambiguous word *organic* and the metaphorical phrase "raised to a higher level," the present writer prefers his own more literal verbiage in his *Religion, Reason, and Revelation.*

† Quoted by J. Theodore Mueller. "Luther and the Bible," III, 96, *Inspiration and Interpretation.* edited by John W. Walvoord (Eerdmans, 1957).

ing that Luther had previously said, in various places, every point in this quotation from Quenstedt. Kenneth Kantzer in the next chapter of the book, "Calvin and the Holy Scriptures," shows that Calvin accepted the same view. These references to Luther and Calvin and Quenstedt are not meant to belittle Warfield. The aim is to show that *sola scriptura* is as much essential to evangelical Christianity as *sola fide*, and *soli Deo gloria*.

Not only are many liberals ignorant of the history of doctrine, some are logically deficient in exegeting the Scripture. Several say that the Bible itself does not claim infallibility.

Incidentally, the recent attempt to differentiate between infallibility and inerrancy, accepting the first and repudiating the second, does not recommend their honesty to one who knows English. A text that is infallible is one that is inerrant.

Would falsehoods be useful for teaching, for instruction in righteousness?

Does then the Bible claim to be inerrant? The passage before us says that every scripture, distributively every verse, has been breathed out by God. Is that not an assertion of inerrancy? Every verse is also useful for teaching, correction, for refutation of falsehoods, and so on. Would falsehoods be useful for teaching, for instruction in righteousness? The liberals, or semi-liberals who call themselves evangelicals, would be more honest if they simply said, "The Bible contains errors, and this is one of them."

The inerrancy of Scripture, as Quenstedt so carefully detailed it, is of fundamental importance. Nowhere else could we learn of salvation. Nowhere else could we learn of justification by faith. Nowhere else is there any information about Jesus Christ. Whatever later Christian authors have written about the virgin birth, the atonement, and the resurrection has its source in Scripture. If the Scripture is in error here and there, it is possible that it is in error here. Then, too, from the standpoint of logic, there is a question the new so-called evangelicals are reluctant to answer. It is this: If the Bible contains falsehoods here and there, the theologian must have a criterion to distinguish the parts that are true from the parts that are false: What is that criterion? In a court of law if the judge and jury detect a witness perjuring himself two or three times, or even once, they cannot accept any of the remainder of his testimony. If some things he says happen to be true, they must be proved by other witnesses. Therefore, attacks on the evangelical position are obliged to state the criterion they use in separating the truths of the Bible from its falsehoods. What is this criterion by which from its superior position it convicts the Scripture of error? Are the Assyrian inscriptions infallible in matters of history? Is Swedenborg an inerrant authority on Heaven and Hell? Bultmann at least has the consistency to say we do not know a single thing Jesus ever said or did.

Because God breathed out the words through Paul's mind onto the manuscript, Timothy knows what he is obliged to teach, refute, correct, and instruct. Otherwise, neither Timothy nor any other minister down to the present day could provide his parishioners with anything better than his own personal prejudices. In fact, this is precisely what happens in much contemporary pastoral counseling. Take three neo-evangelicals and present them with a domestic problem: There will be two contrasting recommendations, while the third pastor smiles, says nothing, and pats the parishioner on the shoulder. What the many troubled people in this society need is the Word of God. Nothing else is needed. Note that the final verse ends with the statement, "that the man of God may be competent, furnished [or, equipped] for every good work." Those who do not hold the Bible in high repute, and many who do, will demur. Does the Bible, they ask, inform us what to buy in the stock market? Asks a young man, Which of these two, or three, girls should I marry? Well, if a young man has to ask that question, I think the best answer would be, None. More strictly, the Biblical answer is, any one, providing they are all Christians.

Take three neo-evangelicals and present them with a domestic problem: There will be two contrasting recommendations, while the third pastor smiles.

But there are so many questions the Bible does not answer. Is this verse therefore a falsehood? No, but the questioner has missed the implication. The questioner thinks that buying AT&T is a good work and that buying XY&Z is bad. The Biblical view is that neither is either. Scripture tells us that we should work and invest in the stock market (*Matthew* 25:27) in order to make our living. But in God's providence it might be good for us to make a bad investment. If we are greedy, if we worship wealth, a loss might teach us a spiritual lesson. But though investment is proper for those who have money to invest, there is no moral problem in deciding between two honest businesses. In such matters the question of morality is the internal motive. Giving a cup of cold water to a thirsty traveler is neither good nor bad as an external action. To give it "in my name" is a good action.

If someone claims that overt actions such as murder, adultery, and theft are always evil, the answer is that these are not precisely overt actions. The terms used include both motive and various other circumstances. The overt act of killing a man is not always murder. Under certain circumstances this overt act is a good act. Sexual intercourse is legitimate for a married couple. Adultery already has the idea contained that the couple is not married the one to the other. Picking up some money and putting it into one's pocket is an overt act, but it is not necessarily theft. The three terms include ideas of motive and other circumstances, and when these conditions obtain, the act is wrong. But it is the motive, not the motions, that make it wrong. In other circumstances an act is neither right nor wrong. When all this is sorted out, we find no reason to deny that Scripture equips us *completely* for every *good* act.

Chapter Four

4:1, 2

I charge [you] before God and Christ Jesus, who is about to judge living and dead, at his appearing and his kingdom, preach the doctrine, be attentive in season, out of season, refute, censure, exhort, in all patience and instruction.

It is unlikely enough that a second-century Christian would fraudulently plan such a great emphasis on teaching, truth, reproof, inerrancy, and righteousness; but this solemn adjuration, unless from Paul himself, would require an exceptional degree of depravity.

The present commentary proceeds throughout on the basis that the pastoral epistles are genuine letters of Paul. It has mentioned a few supporting evidences. Those interested in this question should consider these two verses. Forgeries have occurred. The name Dionysius the Areopagite was attached to a fifth-century composition, deceiving the church for centuries. This procedure goes by the name of "pious fraud." How pious? Since Christians as well as non-Christians are sinners, one cannot deny *a priori* that nothing fraudulent has been published. But how likely is it that even a semi-pious Christian would forge this solemn oath at the beginning of chapter four? It is unlikely enough that a second-century Christian would fraudulently plan such a great emphasis on teaching, truth, reproof, inerrancy, and righteousness; but this solemn adjuration, unless from Paul himself, would require an exceptional degree of depravity. Conzelmann wisely ignores the difficulty.

From the Gospels we learn that the Jews took oaths, appealed to God as a witness to the truth of what they were saying, not only frequently, but on trivial matters. They would swear by the Earth, by Jerusalem, by their head (*Matthew* 5:33-37). They made queer distinctions: An oath by the temple was not binding, but an oath by the gold in the temple was; an oath by the altar is nothing, but an oath by the sacrifice on it, is (*Matthew* 23:16-22). Christ, however, while he condemned these evasions and trivialities, took an oath on a most important occasion. Here Paul is not strictly taking an oath; but since he seems to suggest that Timothy take, or intend the meaning of, an oath, the same principles apply. The situation is not trivial, but serious. Timothy cannot be light-hearted; he must be altogether sincere.

Accordingly, Paul adjures Timothy in the name of God and Christ. A theologian could use this verse to support the doctrine of the deity of Christ—of course with other material also. Here Paul describes Christ as the one who will judge the living and the dead. All this is solemn enough.

Now an exegetical difficulty appears. Paul has obviously appealed to God and Christ. Does he also appeal to something else, like the gold on the temple? The critical text and many exegetes say that Paul adjures Timothy by Christ's *epiphaneian* and *basileian:* his appearing and his kingdom. These two nouns are accusatives, and oaths regularly require the accusative. The critical text reads, "in the presence of . . . Christ Jesus . . . and by his appearing and kingdom." But a great many manuscripts, indeed the majority, instead of "and by" *(kai),* read *kata* (at his appearing). This makes much better sense: Christ will judge all people at his appearing. It seems queer to swear *by* his appearing. Alford agrees.

The actions which Paul wants Timothy to perform are now listed. Note again, for the umpteenth time, the strong emphasis on the intellectual and intelligible content. Timothy, and his conscientious successors, must preach the doctrine, in season and out of season, that is, always. That is their main business.

Not only must they preach positively; they must also refute false doctrine: *Elegxon* can mean *expose, set forth, convince, reprove, put to shame, cross-examine, accuse*; the noun *elegchos* means *reproach, disproof, refutation, scrutiny*. In twentieth-century preaching these terms and actions are conspicuously absent. The power of positive thinking brands negative thinking a sin. But Paul denounced heretics publicly by name. It is not enough to give diplomatic, spineless, uninformative warnings against unidentified errors. They must be clearly explained and clearly refuted. Some in the congregation may think refutation is useless and tedious. But Paul commands the preachers to persevere in their instruction with all patience. The neo-evangelicals, the new modernists, those who reject *sola scriptura,* dismiss these verses as another Biblical error.

It is not enough to give diplomatic, spineless, uninformative warnings against unidentified errors. They must be clearly explained and clearly refuted.

The neo-evangelicals are the new modernists.

4:3, 4

For there will come a time when they will not endure sound doctrine; but according to their own desires and having an itch in their ears, they will gather teachers for themselves, turn their ears away from the truth, and will turn toward their myths.

Whatever troubles beset the Ephesian church, Paul here suggests that the future will be worse. This prophecy has been fulfilled to some degree in every age. But looking back into the past through a romantic fog of nostalgia does not explain away the judgment that the world is worse since World War II. By the end of the sixteenth century the Roman church was not only corrupt—it was apostate; yet it professed (no doubt unprofitably) the doctrine of the Trinity. In the eighteenth century Deists in England largely rejected the Trinity, but they still believed in some sort of god. Today not merely practical atheism but theoretical atheism is rampant. Fornication and adultery have always been common, but today's society is approximating the homosexuality of Sodom and Gomorrah. The blind optimism of Herbert Spencer has become the unyielding despair of Bertrand Russell. Truth is nowhere and irrational existentialism reigns.

Descending from heights of pessimistic generality, we may dull our pain with a bit of grammatical laudanum. The *New English Bible* is mistaken when it says "gather together a crowd of teachers to tickle their ears." The idea is not that they want someone to tickle them; but rather their ears are already itching and they want someone to come and scratch them.

By the end of the sixteenth century the Roman church was not only corrupt—it was apostate; yet it professed (no doubt unprofitably) the doctrine of the Trinity.

How many popular evangelists attack, refute, and oppose false doctrine?

4:5

But you exercise self-control in all things, endure evil, do the work of an evangelist, fulfill your ministry.

This admonition to Timothy forms a contrast between his actions and those of the false teachers. One may note that the endurance of evil, here mentioned, is not particularly connected with pagan persecutions, but with the doctrinal attacks by the heretics. Had Paul been referring to Roman persecution, he might have said, When persecution arises in one city, flee to another. What he actually wrote was, "Do the work of an evangelist." How many popular evangelists attack, refute, and oppose false doctrine? Why, some of the most popular seem to be unable to get very much true doctrine into their harangues. Naturally, Timothy had other obligations in addition to refuting falsehoods; but instead of listing and emphasizing them, Paul merely sums them up in the phrase, "fulfill your diaconate" (service).

4:6

For I myself am already being poured out as a libation [spendomai], and the moment of my dissolution (departure, death) has arrived.

In *Philippians* 2:17 Paul regards *spendomai* as a future possibility; here he sees it as imminent. In *Philippians* 1:23 the noun *analusis* is also found. Now as the soldiers are coming to behead him, as we may imagine, he can burst out and exclaim,

4:7

I have fought the good fight, I have finished the race, I have kept the faith.

This is a well known verse, often quoted, in tones of great devotion.

But in spite of its simplicity many Christians miss its meaning. The term *race* is obviously metaphorical. Paul was no Olympic athlete. The term *fight* is more literal, for not all fights are those of boxers or gladiators. Athanasius for more than fifty years fought *contra mundum.* Augustine fought Pelagius and the Donatists. But the completely literal term, which here characterizes Paul's fight, is "the faith." The several actions on various fronts or in different rings naturally differed in several particulars, but they were all fights for the faith. Note that Paul did not say, I have fought a good fight, nor, I have kept faith. Heydenreich and Barrett thoughtlessly expound *pistis* to mean fidelity in observing the rules of the game. But "the faith" is the doctrinal content of Christianity, the deposit which God deposited with Paul and Timothy. As Alford says, "The constant use of *ē pistis* in these epistles in the objective technical sense must rule the expression here." How can anyone think that Paul is boasting of his personal fidelity, on which will be based in the following verse his receiving the crown of righteousness? In our present subjectivist milieu we may imagine the great apostle as worthy by his own righteousness, but the great apostle himself ever denied and combatted this opinion. Paul kept *the faith.*

"The faith" is the doctrinal content of Christianity, the deposit which God deposited with Paul and Timothy.

Paul is not boasting of his personal attainments.

4:8

For the rest there is reserved for me the crown of righteousness which the Lord will give me on that day, the righteous Judge, and not only to me but also to all who have loved his appearing.

That Paul is not boasting of his personal attainments, as indicated in the previous comment, is clear here in its application to all who have loved his appearing. The crown itself cannot be regarded as the righteousness, particularly not the righteousness of Christ imputed to us. Paul had already received that righteousness. At this point Calvin vigorously attacks the papists with their theory of personal merit and free will, which puts God in our debt. God certainly does not become or even remain just by paying any debts. Perhaps the righteousness is the personal subjective righteousness a Christian receives upon death, in contrast with our present incomplete sanctification. We may also consider the idea, found in 1 Corinthians 3:14, where "rewards" are given in proportion to, but not because of, our good works. However, here in Timothy, Paul has more in mind the similarity of the crown given to Christians rather than any differences among the awards.

This ends the main message of the epistle. The remaining verses are personal in nature, yet, though less applicable to our twentieth-century problems, they are not without value.

4:9

Hurry and come to me quickly;

Here begins the final section of the epistle: some personal matters (verses 9-18) and then a final greeting.

First, Paul urges Timothy to visit him. Although he surmised that his death was near, he apparently thought that Timothy could get to him before the end.

4:10

for Demas has deserted me, because he loved the present age, and has gone to Thessalonica; Crescens to Galatia; Titus to Dalmatia.

Some nonsense has become prevalent to the effect that agapaō means a high, exalted, spiritual love of God, and that phileō, not to mention disreputable eraō, which does not occur in the New Testament anyway, means some lower form of human love.

Aside from his approaching death, the reason Paul wants Timothy to come to him is that he is almost alone. Demas deserted; whether he later repented is not known. Crescens and Titus did not desert: They went off on legitimate evangelistic missions. There is an interesting textual reading that Crescens went, not to Galatia, but to Gaul. One must remember that in 278 B.C. some 20,000 Gauls from what we now call France settled in *Galatia* (hence the name). Galatia is the better reading. In any case we know nothing further about Crescens.

It is linguistically interesting to note that Demas loved the present world. The verb (participle) is *agapēsas.* In recent days some nonsense has become prevalent to the effect that *agapāo* means a high, exalted, spiritual love of God, and that *philēo,* not to mention disreputable *eraō,* which does not occur in the New Testament anyway, means some lower form of human love. This verse is a case where *agapaō* is unmistakably contrasted with love for God. Demas loved the present world. Who would have thought that this innocuous phrase in this verse destroys the work of several learned but too ingenious theologians?

Also interesting is Barrett's attempt to discredit the authenticity of the epistle by arguing (120) that "the present age" is not sufficiently eschatological in tone and therefore Paul could not have written it. These destructive critics are nothing if not ingenious.

4:11

Only Luke is with me. Get Mark and bring him with you, for he is useful for me in the service.

The dismal picture has one spot of light. Mark, whom Paul thought was cowardly on a previous occasion, now reappears as a faithful and useful servant. The word *diaconian,* of course, does not mean "deacon" in our official sense: It simply means *service* in some sense or other, as it was used of Phoebe in *Romans* 16:1. The technical sense of the term (described but hardly used in *Acts* 6:1, 2) is rare in the New Testament. Meyer wants it to mean "the apostolic office" in the present verse.

4:12, 13

I have sent Tychicus to Ephesus. The cloak I left in Troas with Carpus, bring when you come, and the books, especially the parchments.

Some commentators want to make *philonēn* a bag for carrying books; but the mention of winter in verse 21 favors the translation cloak. Instead of *parchments* the *New English Bible* has "above all my notebooks." Even Barrett sees that parchments were too expensive for notes. The papyrus books may have been parts of the Old Testament. One commentator suggests that the parchments were legal documents relative to Paul's Roman citizenship. Of course this is all guesswork.

4:14, 15

Alexander the coppersmith did me a great deal of harm [showed me many evils]; the Lord will give back to him according to his works; you watch out for him, for he very much opposed our doctrines.

Alexander was a common Greek name, and one has difficulty in identifying this Alexander with any other. Timothy knew whom Paul had in mind, and it makes no difference to us. We simply realize that God will give back evil to those who oppose sound doctrine.

Indications of Peter's whereabouts in the New Testament show that Peter could never have spent much time in Rome: He always seems to be somewhere else.

4:16

In my first defense no one stood by me, but all deserted me; may it not be imputed to them.

This verse, as to its historical references, must be taken with the following two. But one side issue, not without considerable importance in itself, deserves a comment. If all his friends in Rome deserted Paul, could Peter have been in Rome at that time and have been among the deserters? This would be incredible. Peter denied Christ on one occasion; he even succumbed to hypocrisy on a later occasion; but no one can convince us that Peter would have deserted Paul when Paul was on trial for his life. It follows, therefore, that Peter was not in Rome at that time. In fact, indications of Peter's whereabouts in the New Testament show that Peter could never have spent much time in Rome: He always seems to be somewhere else. Some Protestants have gone beyond the evidence and have asserted that Peter was never in Rome. This is unlikely. But that Peter was pope and bishop of Rome for twenty-five years, as the Romanists claim, has no evidence to support it.

4:17, 18

But the Lord stood by me and strengthened me in order that through me the preaching [the message] might be fully completed and that all the nations might hear it, and I was delivered from the mouth of the lion. The Lord will deliver me from every evil and will save [me] to his heavenly kingdom, to whom the glory for ever and ever, Amen.

It is clear from verse 16 that Paul had two appearances in court. They must have both been in Rome, for the statement that no one stood by him does not fit his trial in Caesarea. Since there were two trials, therefore, either he was acquitted and later arrested again, or the trial was not completed and Paul remained a prisoner. It is at least likely that he was acquitted, for the Jews' case against him in Caesarea was very weak. If he was acquitted, he could have gone to Spain. One New Testament scholar argued that he probably went to England, for Spain contains no evidence of any visit by Paul; and though England furnishes none either, the chaotic conditions in England through the early Middle Ages could have easily destroyed the evidence, while destruction was less likely in more civilized Spain.

It is clear from verse 16 that Paul had two appearances in court. They must have both been in Rome, for the statement that no one stood by him does not fit his trial in Caesarea.

Whether England or Spain, the phrase "that through me the preaching might be fully completed and that all nations might hear it" certainly suggests a missionary journey to the western end of the Roman Empire. The explanation of some liberal scholars that all nations heard by reason of a public trial in Rome (no acquittal) is unconvincing.

Then, too, the phrase "I was delivered from the mouth of the lion" strongly suggests acquittal. Furthermore, verse 18 can easily be interpreted to refer to a later trial. Previously he was delivered from the lion (Nero?); but now God will bring him into the heavenly kingdom. The conclusion may not be apodeictically certain, but the text lends more favor to an acquittal, an intervening missionary journey, and a final arrest and execution. Hendriksen defends this position at length (325-330).

4:19-22

Greet Prisca and Aquila and the house of Onesiphorus. Erastus remained in Corinth; I left Trophimus sick in Miletus. Hurry and come before winter. Eubulos greets you, and Pudens and Linus, and all the brethren. The Lord be with thy spirit. Grace be with you.

Titus

Chapter One

1:1-4

Paul, slave of God, but apostle of Jesus Christ, according to [the] faith of God's elect and [the] knowledge of the truth which is according to piety on the hope of eternal life which the non-lying God promised before times of ages, but at his own times published as his word by preaching, with which I was entrusted according to the decree of God our Savior: to Titus, legitimate child according to [the] common faith; Grace and peace from God, Father, and Christ Jesus our Savior.

The phrases and the lengthy complicated grammar are so Pauline that no telltale evidence of forgery remains. Paul was adept at forging his own letters.

Obviously this translation of mine is not designed for public reading in the pulpit; but it is what the Greek says.

The *New English Bible* turns it into:

> From Paul, servant of God and apostle of Jesus Christ, marked as such by faith and knowledge and hope—the faith of God's chosen people, knowledge of the truth as our religion has it, and the hope of eternal life. Yes, it is eternal life that God, who cannot lie, promised long ago, and now in his own good time he has openly declared himself in the proclamation which was entrusted to me by ordinance of God our Savior.

Undoubtedly the *New English Bible* uses good English. This address or salutation is twice as long as those in the two *Timothys*. Unfriendly critics have accused a forger with having heaped up Pauline phrases to make the letter look genuine. He succeeded: The phrases and the lengthy complicated grammar are so Pauline that no telltale evidence of forgery remains. Paul was adept at forging his own letters.

We must now work our way through the complications. That Paul was the slave, the bond-slave, or more delicately the servant, of

God hardly needs comment. In *Romans* and *Philippians* he calls himself the slave of Christ. A forger would have used *Christ* instead of *God*.

The word *but* (*de*) is weak, not a strong adversative. Yet though it is weak, it should not be reduced to the colorless *and* of the *New English Bible* and *New International Version*. There is a contrast between slave and apostle. The real difficulty, however, begins with the word *kata* (*according to*). The text clearly says, "an apostle . . . according to the faith of God's elect." But how can this be? How can our believing be that according to which Paul became an apostle? Did God make Paul a slave and an apostle just because we believe he did? Hardly. The difficulty arises because of a mistaken notion of faith. *Faith* here, and usually, is not our subjective activity of believing. Subjectivizing Christianity is a modern evil. *Faith* is not our believing: It is the truth we believe. That Paul was an apostle is one of the doctrines we believe.

Faith here, and usually, is not our subjective activity of believing. Subjectivizing Christianity is a modern evil. Faith is not our believing: It is the truth we believe. That Paul was an apostle is one of the doctrines we believe.

Calvin in his commentary makes this quite clear by saying that "there is a mutual relationship between my [Paul's] apostleship and the faith of God's elect, so that nobody can reject it without being a reprobate and a stranger from the faith."

Alford rejects Calvin's explanation. He gives two reasons. First, he alleges that Calvin is "setting up a standard which the Apostle would not have acknowledged for his apostleship." But if Alford has correctly expressed himself, we are forced to say that his words contradict what Paul himself said in his Galatian letter. His apostleship and the truth of his message were inextricably intertwined. Alford's second reason is that the following word *epignōsis* (*knowledge*) also belongs to *kata* (*according to*) and therefore rules out Calvin's view.

On the contrary, Calvin set up a standard which the Apostle explicitly acknowledged and which admirably suits *epignōsis* below. Let us see. If Paul had meant that his apostolic preaching was *for the purpose of* extending faith and knowledge to God's elect—and this is what the *New American Standard* and the *New International Version* seem to suggest—one would have expected the preposition *eis* (*for the purpose of*) instead of *kata* (*according to*). Hendriksen defends the purpose position. He says, "The service and apostleship are exercised 'in the interest of' (that seems to be the meaning of *kata* here; cf. John 2:6; 2 Cor. 11:21) the faith of God's elect." The idea of purpose is plausible in *John* 2:6, but that does not determine the meaning in *Titus*. In *2 Corinthians* 11:21 it is impossible, for there Paul did not speak *in order to* produce shame.

One might say that Paul was an apostle "according to faith" in the sense that his apostleship presupposed the truth which God's elect believe; and even presupposes their knowledge—not so much their subjective knowing, but the truth they know. That is to say, Paul was an apostle in conformity with the revealed information God has given his elect.

This interpretation, essentially Calvin's, accords well with the next three words: "and knowledge of the truth." The body of knowledge and information, that is, the truth, and the faith are identical. In this regard one should pay particular attention to the word *elect.* God's elect are the Christians themselves. Men and women are Christians because God elected them before all ages. They come to believe at a point in time, but God's election or choice of them is eternal. The faith and the truth are themselves as eternal as election. Hence we may understand Paul to mean that his historical induction into the apostleship was a part of God's eternal plan.

If one wishes to find a subjective element in these verses, it is better to pass beyond *epignōsis* (*knowledge*) and *alētheia* (*truth*) to *eusebian* (*piety*). Piety is surely a subjective or individual state of mind. Even so, piety is according to or determined by truth, rather than vice versa. But in congregations where few are professional theologians, it often happens that certain men are recognized as eminently pious. Assuming that this judgment is correct, Paul joins truth and piety together. The people may not too well understand the truth, but they see the piety. As is customary in the epistles, the congregation is regarded as ideal, and the possibility of a mistaken judgment on a man's piety is disregarded.

God's elect are the Christians themselves. Men and women are Christians because God elected them before all ages. They come to believe at a point in time, but God's election or choice of them is eternal. The faith and the truth are themselves as eternal as election.

Verse 2 begins with a different preposition: *epi* rather than *kata. Epi* means *on*. But with what antecedent shall we connect this preposition? There are three possibilities: (1) Paul . . . upon the hope of eternal life; (2) piety in the hope of eternal life; or (3) knowledge of the truth in or upon the hope.

As an antecedent, *Paul* is some words distant; but distance in such a complicated sentence is not a decisive objection. Is it *piety* in the hope of eternal life? At least *piety* immediately precedes *upon*. But as distance does not eliminate *Paul*, so proximity does not necessitate *piety*. Could it be *knowledge of the truth* in or upon the hope? That hardly makes good sense; yet at least two German exegetes endorse it, while another reverses it and makes faith and knowledge depend on hope. The first possibility seems to be the best. Paul's apostleship is subjectively founded on his hope of eternal life.

Alford, however, denies that this hope refers to Paul's apostleship and makes it modify the compound clause "according to faith . . . according to piety." The meaning of the resulting sentence, however, is not clear. Alford favors it because it fits his understanding of *kata* as *eis:* of *according to* as *for the purpose of.* But if one rejects this initial point, as we have done, one cannot accept Alford's consequence.

"Eternal life which God has promised" poses no problems. Strange, isn't it, that Paul can write five words so easily understood. Yet (would you believe it?) some German commentators connect "which God promised" with "truth" rather than with "eternal life." One of them seems to have "hope" the antecedent.

Next comes *apseudēs,* which the *King James* and the *New American*

Standard translate as "God who cannot lie." *The New International Version* is better, "God who does not lie."

The translation "cannot lie" has induced some unwary Arminians to doubt divine omnipotence: Here is something, they say, that God cannot do. Of course, Arminians were never favorably predisposed to exalt divine omnipotence. Whether they realize it or not—probably not, for they are neither philosophers nor particularly bright—their view logically posits a moral principle superior to God, which he cannot disobey. Leibniz, not an Arminian, but a Lutheran and a brilliant philosopher, worked out this theme under the phrase "the best of all possible worlds." Its goodness is independent of God's choice. Descartes held the opposite view, namely, that the world is good because God chose it. Similarly, God "cannot" lie because whatever he says *ipso facto* determines the truth. Therefore, instead of using the phrase "cannot lie," it is both clearer and grammatically correct to translate the word *apseudēs* as "does not lie," or more literally, "the unlying God."

Since God is eternal and since his mind is the truth, the promise of eternal life has stood from before all ages, before eternal times. Twice now in three lines Paul has adverted to God's eternal and immutable decree. The assurance of hope depends on the doctrine of predestination.

Twice now in three lines Paul has adverted to God's eternal and immutable decree. The assurance of hope depends on the doctrine of predestination.

An Arminian cannot logically be assured he will get to Heaven, for his free will may ruin him tomorrow.

On one occasion I made this remark to a gentleman whom I did not know to be an Arminian. I was immediately disillusioned. He became irate. Our salvation, he vigorously asserted, depends on Christ's sacrifice and on nothing else. Of course the gentleman with his Arminian mind-set never heard what I had said. Acceptance with God, forgiveness of sins, entrance into Heaven is based entirely upon Christ's merits. To put faith in anything other than or anything additional to the merits of Christ renders void a man's relation to Christ. But I had not been talking about the meritorious cause of our salvation. I was talking about our assurance of salvation. An Arminian cannot logically be assured he will get to Heaven, for his free will may ruin him tomorrow. An assured hope depends on God's faithfulness to his predestinating, irresistible, and irreversible call.

Although the promise "dates" from eternity, it was proclaimed at chosen times. First came the promise to Eve, then elaborated to Moses and David, and temporally made effective by Christ's death and resurrection. It was further promulgated by Paul's preaching "his doctrine" (*ton logon autou*), with which Paul was entrusted. "His doctrine" is essentially a synonym for the promise. The promise was hidden and then proclaimed. God entrusted the doctrine to Paul. Not that God refused to entrust his word to Peter, Matthew, or Jude; but that this is Paul's epistle and he wants Titus and us to know that his preaching was in obedience to God's command. Incidentally, here is another instance of *kata, in accordance with*. It does not mean *eis, for the purpose of*. The latter makes no sense at all.

Barrett refers to "the clumsy Greek" of these verses. Well, Paul often uses complicated sentences; but here one should realize that these four verses are not a sentence. Essentially they say, "Paul . . . to Titus . . . Greetings." Hence there is no point in trying to find a main verb with a subject and predicate. Verse 4, accordingly, begins with "To Titus"; whom Paul recognizes as his "legitimate" spiritual son, because the two men hold a definite faith in common.

Finally comes the greeting: Grace and peace from God the Father and from Christ Jesus our Savior.

1:5, 6

On account of this I left you in Crete in order that you might set right what remained [to be done] and establish elders in every city, as I ordered you, if any is irreproachable, the husband of one wife, having believing children, not accused of dissipation or insubordination.

Usually the phrase "on account of this" refers to what preceded it; and such a backward glance is not completely impossible here, if we take the first four verses broadly as including the proclamation of the Gospel in general. The definite purpose however, does not come in the preceding but in the following phrases. Paul, sometime before writing this letter, had established Christianity in Crete, along with Titus, whom he left there to finish the work. Apparently Paul had to leave before the organization of churches had proceeded very far. So he left Titus there to finish what remained to be done. The most important task was to ordain elders in every city.

The second flaw in the prelatical view is that bishops are regarded as a higher order of clergy. Only two verses below we shall see that bishop and elder are synonymous terms.

Episcopally and prelatically inclined churchmen, in opposition to Presbyterians, will point out that these new elders were not elected by the congregations, but were chosen and ordained by Titus in his role of bishop. There are two defects in this argument. The text indeed says that Titus is to set up, or ordain, elders; but the text does not deny a prior election by the congregations. Or, for that matter, Titus may have supplied new congregations with provisional elders from earlier established churches. One does not need to assume that Paul, however brief his stay in Crete, organized no congregations at all. The second flaw in the prelatical view is that bishops are regarded as a higher order of clergy. Only two verses below we shall see that *bishop* and *elder* are synonymous terms.

On the other extreme from prelatic hierarchies are those anti-establishment libertarians, or anarchists we might say, who denounce all government for the church. I know well one group that objected even to having a church roll. There should be no membership at all. How they could hold property is a mystery. In choosing a minister or in any other business anybody off the street could come in and vote, if such an organized activity as voting were allowed. After that hurdle had been surmounted and an embryo organization had been established, several who had been attending the chaotic group refused to become members because the existence of officers made everyone else second class citizens. But more important than the legal difficulties of operating without members and officers was the refusal of these anti-establishment people to obey the organizational instructions, not only in the pastoral epistles, but in the Gospels as well—organizational directions given by Christ himself.

In this last quarter of the twentieth century, when the liberal denominational officers are forcing reluctant congregations to elect teen-agers as elders, emphasis should be placed on the Scriptural requirements that elders must be married, have children, and rule their households well. No teen-ager is eligible. Remember that some people despised Timothy because he was only forty years of age. Paul defended Timothy, but he never approved of childless singles.

This requirement of marriage, so deliberately violated by Roman Catholicism, is also largely forgotten among Protestants. Paul gives a reason for his requirement in the next verse.

Elders must be married, have children, and rule their households well.

This requirement of marriage, so deliberately violated by Roman Catholicism, is also largely forgotten among Protestants.

It is not enough to warn people against drinking poison: One must add, "That bottle of nitric acid is a poison." The heretics and heresies must be identified by name.

1:7, 8, 9

For it is necessary that the bishop be irreproachable as a steward of God, not stubborn [arrogant], not inclined to anger, not addicted to wine, not a brawler [striker], not greedy, but hospitable, a lover of good, prudent, just, pious, self-controlled, holding the faithful [pure?] word according to the [our?] teaching, in order that he may be capable both of exhorting in the sound doctrine and refuting those who contradict it.

First, as previously indicated, the *episcopos* of this verse and the *presbuteros* of verse 5 are the same official. Even Anglicans admit that the term *bishop* in the New Testament does not bear the High Anglican meaning of the word.

Next, the qualifications for the office are divided into two sections. General moral qualifications come first, most of which are also qualifications for church membership, even if not so strictly enforced. Then come the doctrinal requirements.

The man must be sound in his theology. He must be convinced of the truth of Paul's teaching. Otherwise he would be incompetent for exhorting. Note that exhortation is not a simple invitation to "come to Christ." Paul says, "exhorting in the sound doctrine." A Greek peculiarity is interesting here. Paul did not say, "exhorting in sound doctrine." There is a double emphasis that is usually missed in English. The literal translation would be "exhorting in the teaching the sound." The repeated article adds emphasis. Nor is the obligation limited to so-called "positive" instruction. Specifically included is the refutation of heretical or heterodox arguments. The elder or bishop must analyze what is "said against" (*antilegontas*) the teaching and explain its fallacies and falsehoods. It is not enough to warn people against drinking poison: One must add, "That bottle of nitric acid is a poison." The heretics and heresies must be identified by name.

1:10, 11, 12

For many are insubordinate, fallacious reasoners and deceivers, especially those of the Jewish party [those of the circumcision], whom it is necessary to silence, who upset whole families, teaching what they should not for the sake of shameful profit. One of them, one of their own prophets, said, "Cretans are always liars, evil beasts, useless gluttons."

These three verses reflect a complicated congregational or presbyterial situation, inattention to which results in some confusion. No confusion results from the simple idea that insubordinate church members are a nuisance in any congregation, and deliberate deceivers, or even sincere deceivers, are worse. Fallacious reasoning, on the part of elders especially, and as well on the part of conceited members, is also an obvious disadvantage. But behind the easily observed difficulties there are hidden reasons why Paul should include fallacious reasoning in this list.

Before his fall into sin Adam had never proposed a syllogism with two undistributed middle terms; his universal conclusions never had a particular premise. Of course Adam did not know these technical Aristotelian designations. He had never taken a college course in logic. He escaped all fallacies by instinct. Adam was the image of God, and since logic is the form of God's mind, Adam's mind functioned logically automatically. When he sinned, God's image was distorted. God did not degrade him to the level of an irrational animal; he was still human, a rational creature, but an imperfect one. He occasionally committed fallacies. Things got so bad that now college students ought to take a course in logic. Why? Because all sinning is the result of fallacious thinking. Sometimes the fallacy does not lie on the surface. Evil men can run through a long series of valid syllogisms. But away back somewhere they have had a wrong thought. The Scriptures teach that out of the heart, or mind, come all the issues of life; as a man thinks, so is he. Those who disturbed Paul's congregations were fallacious reasoners. And churches still have too many. Make sure you never use a distributed term in the conclusion, if it was undistributed in a premise.

Before his fall into sin Adam had never proposed a syllogism with two undistributed middle terms; his universal conclusions never had a particular premise.

Adam was the image of God, and since logic is the form of God's mind, Adam's mind functioned logically automatically.

All sinning is the result of fallacious thinking.

An American of the twentieth century is likely to be surprised that those who caused the most trouble in Crete, and elsewhere, were not polytheistic pagans: They were Jews. But then how does the proverb apply? The proverb "Cretans are always liars" was first formulated by Epimenides some centuries earlier. How then can Paul use it as a retort to the Jews of his day? Since it was said by a Cretan, it could be turned back upon Cretans, but hardly upon Jews. One might not be so surprised that the trouble in the church was not pagan sexual immorality, but Jewish greed for money. Jews are often thought of as greedy, yet Jews do not have the reputation of being gluttons. Gluttony was a pagan vice. The solution to this puzzle is embedded in the verses themselves. The Cretan churches contained both Jews and native Cretans. Here the Jews caused the most trouble. They above all could be called fallacious reasoners. But the Christians converted from paganism also had their faults. Paul addresses both groups. Though he has the Jews chiefly in mind, he includes the others too, and because his censure is condensed into only three verses, it can puzzle a speed reader.

There is the additional possibility that even some Jews, after having lived in Crete for a generation or two, may have succumbed to Cretan characteristics and so merited Epimenides' condemnation.

After reading this denunciation, one may ask, Do pastors today imitate Paul? Few dare to do so. Yet Paul in *1 Corinthians* 11:1 commands us to imitate him. The *King James* softens *imitator* to *follower,* but *imitator* is the correct translation.

1:13

This testimony is true. For which reason rebuke [refute] them sharply in order that they may recover their health in the faith,

Epimenides' adage was true: Therefore, rebuke them. The verb *elegcho,* previously found in verse 9, means: *to put to shame, to treat with contempt, cross-examine, accuse, prove, refute, decide a dispute*. There is an instance of this last meaning in the *Septuagint*, *Genesis* 31:37. Aristotle used it in the sense of *refute* or *disprove*. One is free to choose whichever of these meanings best fits the context.

Meyer identifies the people to be rebuked as "not so much the heretics as the Cretans who were exposed to their misleading influence." This is not likely, especially if we take the word *Cretan* as Epimenides used it. Surely Paul had the church community in mind, not all Crete. Alford is little better: "the Krētes indicated here, who are thus rebuked in order to their soundness in the faith, are manifestly not the false teachers, but ordinary believers." But if we assume, and it is a most likely assumption, that the false teachers operated from within the congregations, as the Judaizers in Galatia, surely Paul would have had Titus reprimand them even more severely than some befuddled simpletons. Nor does Alford's appeal to the next verse justify his interpretation.

One thing, however, is clear: the importance of the orthodox faith. In the present decadent age I frequently hear condemnations of "dead orthodoxy." There is so little orthodoxy today that even dead orthodoxy seems preferable to living heresy. For myself, in my various travels, I have never discovered any dead orthodoxy. Furthermore the Scriptures, which make sanctification an inevitable result of justification, teach that orthodoxy is never dead. Finally, those who use the phrase neither define nor instantiate it. If they are not deceitful, they are befuddled. At any rate, the pastorals place great emphasis on sound doctrine.

In the present decadent age I frequently hear condemnations of "dead orthodoxy." There is so little orthodoxy today that even dead orthodoxy seems preferable to living heresy.

The Scriptures, which make sanctification an inevitable result of justification, teach that orthodoxy is never dead.

1:14

and not pay attention to Jewish myths and commandments of men who turn away from the truth.

Meyer's American editor (294) asserts that these Jewish myths were "greatly affected by Greek or Oriental philosophy." Guthrie, Hendriksen, and even Barrett correctly note that the following verse suggests the Jewish food laws, and that *1 Timothy* 1:4 mentioned (allegorical interpretations of) Old Testament genealogies. Therefore, instead of looking backward to Greece and Oriental philosophizing, we do better to look forward to a developing *Talmud*. Be that as it may, no matter what the details of the heresy were, the Christian emphasis is on doctrinal truth.

1:15, 16

All things are pure for those who are pure; but to those who are defiled and unbelieving, nothing is pure; on the contrary, their mind and conscience are defiled. They profess to know God, but by their deeds they deny him, for they are detestable, disobedient, and with respect to any good work, disqualified.

Paul, however, is not talking about human actions. He is talking about things.

Some carping ignoramus may ask, If all things are pure for Christians, are murder, adultery, and theft pure? Are these actions evil only when done by unbelievers? There have been some professing Christians who hold that the Law, the Ten Commandments, do not bind believers. Since all things are pure, and since Christians are not under the Law, disobedience to the Ten Commandments is pious activity. The converse stupidity also occurs, namely, that the Ten Commandments bind Christians, but place no obligation on unbelievers.

Paul, however, is not talking about human actions. He is talking about things: pork, oysters, and meat offered to idols. The term *pure*, though used in a spiritual sense in its second occurrence, refers in its first instance to the food laws that distinguished between clean and unclean foods. Jesus, while he himself observed the Mosaic restrictions, anticipated their revocation. *Mark* 7:15 is a hint, and four verses later Mark recognizes that Jesus was about to abrogate these food laws. Paul had expressed the main idea in *1 Timothy* 4:4. The context in Titus has to do with Jewish asceticism, not with Gentile licentiousness.

Though all things are pure to the pure, and every creature of God is good, it does not follow that to the pure every action is good. Men can use good things sinfully. A bow and arrow, or a slingshot, can legitimately kill a lion, or even Goliath, but to murder an innocent person is still sin. Not only so, but even activities innocent in themselves, like ploughing a field, are sinful when done by the unregenerate. The morality of an act depends not so much, perhaps not at all on the describable, physical motions, but on the circumstances and intention. Picking up a valuable item, even if it belongs to someone else, and walking away with it is not always theft. Pronouncing the name of God may or may not be profanity. It is the motivation that counts. Since the motivation of unbelievers is always wrong, their actions are always sinful.

The second and greater error in trichotomy is that it ignores the one place in the Bible where the composition of man is explicitly described. The account of creation in Genesis clearly imposes a dichotomy.

This explains the next phrase. Paul says, "their mind and conscience are defiled." Yet Paul really says two things at once. We might have expected him to say, "to unbelievers nothing is pure *because* their minds are defiled." And this would be true. Defilement is the reason why eating roast lamb and ploughing a field are sinful. However, instead of the conjunction *because,* Paul uses the strong adversative *but,* or *on the contrary.* Paul actually makes a contrast rather than giving a reason. The contrast is between believers and unbelievers. Nevertheless, defilement is a reason because the believers are pure and the unbelievers are impure. Paul has spoken in a condensed manner, merging contrast and reason. We need both ideas.

Paul says that the impure are defiled in mind and conscience. These two words raise a point about Biblical psychology. The Greek words are *nous* and *suneidēsis; mind* and *conscience* are perfectly good translations. But do the two words require us to suppose that they designate two parts or functions of the soul? There is good reason for observing what the Bible says about human psychology, for the Bible is God's Word, and since God made man, he knows what man is. Furthermore, the nature of man has implications for any view of regeneration, sanctification, and all Christian life. If man is a mechanism without a soul, the statements in the Bible cannot be true; and conversely, if man is what the Bible says he is, behaviorism must be false. In the present passage the question is not so broad; we want to know whether mind and conscience are two parts of the soul or whether the words are synonyms.

Several times in the history of theology a view called trichotomy has gathered some prominence. In the United States during the first three decades of this century the view was widespread, and more recently, a few popular evangelists have continued it. Trichotomy is the theory that man is a threefold being, composed of body, soul, and spirit. Its advocates regularly appeal to *1 Thessalonians* 5:23 in which occurs the phrase "your spirit, soul, and body." But why should not someone appeal to *Mark* 12:30 to support a quadripartite theory of heart, soul, mind, and strength? Or, if the Trinity requires that man be three-fold, Mark only a few verses later gives us the division of heart, understanding, and strength. The present verse in Titus also gives a tripartite division of body (though it is not mentioned here), mind, and conscience. The common error in these conflicting views is that they all assume the terms to be mutually exclusive and distinct. We ask, why cannot they either overlap in meaning or even (some of them) be synonymous? The second and greater error in trichotomy is that it ignores the one place in the Bible where the composition of man is explicitly described. The account of creation in *Genesis* clearly imposes a dichotomy. God formed man's body out of the earth and breathed his spirit into that body. There are precisely two components.

Therefore, conscience cannot be a part or function different from mind. There is indeed a popular connotative difference. But first let us see what English words the lexicon gives for the Greek term *suneidēsis.* Liddell and Scott list: *knowledge shared with another, communication, information, knowledge, consciousness, consciousness of right and wrong, conscience, complicity, guilt,* and *crime.* In translating the New Testament, the choice from these possibilities depends on the context. In popular thought, when *mind* is mentioned, the idea of mathematics or even theology arises, but not specifically the idea of morality. The term *conscience* carries a strong moral connotation. Psychologically the function is the same. It is the intellectual function of judging. We may judge that a certain solution to a mathematical equation is correct, or we may judge that murdering innocent unborn babies is wrong. Both are judgments. If we needed separate parts of the soul for every different matter of judgment, we should have not trichotomy, but muriachotomy plus.

Anyone who tries to supplement the merit of Christ deprives himself of Christ's merit.

We pass on to later words: *detestable, disobedient, worthless.* Today many preachers would not condemn ascetics so harshly. Is it such a sin not to eat pork? Yes, it is: Avoiding pork is a major sin if we put more trust in not eating pork than we put in Jesus Christ. Anyone who tries to supplement the merit of Christ deprives himself of Christ's merit. That is why Paul was so angry in his epistle to the Galatians. Then, too, one should remember that the Judaizers in Crete were using their religion for financial advantage—a sin not completely unheard of in this age, too. Then, strangely, Paul refers to the false teachers as lazy gluttons. This is a strange charge to bring against ascetics. Guthrie believes it to be a metaphorical expression for financial greed. This would solve the puzzle. Otherwise we should have to admit—as we must many times—that we do not know very much about the social conditions in the Cretan churches.

Chapter Two

2:1

But you [must] speak what fits sound doctrine.

This stress on theological orthodoxy does not in any way belittle moral conduct. On the contrary, the theology is the foundation of the conduct.

Instead of heresy, indeed instead of pious irrelevancies, Titus must teach sound theology. The reader may be getting tired of this commentary's insistence on sound theology; but if so, he is getting tired of Paul's inspired commands. The liberal churches preach anti-Christian Marxism. They advocate a totalitarian state—provided it does not prohibit the murder of infants. The so-called evangelicals sell Norman Vincent Pills as tranquilizers. Primitive Baptists, bless their heterodox souls, still retain a large proportion of the Gospel. The Sovereign Grace Baptists are still better. But Christianity needs another Calvin, Knox, Turretin, and a George Gillespie as well.

2:2

Older men must be sober, pious, prudent, sound in the faith, in love, in perseverance.

The first word here means "older men," not elders or presbyters. They are to be temperate, not given to wine. This repeats some of the directions given in the previous epistles. They must also be sound in the faith. This stress on theological orthodoxy does not in any way belittle moral conduct. On the contrary, the theology is the foundation of the conduct. A different theology would result in different actions. Once a man begins to depart from the faith, one may expect him gradually to alter his conduct, too. Conversely, when a pagan repents (changes his mind, *metanoieō)* and believes Gospel truth, he begins to alter his conduct in a slow process of persevering sanctification.

2:3, 4, 5

Older women likewise in reverent demeanor, not slanderers nor enslaved to much wine, teachers of what is good, in order that they may encourage the young women to love their husbands, their children, to be prudent, chaste, homemakers, kind, subject to their own husbands, in order that the Word of God may not be blasphemed.

The mention of elderly women, young women, children, and husbands confirms the fact that Paul is speaking about families, and not church officers. The triple note of husbands, children, homemakers, and husbands again may have been motivated by the fact that the false teachers were invading and breaking up households, indicated in 1:11. The exhortation, however, is universally applicable.

The triple note of husbands, children, homemakers, and husbands again may have been motivated by the fact that the false teachers were invading and breaking up households.

One commentator restricts the term *katastēmati* to *clothing*; but the regular meaning is *demeanor*, or *deportment* in general. The other items also are most ordinary and pose no difficulty.

The commentary on *1 Timothy* 2:12 remarked that women were not forbidden to teach their children. Here the words, "teachers of what is good," confirm the comment.

The verb here translated "encourage" and the adjective "prudent" in the next line have the same root. We might have paraphrased it as: Give the young women the common sense to love their husbands and to show common sense. *Advise* or *urge*, however, are satisfactory translations.

Many particular or subordinate reasons support the moral injunctions of Scripture. The first and basic reason is the glory of God. A much inferior reason would be to avoid unpleasantness with one's neighbors. Here the reason is, "that the Word of God be not blasphemed." When a church member is discovered to be guilty of some infraction of the moral law, unbelievers revile the Gospel and conclude that all church members are hypocrites. The inference, of course, is a logical fallacy, but it damages the church nonetheless. In one case, a minister took off with the attractive organist, and the congregation suffered from a bad reputation for twenty years afterward. Hence, Paul urges the young women to observe a reverent demeanor in order that the Gospel should not be maligned.

2:6

Similarly urge the young men to be prudent [also].

One should not suppose that young women are the only or the chief evil examples in a congregation. Possibly women are more given to gossip than men are; and obviously adultery requires both. Probably men are more inclined to drunkenness than women, and they may be less kind. Hence, Paul says "Likewise," and with this word he applies the same injunctions to men. Hendriksen and some others want to add the first two words of verse 7 so as to urge young men to be prudent "in every respect." This is not needed to secure the application of the injunctions to the young men, and it makes the following sentence too abrupt.

2:7, 8

In all respects, present yourself [Titus] as an example of good works, incorruptible in teaching, reverent, irreproachable in healthful doctrine, in order that the opponent may be put to shame, having nothing evil to say about us.

Here, as everyone can see, Paul turns from instructions designed for the communicant members to instructions for Titus himself. They are essentially the same: sound doctrine and good works. As for *teaching* and *doctrine,* one might take the former to refer to the activity of teaching and the latter to the material taught.

The opponents cannot have anything evil, cannot point to any evil behavior on our part, with which to condemn us.

There is a difficulty for us in the last phrase of verse 8. How can Paul promise that our opponents can say nothing evil about us, when they are always ready to say something evil about us? There are two possible answers to this question. First, we may insert an implicit adverb, "justifiably." If we do good, and are irreproachable, our enemies will have no justifiable basis for any accusation. This answer, though it would remove the objection, and though it would correctly describe the opponent's slanders, is weak, for we are not justified in inserting an allegedly implicit *justifiably* into the text. The answer is weak also because it attaches the idea of evil to the wrong object. The second answer will therefore be better. Alford asserts that the New Testament never refers this term for evil (*phaulon*) to words, but always to behavior. It connotes evil deeds rather than slanderous words. Hence the idea is that the opponents cannot have anything evil, cannot point to any evil behavior on our part, with which to condemn us. Their slanders are *kaka* (evil) but not *phaula* (evil).

There is an interesting personal note in the words "about us." The opponents will not only slander the church members, they will also attack Titus, and even further, they will blaspheme Paul himself.

2:9, 10

Slaves should be subject to their own masters in all respects, acceptable, not contradicting them, not stealing [from them], but exhibiting all good faith, that they may adorn the doctrine of our Savior God in every way.

After the instructions relative to older men and women, and to young men and women, Paul adds these two verses about slaves. First, an incidental linguistic note. Should we say that Paul urges the slaves to be subject to their own masters and not to some other slave's master? Back in 2:4, 5 young women are told to love their husbands. The first instance is a compound word *husband-lover;* the second instance is "be subject to your *own* husband." Is the force of the phrase that the young women should not be subject to some other woman's husband? If one examines every instance of the term *idios* in the pastorals, one will discover that it does not have the force the English word *own* has. Indeed it can well be dropped in this translation. *Their own husbands* in Greek means no more than *their husbands* in English. Hence Paul does not have in mind a slave's possible attraction to a master other than his own. He simply wants the slave to obey his master.

The topic now is slavery. The epistle to Philemon considers another aspect of the problem. Here Paul may have had in mind the possibility that Christian slaves, enamored of Christian liberty, might unite in riots, or on a lesser level sabotage their masters' interests. Such activity could not fail to aggravate the slaves' condition and, even worse, hinder the spread of Christianity. If, on the other hand, a pagan master saw that his slave's acceptance of Christ made him a more faithful workman, not only would the slave profit personally, but possibly the master might become a Christian, too.

Their own husbands in Greek means no more than their husbands in English.

Paul states his motivation more forcefully than the explanation just given. He says, "in order that they may adorn the doctrine of our Savior God in every way." Perhaps the master will be converted, perhaps not; but the theology, the doctrine, the teaching that controls the slave's changed behavior has received adornment. Although the text uses the term *Savior* in the phrase "God our Savior," the reference, as in 1 Timothy 1:1, is rather to the Father than to the Son. God is glorified by the slave's conduct.

Here there seems to be an assertion of universalism, and this would contradict other verses in the Gospels.

2:11

For the saving grace of God has appeared to all men,

There is a difference of opinion concerning the translation of verse 11. The *New American Standard* has, "For the grace of God has appeared bringing salvation to all men." The *Revised Standard Version* has, "For the grace of God has appeared for the salvation of all men." Both of these suggest universalism: No one is lost; Hitler and Stalin will both sit down at the marriage supper of the Lamb.

This presents us with two problems of tremendous importance. There is the universalism; but there is also a question about the inerrancy of Scripture. Many higher critics reject the truthfulness of the Bible on the ground that some Assyrian inscriptions contradict a small detail in *2 Chronicles* or elsewhere. One after another of these alleged errors has been exploded. The more serious problems are those concerning statements other than historical data. Here there seems to be an assertion of universalism, and this would contradict other verses in the Gospels. Just three verses ago it seemed impossible that Paul could have told the truth: He said, or it looked as if he said, that his opponents could not say anything evil about him. Here it says, or it looks as if it says, that all men will be saved. But if so, the Bible is not the Word of God.

Perhaps the translations are wrong. In contrast with the *New American Standard*, the *New International Version* is better, "For the grace of God that brings salvation has appeared to all men." The

King James has essentially the same thing. We may note in favor of the last two translations that the idea of "bringing salvation" is expressed by one word, *soterios*. This is a feminine adjective, modifying the noun *grace*. This is why I translated it "For the saving grace of God has appeared to all men." This says something less than "bringing salvation to all men," as the *New American Standard* has it. Indeed, I would say that the *New American Standard* had mistranslated the verse.

Before considering the universalistic interpretation, one may note that Barrett uses the wording to deny the Pauline authorship: "the verb 'has dawned' (*epephanē*, cp. 3:4, and the use of the cognate *epiphaneia* in I Tim. 6:14; II Tim. 1:10; 4:1, 8; Tit. 2:13) is not Pauline" (136).

Paul clearly has been talking of classes of people rather than individuals.

While there are other questions of interpretation in these two verses, most ordinary Bible readers will find the subject of universalism the most interesting and most important. Does this passage teach that every last human being who has ever lived or ever will live on Earth is assured of entrance into Heaven? Those who have conscientiously examined the preceding context can hardly answer, Yes. Paul clearly has been talking of classes of people rather than individuals. He talks about elderly women, not the widow Smith; he talks about young women, not about beautiful Katie. He talks about slaves as a class, and not about Onesimus. Onesimus comes in the following epistle.

Furthermore, the verse says that God's grace has appeared to all men. It does not say that saving grace has been applied to every human individual.

Furthermore, the verse says that God's grace has *appeared* to all men. It does not say that saving grace has been applied to every human individual. This may mean that the general populace can see that grace has been applied to men of every class and rank. Possibly this stretches the meaning of the verse too far, for although the Roman and Greek populaces could see that men of every rank had become Christians, they would not likely have attributed it to the grace of God. The disregard of class and race, however, was and is important, more important in Paul's day than now, for the Greeks, at least in earlier centuries, regarded the rest of the human race, that is, the barbarians, as natural slaves, as Aristotle testifies, and the Greeks were natural masters. The Romans, on the other hand, held no high opinion of the Greeks, though they admitted some to Roman citizenship. Neither Greeks nor Romans had much regard for slaves. But God did. His grace not only appeared publicly, but it was actually applied to every class—Roman officer, Corinthian adulterer, swinish slave, and even stiff-necked Jew. With the almost total absence of class distinctions in most of the world today (some remain in India) we forget how important they were in earlier days, and how revolutionary the Gospel.

Individually taken, it is false that the Gospel has even appeared to all men.

That Paul did not mean individuals, but classes, is evident from another consideration. Individually taken, it is false that the Gospel has even appeared to all men. It cannot have already appeared to future generations, though future generations are included in the individual or denotative concept of all men. Nor had this grace previously appeared to the Negroes of central Africa and the Chinese beyond the Gobi Desert. It had not appeared to the Druids of England, the savage Picts and Scots, nor to the miserable creatures on the Emerald Isle.

Furthermore, to be as exact as possible, one should not hastily assume that this grace necessarily brought salvation to all the members of Titus' congregation. I do not deny that God's grace (in a different sense) had regenerated many of the people to whom Titus ministered; but what Paul refers to as having appeared is the Gospel preached. Paul is not speaking of the internal irresistible grace of God, but of the external call heard by all in the audience. The grace has been preached to all classes of men. However, he does not dwell further on this thought, but immediately proceeds to its intended effects on those who believe it.

The grace has been preached to all classes of men.

2:12

teaching us, in order that, denying impiety and worldly desires, we may live prudently, righteously, and piously in the present age,

Note that Paul has turned from "all men" to "us." He does not say, "teaching them." The always liberal Barrett takes this opportunity to deny the Pauline authorship again: "The author further diverges from Pauline usage when he adds that by this grace *we are disciplined.* In Paul grace is not educative, but liberating" (137). Barrett fails to recognize that liberating grace liberates Christians not only from the final penalty of sin immediately, but also gradually from the reigning power of sin.

The translation "teaching us" or "instructing us" may not express the full meaning of the Greek participle. *Paideuousa, a* feminine in agreement with*grace,* conveys the idea of a tutor who not only teaches Latin and math, but who also disciplines in morals and courtesy. Luther translated it "chastizes us."

Meyer, in enforcing this disciplinary idea, rejects the purposive sense of the following clause to make it an object clause: not "teaching us in order that we may live a godly life," but "teaching us to live a godly life." In this case, however, the difference between purpose and object is miniscule.

The particular sins and virtues here enumerated in rather general terms hardly need any explanation. Indeed, it is not really an enumeration of separate sins, but rather of qualities found in every sin, as also *dikaiōs* and *eusebōs* describe all godly living. If anything needs pointing out, it is the contrast between the present age and the future age next to be alluded to.

2:13

waiting for the blessed hope and appearing of the glory of the great God and our Savior Jesus Christ,

In this present age we must wait for the blessed hope. Obviously *hope* does not refer to our hoping, but to the thing hoped for. Subjectivity, so emphasized by popular evangelists today, cannot possibly be substituted here. The hope is defined as the appearing of the glory of God. The Greek verb and the noun (*prosdechomai* and *elpis*) are also found in *Acts* 24:15 and *Galatians* 5:5. Since *Acts* was written by Paul's companion, and since even the most hostile critics cannot deny the authenticity of *Galatians*, we may assert that this phraseology is decidedly Pauline.

The main difficulty in the verse, and one which commentators have discussed since the early centuries, is whether "the great God and our Savior" refers to the Father and the Son, or to the Son alone. The problem is perplexing, for it involves Greek grammar, theological bias, and the authority of the epistle. Let us get rid of this last matter first.

In this present age we must wait for the blessed hope. Obviously hope does not refer to our hoping, but to the thing hoped for. Subjectivity, so emphasized by popular evangelists today, cannot possibly be substituted here.

Barrett as usual attacks authenticity. Textually and grammatically he prefers the identification of the great God with Jesus Christ our Savior. But this identification, so he holds, is a later development, one that Paul himself would not have made, one that "post-Pauline writers occasionally do . . . and the author of Titus is to be counted among them" (138).

Alford notes that the one-person view (that is, the great God is Jesus Christ himself) is the view of the Greek Orthodox fathers in their struggle against Arianism. That it can be so used, however, does not prove the one-person theory. To defend the doctrine of the Trinity, many other verses are sufficient, and this one is not needed. The proper procedure is to determine first, if possible, what the verse means, and then apply it in any relevant way. One may also note, if my information is correct, that while the Orthodox fathers referred the verse to the Son, several early versions (translations into other languages) referred the first half to the Father.

A more doctrinal argument is that only Christ *appears*—the second coming is not a coming of the Father; therefore the great God who appears must be Christ. This certainly favors the one-person theory, but it falls short of being decisive. The text does not clearly say that the great God, understood as the Father, appears. It says that the glory of the great God appears; and surely one may say that the appearance or return of Christ exhibits the glory of God the Father. If the heavens declare the glory of God, why not the second advent as well, and better? The genitive *sōtēros* is not dependent on *epephaneian,* but on *doxēs.*

There is another textual hint. This very verse has just said, "the blessed hope and appearing." Here we have one article, not two, with the conjunction *and*, so that *hope* and *appearing* are identified. Hence the article with the great God, followed by the same conjunction, identifies the great God as Jesus Christ. Certainly this is possible, probable, but is it conclusive?

Most readers of commentaries do not like authors to suspend judgment: They want a decision. Here the decision is that the various considerations give strong support to the view that Jesus Christ is God, as Paul also said in *Romans* 9:5. There still remains some grammatical ambiguity, but not enough to justify an assertion of the contrary view.

It seems to me that the above considerations are sufficient; but such has been the interest in this passage that some further grammatical observations are permissible. Those who care to, may continue with this addition; others are at liberty to skip it and go on to the next verse, for the argument will be somewhat technical. The material comes from Meyer's American editor, with some alterations.

In favor of understanding Christ alone and not the Father, grammarians insist that two appellative words, united by *and,* belong to the same subject. *(Appellative* means a common noun determinative of a class rather than a proper noun or name.) Since *theos* and *sōtēr* are appellatives, the reference is to Christ alone. Some critics reject this grammatical argument on the ground that *theos* and *sōtēr* are not clearly appellatives. They object that these two words are proper names. Originally they may have been common nouns, but in Paul they became names. This is said to defend a reference to God the Father. But this defense is imperfect. *Sōtēr* did indeed become a proper name, but in the New Testament it still seems to be an appellation.

Speak these things and exhort and refute with all authority. Let no one despise you.
Titus 2:15

Another indication that only Christ is referred to is the singular relative pronoun in verse 14: "Jesus Christ who . . ." with a singular verb. Those who want the reference to include the Father reply that after two persons are mentioned, it is perfectly allowable to add a relative clause concerning the second person. A specific case is *Galatians* 1:3, 4. But in this passage the term *patros* explicitly distinguishes between the two.

A further argument to support reference to the Father is that *theos* in verse 11 clearly means the Father, and therefore it is improbable that the same word in verse 13 means anyone else. The reply is that the intervening material is sufficient to remove the improbability. Such is a selection of considerations given by Meyer's American editor.

2:14, 15

who gave himself for us in order to redeem us from all lawlessness and to cleanse, for himself, a chosen people, zealous of good works. Speak these things and exhort and refute with all authority. Let no one despise you.

The first part of these two verses concludes the sentence begun in verse 11. If the destructive critics can contend that this verse or that verse is not linguistically Pauline, others can better contend that such a complicated sentence is very Pauline.

An important point is the word *for* in the phrase, "gave himself for us." The English word *for* has at least two different meanings: *on behalf of*, and *instead of*. The difference can be illustrated from a situation in baseball. A sacrifice bunt is for or on the behalf of a runner on first or second. But a pinch hitter goes to bat for or instead of another player. Before the papyri were discovered, the liberals contended that *huper hēmon* could not mean *instead of*: It could only mean *on behalf of*. *Huper* they said, simply means "for the benefit of." Thus they concluded that Paul or even the New Testament as a whole did not teach a vicarious atonement. Of course, this was bad logic. Even if *huper* itself cannot signify substitution, it does not follow that substitution is unscriptural. Other verses could more fully explain how the benefit was obtained. The liberals can be faulted for their poor reasoning, but they could be somewhat excused for their ignorance of Greek. They were unaware that the Hellenistic meaning of *huper* was different from the classical meaning. The papyri, which began to appear at the beginning of the century, show that *huper* can and often does mean substitution. *Lutrōsētai* means the payment of a ransom, and Christ not only paid the ransom, he was himself the ransom paid: He gave himself for his people. The *Septuagint* in *Psalm* 130:8 has the same verb.

One cannot divorce New Testament sanctification from the Ten Commandments.

Twentieth century so-called evangelicalism is an emaciated shadow of sixteenth and seventeenth century Calvinism.

Christ then redeems us from all lawlessness. The adjective *all* includes the guilt of sin as well as the actual transgressions, though *cleanse* emphasizes Christ's freeing us from sinful practices. It must always be kept in mind that sin is any want of conformity unto or transgression of the law of God. Where there is no law, there is no sin. Sin is lawlessness. One cannot divorce New Testament sanctification from the Ten Commandments. One of the excellencies of the Reformed faith, especially in contrast with Arminianism, is Calvin's insistence on the Ten Commmandments and the *Westminster Larger Catechism*'s exposition of them. Twentieth century so-called evangelicalism is an emaciated shadow of sixteenth and seventeenth century Calvinism.

The idea of a chosen people, a people whom Christ chose to cleanse for himself, echoes *Exodus* 19:5 and *Deuteronomy* 7:6 and elsewhere. The Old Testament in many passages emphasizes predestination.* Christ by his death not only redeems his chosen people but cleanses them so that they become zealous of good works. Fuzzy minds, regardless of what the subject is, often fall into the fallacy of false disjunction. A father will say to his small son, Do you want ice cream or apple pie? The logical youngster replies, Both. Fundamentalists have, at least sometimes, emphasized the atonement and, if they know the terminology, justification by faith alone. The liberals, more particularly the modernists early in this century, emphasized morality and good works, though perhaps not sanctification. However, it is not either-or; it is both-and. What passes so apparently as good works are not good unless preceded by justification and sanctification; and if a claimed justification does not inevitably produce sanctification and good works, it simply was not justification.

* Compare Clark, "Predestination in the Old Testament," in *Predestination*, 1978.

These are the things that Paul wants Titus to speak and enforce, rebutting all contrary views.

Before continuing with chapter three, the reader who is interested in the authenticity of these epistles will be glad to know that Hendriksen at this point gives a lengthy analysis of one of the important contentions of the liberal critics. Their argument is that the pastorals contain so many *hapax legomena* that Paul cannot have been the author. A *hapax legomenon* is a word that occurs only once in an epistle, in all of an author's works, or in all the New Testament. The second chapter of *Titus* contains an extra large proportion of these. Hendriksen aims "to show that *every word* of this chapter is of such a character that no one has a right to say, 'Paul cannot have written it.' " To support this conclusion Hendriksen offers four pages in small type.

These are the things that Paul wants Titus to speak and enforce, rebutting all contrary views.

Chapter Three

3:1, 2

Remind them to be subject to rulers and authorities, to obey, to be ready for every good work, to slander [blaspheme] no one, to be peaceable, gentle, showing all humility to all men.

These various facets of Christian behavior are appropriate in every age and country, but they may have needed particular emphasis among the crude Cretans. If there were many Jews in these churches, Jews with an inbred hostility to Roman authority, and if they had also adopted some Cretan unpleasantnesses, we can easily understand Paul's motives. I doubt that the unworthy conduct here condemned is especially prominent in evangelical congregations today. There may be some gossip, but not likely much malevolence. Most nominal Christians do not advocate lawlessness or disobedience. This is generally restricted to the lunatic left. But thoughtlessness and preoccupation may lower the level of gentleness and humility toward all men. There are a few obnoxiously humble, and efforts at being helpful can be unwarranted intrusions. It is really difficult to be a perfect Christian.

3:3

For even we were once mindless, disobedient, erring, enslaved to desires and variegated pleasures, proceeding in evil and envy, hateful, hating each other.

Verse 3 is the reason for the exhortation in verse 2, but not verse 3 by itself; the full reason for verse 2 is verses 3 and 4 together.

Verse 3 paints a pretty miserable picture, especially since it includes Titus and even Paul himself. We have little information on the sins of Titus; but Paul's are clearly reported. First of all, he was "mindless"; "ignorant, senseless, without understanding," are more colloquial translations. This refers to his failure to see the truth of the Gospel. Being thus in error, he was naturally disobedient. We hardly think of Paul as having been enslaved to "many colored" pleasures. On the contrary, as a persecutor, he drove himself with the same degree of zeal which he later showed as an apostle. But since "we" includes not only Titus, but the Cretans and others in general, the term is appropriately inserted. Paul clearly succumbed to malice; and if not to envy, he certainly hated and was hated. Maybe the persecuted Christians should not have hated him, but we suspect they did. Or, perhaps, we can more easily attribute hatred to the not-so-sanctified Cretans. Let us not confine our attention to the disreputable Cretans; "even we" includes us Americans as well.

Readers who are interested in literary embellishment may notice Paul's somewhat cumbersome (by modern standards) balancing of seven virtues against seven vices. Verses 1 and 2 mention submission, obedience, good works, no slandering, peace, gentleness, and humility. The reader can count the evils in verse 3.

Let us not confine our attention to the disreputable Cretans; "even we" includes us Americans as well.

3:4, 5

But when the goodness and philanthropy of our Savior God appeared, not of works which in righteousness we did, but according to his mercy, he saved us by the washing of palingenesis and renewing of the Holy Spirit,

Here begins another of Paul's complicated sentences, extending to the end of verse 7. In studying a commentary such as this, and some others are even worse, the reader succumbs to the danger of getting lost in the details. Puzzling out the meaning of a phrase, he forgets, if not the preceding phrase, the one before that. Of those who read the Bible with some regularity, most miss the details and must do with a vague, general idea. What is needed is to see how the minute details fit together to produce an extended argument—the message of a paragraph, a chapter, a complete epistle.

What is needed is to see how the minute details fit together to produce an extended argument—the message of a paragraph, a chapter, a complete epistle.

This fourth verse begins a contrast with the third. The contrast is that between the life of an unregenerate sinner and, if not the life of a regenerate sinner, at least the goodness of the regenerating God. Above in 2:13 we discussed the deity of Christ—could Christ be called "the great God?" Here the reverse question appears: Can God be called Savior? Remember the first verse of this commentary, *1 Timothy* 1:1, "Paul an apostle of Christ Jesus by the command of our Savior God and of Christ Jesus our hope." When we see that Jesus is the great God and the Father is the Savior, we begin to enter upon the doctrine of the Trinity. How long ago was it that you heard a sermon on this verse or on the Trinity? Some pastors ride a hobby horse that never seems to get on the Trinity track.

There was a time when the Father's goodness and his love of mankind appeared. In one sense his goodness and love appeared one marvelous night in Bethlehem. They also appeared one terrible midday on Golgotha. But here the prominent idea is the appearing of his goodness to each individual, his appearing to a definite number of Cretans and to a definite number of Americans.

This goodness was not extended on the ground that the Cretans had done anything righteous. They had been dead in sin and were incapable of doing anything righteous. The love was extended by God's mercy. He saved us in spite of what we had done, and saved us from what we had done.

Alford correctly insists that the verb *epoiēsamen* is aorist and should be translated *did*. He thinks that *had done* so obscures the meaning as to allow the idea "not on the ground of what we had done, but on the ground of what we are doing and will do." This is an unnecessary caution, for the verse itself specifies grace or mercy, and this excludes future works as well as past. Furthermore, Alford's insistence, even on its own basis, is not successful, for the aorist *did* could as well allow future works to be the ground of justification, for *did* is as past as the pluperfect. Alford really wants Paul to have written Toplady's excellent lines:

God loved the world to the degree of sending his Son to save believers. He did not love the world so as to save every human being.

But not for works which we have done
Or shall hereafter do.

When the text says that God saved *us,* the *us* is defined by the previous pronouns. Verse 3 said, "We also"; that is to say, Paul, Titus, and the Cretan Christians were also sinners as other people were. Now, God had a certain love of man, or of mankind in general, but he saved us, not mankind as a whole. Verses 6 and 7 will make this still clearer.

Universalistic interpretations of such verses fail to consider the exact wording. The best known example is *John* 3:16. It says, "God so loved the world." Now, aside from the meaning of the term *world*, which itself has several different referents in the New Testament, the word *so* indicates a certain degree, restriction, or qualification. God loved the world to the degree of sending his Son to save believers. He did not love the world so as to save every human being. But have we not all heard ignorant evangelists who with swelling volume proclaim, "God so-o-o loved the *world*!"? But the word they emphasize is precisely the word they do not understand.

Our present text now says that God saved us by the washing of regeneration (*palingenesis*). This phrase too excludes past and future works, for clearly it is God who washes, and we are passively washed.

What is this washing? Although Calvinists quote Calvin with awe and reverence, we are not required to follow him in his few minor infelicities. On this phrase his commentary says, "I have no objection to the explanation of the whole passage in terms of baptism." No doubt the word *washing* suggests baptism. (It does not suggest immersion.) Nevertheless, one can hardly explain the whole passage in terms of baptism. This should all the more be avoided in order to show that the passage does not teach baptismal regeneration.

Meyer is more objectionable than Calvin: "From Ephesians 5:26 it is clear that it can mean nothing else than baptism." Ephesians 5:26 says, "as Christ also loved the church . . . having cleansed her by the washing of water with the Word." And a few lines below he adds, "Paul uses that name for it as the bath by means of which God *actually* brings about the new birth."

If Meyer is more objectionable than Calvin, Alford is more so than Meyer. We shall take Alford in two steps. First, he rejects the term *washing* and inserts the term *laver:* "by means of the laver (not washing as E. V.) . . . always a vessel or pool . . . here the baptismal font." To this first point Guthrie replies, "In the LXX the word, which occurs only three times (Ct. iv. 2, vi. 5, and Ecclesus xxxi, 25), on each occasion seems to represent not the receptacle but the washing itself" (205).

Second, Alford continues:

> The font is the laver of regeneration because it is the vessel consecrated to the use of that Sacrament whereby, in its *completeness* as a Sacrament, the new life unto God is conveyed. And inasmuch as it is in that font, and when we are in it, that the first breath of that life is drawn, it is the laver *of*—belonging to, pertaining to, setting forth—regeneration. Observe, there is here no figure: the words are literal. Baptism is taken as in all its completion—the outward visible sign accompanied by the inward spiritual grace; and as thus *complete* it not only represents, but *is* the new birth (424).

If baptism caused, or was, regeneration, the phrase should have been "the regeneration of washing."

In reply to this sacramentarianism several points are pertinent. First, let us ask whether the language is figurative or literal. This is a difficult question and incapable of solution if we attend only to the wording of a single sentence. Presumably everyone would acknowledge that "I am the door" is a figure of speech. But "this is my body" has generated endless controversy. Luther sided with the Romanist interpretation (with one modification) against Zwingli. Calvinists, of course, consider *body* to be a metaphorical expression. And why not? When Paul says that the church is the *body* of Christ, can anyone take it literally? Some conservative exegetes take "I am the truth" to be figurative. The present writer to their dismay regards it as philosophically and theologically literal. We must therefore go beyond such phrases in isolation and fit them into the Scriptural system as a whole. Scripture must be interpreted by Scripture.

A second consideration, confined to the verse itself, is that if baptism caused, or was, regeneration, the phrase should have been "the regeneration of washing." The actual phrase "the washing of regeneration" indicates that regeneration washes, not that washing regenerates.

A third point, though these numbers do not necessarily follow in any strict logical order, is that if baptism regenerates, and baptism alone, then Paul was regenerated, not when he saw Christ on the Damascus road, but after Ananias had come to visit him. Perhaps this could be stubbornly maintained, but only by denying that regeneration is a subjective change. Surely Paul "changed his mind" that is, repented, and became a "new man" before he reached the city. Similarly, the thief on the cross was regenerated, but never baptized. But if baptism is regeneration, the thief could not have been in Paradise with Christ that evening.

Some defenders of sacramentarianism, if not stubbornly, at least confusedly, deny that regeneration is a subjective change of mind. In a footnote (*Systematic Theology*, III, 597) Hodge refers to one who made it a purely legal term such as adoption or justification. To quote: "Regeneration on the part of the grantor, God Almighty, means admission or adoption into sonship or spiritual citizenship; and on the part of the grantee, namely man, it means his birth or entrance into the state of sonship or citizenship." In the case of Paul it would mean that he underwent a subjective change of mind on the road, but became a son of God a number of days later. This view insists that *Titus* 3:5 distinguishes between *regeneration* and the *renewal* of the Spirit. A second *dia* (by means of) or a second article would have clearly distinguished between the two; but the actual text is more plausibly a case of apposition. The washing effected by regeneration is the renewal, that is, the renewing the Spirit does to us. Those who deny that renewing is in apposition to washing are forced to say, "We are saved by the washing and also by the Spirit's renewal." But this reduces to, "We are saved by regeneration and also by regeneration"; for if the renewing by the Spirit is not regeneration, its identification would be difficult.

If baptism regenerates, and baptism alone, then Paul was regenerated, not when he saw Christ on the Damascus road, but after Ananias had come to visit him.

Faith follows regeneration. The man who believes has already received the grace of God because faith is a gift.

If one admits that "regeneration" is "being saved," baptism cannot be its sole means, for Christ said, "Unless you repent, you will all likewise perish" (*Luke* 13:3). He repeated the sentence two verses later. Many times we read, Believe and be saved. Baptism is not mentioned. After the person is regenerated, then he should be baptized—with water; neither sand nor desire will do. Note that the eunuch first believed, and then Philip baptized him.

This argument is supported by the fact that faith follows regeneration. The man who believes has already received the grace of God because faith is a gift. It is, however, a gift that can be received only by a living mind. Before regeneration a sinner is dead, not alive, and hence can neither receive anything nor act in any way that presupposes a living subject. Baptism is itself a profession of faith; the faith is not obtained by means of baptism. To quote Charles Hodge (III, 601):

> The only way in which Romanists [can] evade this argument is by denying that faith and repentance are the fruits of the Spirit, or of regeneration. They are in their view gracious, but natural works, works which leave the soul in a state of perdi-

tion. But in this they contradict the express words of Christ, who says, Whosoever believes shall be saved.

Further discussion leads into the full doctrine of the sacraments, and this much is enough for a commentary on *Titus*.

3:6, 7

of whom he poured out upon us richly through Jesus Christ our Savior in order that, being justified by that one's grace, we might become heirs according to the hope of eternal life.

Any who talk about the baptism of the Spirit can hardly support immersion by this verse. The Spirit is poured out upon us; we are not immersed or buried in him. The Lutheran practice of pouring is Scriptural; at least Scripture permits it. The pouring of this verse can hardly refer to Pentecost, for here the Spirit is poured out on us, and the "us" includes Titus and his congregations.

The Spirit is poured out upon us; we are not immersed or buried in him.

The pouring of this verse can hardly refer to Pentecost, for here the Spirit is poured out on us, and the "us" includes Titus and his congregations.

There is a disagreement as to the antecedent of the purpose clause. One interpretation holds that "he poured out the Spirit upon us in order that we might become heirs." The other interpretation is, "he saved us in order that we might become heirs." The proximity of the antecedent in the first of these is not definitive, but it contributes a modicum of plausibility. Hendriksen prefers the second of these and says, "the purpose . . . of God in saving us is 'that we might become heirs' . . . [and] have the right as children to look forward to the full possession of that which we now only possess *in principle*" (393). To this Meyer's argument replies, "The structure of the sentence is in favor of the reference to *execheen*. . . . The other view [is] unnecessarily harsh, ignoring the explanatory relation of vv. 6 and 7 to ver. 5, and depriving *execheen* of its necessary definition." Alford, in agreement with Meyer, argues that *esōsen* (saved) has its "full pregnant meaning as it stands and does not require any further statement of aim or purpose; but *execheen* being a word of action is more properly followed by a statement of a reason why the pouring out took place" (495). Perhaps this is enough to favor an uncertain decision. Another possibility is that the purpose clause attaches to both verbs. If God saved us through regeneration and the renewal by the Holy Spirit, and if in particular these two phrases refer to the same thing, then *saved* and *poured out* can both be for the purpose of adopting us as heirs. Why not?

The comments on verse 4 noted how attributes, characteristics, or actions usually ascribed to one member of the Trinity are sometimes assigned to another member. In this verse as well we see the cooperation or unity of the three Persons, in that the Father sends the Spirit through or by means of the Son. This, of course, has nothing to do with the *filioque* clause of the Council of Toledo: It has to do with what theologians call the "economic" Trinity. In plainer words, the present verse alludes to divine actions in dealing with mankind, not with eternal intra-trinitarian relationships. Somewhat as creation is the work of the Father, in some verses, and also the work of the Son, in other verses, so here the outpouring of the Spirit takes place through the Son. Similarly, predestination, usually assigned to the Father, is said to be "in Christ." Some neo-orthodox theologians have seized upon this latter phrase in an effort to modify the full Biblical position, and they try to convey the suggestion that the earlier Reformed theologians had missed this idea. The idea is too prominent for anyone to miss.

We are justified by means of faith and by faith alone.

The versification of the New Testament, except as a method for locating a passage, is a disaster.

The early events of salvation in or for an individual Christian include not only regeneration, repentance, and faith, but also justification. We are justified by means of faith and by faith alone. Justification is a forensic or judicial act of God by which he not only pardons us but also accepts us as righteous in his sight, only for the righteousness of Christ imputed to us and received by faith alone. Accepting us as righteous makes us sons of God and joint-heirs with Christ. The subjective side of this is that we have a hope of eternal life. This phrase could be translated "made heirs of eternal life according to hope." All of which is "by that one's grace."

Who is "that one"? In classical Greek *ekeinos,* particularly when contrasted with *outos* (*this one*), indicates the more remote noun; but the New Testament hardly ever makes this contrast. In John's writing, *ekeinos* frequently does not refer to the more remote noun. In *John* 10:6 *ekeinoi* (plural) simply means *they*, perhaps with slight emphasis. In *John* 9:9, 12, 25, 36 and in *Mark* 16:10, 13, 20, *ekeinos* refers to the immediately preceding subject. So far as grammar goes, therefore, Paul's *ekeinou* here could refer either to the Father, remote, or to the Son, immediately preceding. The term *grace* also is indeterminate: We speak of the grace of God, and in the apostolic benediction we speak of the grace of Christ. But if justification is peculiarly an act of the Father, *ekeinou* must refer to the Father. And although we are joint-heirs with Christ, we are heirs of God the Father, for we are his sons, not sons of Christ.

3:8

Faithful is the saying, and concerning these things I want you to speak confidently, in order that those who believe (have believed and continue to do so) in God may have the mind to be forward in good works. These things are fine and useful to men.

The versification of the New Testament, except as a method for locating a passage, is a disaster. How anyone able to read Greek could be so stupid is a mystery. Modern English readers have fallen into blunders by (for instance) failing to connect *Romans* 7:25 with 8:1. The chapter division deceived them. Here the first three words, "faithful the saying," should have been the conclusion of verse 7.

Nearly all commentators, possibly only one exception, acknowledge that the "saying" is in the preceding verse or verses. They differ as to which. Conzelmann identifies the saying as verses 3 through 7. Guthrie specifies verses 4 through 7 (204). This is not an outright contradiction, but he does not explain how "a Christian hymn . . . is suggested by the opening formula in verse 8." Hendriksen also specifies verses 4 through 7. Others prefer to limit the saying to 5 through 7. The trouble is that "sayings" should be short. Hence some commentators refer indefinitely to some phrase in these verses. The one plausible, and almost certain, conclusion is that verse 3, with its dependence on verse 2, cannot be a part of the saying. Since the "saying" itself, whatever the extent, has been discussed above, we continue with the words that should have been made the beginning of the verse.

"Concerning these things," says Paul, "I want you to speak confidently." The reason given for the need of such confident proclamation is the good works such proclamations produce. But the content of the preaching, certainly its main part, is not an exhortation to good works. The content is God's grace, unmotivated by anything we had done; the theme is salvation or regeneration; the subject-matter is justification, heirs, hope of Heaven. John Sanderson, of Covenant Seminary in St. Louis, has written an excellent book on *The Fruit of the Spirit.* I have nothing but praise for its contents. But in one church the pastor in his sermons, and the session in control of the Sunday School, made the congregation go through the book from beginning to end three times in eighteen months. They had never gone through the *Westminster Confession* once in ten years or more.

This twentieth century usually considers a heretic as a hero, a man to be admired, and imitated by all who have the courage to do so. A heresy-hunter, on the other hand, is the most depraved of all scoundrels.

The verse ends with the phrase, "these things are fine and useful to men." What things? Good works? Not very plausibly. The apostle did not need to say that good works (*kalōn ergōn*) were good (*kala).* Nor is it necessary to keep repeating that evil works are evil, naming them one by one and pointing out how wicked each is. Let there be no misunderstanding. When there is an epidemic of shoplifting, or if the Ku Klux Klan rides through Chattanooga and fires a shotgun at some black women, or if a malicious gossip should threaten the unity of the congregation, these sins should be denounced from the pulpit, by name. But for the most part an occasional reference to these, and more often several general references to sin or sins, seem sufficient. This is more effective than usually thought. Often enough a man in the pews, with a bad conscience, has accused the minister of singling him out for public condemnation, when the minister had no idea that man was guilty of anything in particular. But what is better and more useful, and what should be proclaimed more frequently and with greater confidence, are the contents of the "saying."

3:9

Moronic investigations and genealogies and quarrels and fights about the Law, avoid; for they are useless and in vain.

Once again we see how the sins of the Cretans differed from those of the Corinthians. Clearly there was a large Jewish contingent in the Cretan congregations. Proto-Talmudic hairsplitting, and, seemingly, allegorical adumbrations of genealogical tables were the cause of the trouble. Which group of sins was the worse: the Corinthians' or the Cretans'? I would rather not decide.

3:10, 11

A heretical man after a first and second admonition, reject; knowing that such a man is perverse and sins, for he is self-condemned.

This twentieth century usually considers a heretic as a hero, a man to be admired, and imitated by all who have the courage to do so. A heresy-hunter, on the other hand, is the most depraved of all scoundrels, much worse than the Mafia, the drug addicts, and the prostitutes.

In the Old Testament there are more than forty different words which the Septuagint translates as apostatize.

"By heretics he does not only mean those who embrace and defend known error or some pernicious doctrine, but in general those who do not assent to the sound teaching which he has just laid down."

The New Testament, and the Old Testament too, do not support this view. In the Old Testament there are more than forty different words which the *Septuagint* translates as *apostatize*. But what does the New Testament say? Liberal seminary professors have several times told me that heresy means factiousness and has nothing to do with false doctrine. Though they can cite the first two chapters of *1 Corinthians*, the canons of scholarship would require a more extensive examination of the New Testament. Calvin says, "By heretics he does not only mean those who embrace and defend known error or some pernicious doctrine, but in general those who do not assent to the sound teaching which he has just laid down." A speed reader may find some difficulty in understanding what Calvin means, for the two parts of his sentence seem to say much the same thing. True, the two parts overlap; but it appears that the first part refers to denials of major doctrines—denials so fundamental that hardly anyone could think them unimportant—and the second part indicates matters that most people would consider of less importance. Calvin's definition or description does not exclude the idea of factions or schisms, as Calvin himself notes; but the factions are formed on the basis of false doctrine.

Granted that heresy is basically false doctrine, one next asks, Which false doctrines? Since there is not complete agreement even among the most sincere and orthodox Christians, we hardly exclude from our midst everyone who differs from us on some point or other. For example, there have been disputes as to whether unleavened bread is absolutely necessary for the Lord's Supper, or whether raised bread is permissible.

Many people are thus led to say that a heresy is a denial of some important doctrine. How then can we determine what is important? In 1924 the *Auburn Affirmation*, signed by some 1300 Presbyterian ministers, said that the virgin birth, the miracles, the atonement, and the resurrection were unimportant and not essential.

Years later, three or four ministers of a smaller and more orthodox Presbyterian church, driving home from a meeting, began to discuss heresy. One of them asked, Would you say that it is heresy to deny the third chapter of the *Westminster Confession*? Oh, no, replied one of the group, to be heretical one must deny something important. Since there are only two chapters more important or more basic than the third, the extent of heresy in this way is much reduced.

The adjective *airetikos* occurs just this once in the New Testament. The noun occurs nine times. In *Acts* 5:17 it is translated as "the *sect* of the Sadducees." However factious the Sadducees may have been, they were united by agreement on theological and political principles. *Acts* 15:5 refers to the *sect* of the Pharisees, about whom the same can be said. *Acts* 24:5 speaks about the *sect* of the Nazarenes, that is, the Christians. The context here is Tertullus' accusation against Paul before Felix. In reply (*Acts* 24:14) Paul says, "after the way which they call heresy, so worship I the God of my fathers, believing all things which are written in the law and the prophets." Clearly this usage is strictly theological. The Christians, from Tertullus' point of view, were no doubt a faction, but obviously based on substantial theology. *Acts* 26:5 and 28:22 add nothing further. In *1 Corinthians* 1:10 the theological sense may not be absent, though it is not prominent. The context in *Galatians* 5:20 has to do with various forms of immorality. *2 Peter* 2:1 is unmistakably theological: false teachers, false prophets, damnable heresies, even denying the Lord that bought them. Finally, the adjective in the present passage refers to doctrine more than to immorality or factiousness. It was genealogies and disputes about the Law. Heresy, therefore, is theological deviation.

There is one perfectly clear way to define heresy.

It is simply the adoption of a creed.

As to the degree of deviation, this passage suggests less important points than the atonement and resurrection. The Cretan heretics may have accepted the third chapter of the *Westminster Confession*. Now, there is one perfectly clear way to define heresy. To be sure, it will not settle the differences between Romanists and Protestants, nor between Baptists and Presbyterians. But it provides clarity within each group. It is simply the adoption of a creed. A group of people who realize that they are in substantial agreement gather together and by careful evaluation decide that doctrines *X, Y,* and *Z* are so clearly Scriptural as to be essential. Therefore, deviation from any of them is heresy. Opinions *P, Q,* and *R* may be Biblical or may not, but the case is doubtful; hence the ministers, if they emphasize the Confession, are free to accept or reject *P, Q,* and *R*. If then a heresy trial becomes necessary, the charge will be that Mr. So and So has denied doctrine *Y*.

There is some discussion as to whether Paul wants Titus to excommunicate "the heretical man" or simply admonish and ignore him. The latter would seem to be a stupid and dangerous procedure. The fact that *paraitou* "is not a technical term for excommunication," as the liberal Barrett notes, proves nothing. It certainly does not confirm Alford's opinion that Paul required only "a subjective act" and not an objective ecclesiastical judgment. In the Gospels, Christ tells us to remonstrate with a man privately, then with several witnesses, and then to bring him to trial before the church, after which, if the church condemns him, he is to be treated as a publican and a sinner. Why cannot this be the procedure intended here?

There is also *2 John* 10, "If anyone comes to you and does not bring this teaching [notice the theological emphasis] do not receive him into your house and do not give him a greeting." The word *house* here may or may not refer to the church that meets in someone's house; but if it refers only to a private dwelling and a social visit, or a business visit, how much more must it apply to the house of God?

"If anyone comes to you and does not bring this teaching [notice the theological emphasis] do not receive him into your house and do not give him a greeting."

Ostracism is a part of the required procedure.

In one of my Sunday School classes a very evangelistic lady objected that this would prevent her from trying to reconvert the offender. One should never give up trying to recover that which is lost. The lovely lady failed to realize that there had been previous private expostulation, plus at least two formal admonitions, and that now nothing further than excommunication was possible. If the ostracism does not result in repentance, there is nothing else we can do except pray. But the ostracism is a part of the required procedure.

The verse ends with the statement that we know that the heretic is self-condemned. Meyer says, "He sins with the consciousness of his guilt and of his own condemnation, so that there is no hope of his return." I must confess that I think Meyer is twice wrong here. Admittedly the term "self-condemned" suggests the insincerity and hypocrisy of one who knows he is sinning. It seems that all the commentators take this view. Calvin says, "their sin is voluntary and deliberate and therefore it would be vain to admonish them." A few lines above he had said, "there is no hope of repentance for him."

Now, I must admit that when some young Negro girl, a teen-ager or one in her early twenties, comes to my door and witnesses for Jehovah, denying the deity of Christ (as happened many times when we lived in Indianapolis), I cannot judge her insincere. In fact, I am impressed with her evident sincerity. She is a heretic; if she were a member of a truly Christian church, it should excommunicate her. But Witnesses do not consciously condemn themselves. For that matter, are not the Hasidic Jews very sincere? And many Moslems—in Arabia, if not in California.

Therefore, we may conclude that "self-condemned" (*autokatakritos*) must be taken objectively, in the sense that, to use Calvin's words, their sins are voluntary and deliberate, and hence their sins condemn them, but not that they are all insincere nor that none of them can ever repent. Nearly every commentator disagrees with me on this; but Hendriksen says, "Even when the error is very grievous and dangerous as in the present instance, every effort must be put forth to win the erring one. . . . There must be a second warning. But if even this remedy fails, he must be expelled. Even this extreme measure has as one of its purposes the reclamation of the sinner."

3:12

When I send Artemis to you or Tychicus, make sure to come to me at Nicopolis, for I have decided to spend the winter there.

This verse begins the final paragraph. Since the remarks are very personal, very little exegesis is necessary. There were at least three towns by the name of Nicopolis, and either of two of them might be the one Paul meant. His decision to spend the winter there shows that he was not then a prisoner.

"Even when the error is very grievous and dangerous as in the present instance, every effort must be put forth to win the erring one. . . . There must be a second warning. But if even this remedy fails, he must be expelled. Even this extreme measure has as one of its purposes the reclamation of the sinner."

3:13, 14

Pay the expenses of Zenos the lawyer and Apollos, so that nothing be lacking to them. Let our own people learn to do good works for compelling needs, so as not to be unfruitful.

Here Barrett makes his final attack on the authenticity of the pastorals. He says, "Verse 14 can scarcely be part of a genuine fragment, but it probably accounts for the introduction of vv. 12 ff., whatever their source may have been."

3:15

All those who are with me greet you. Greet those who love us in faith. Grace be with you all.

Greek usage would permit the translation, "Greet those who love us in the faith." Alford prefers this translation and takes it as "a strong corroboration of genuineness." The literal translation above does not make much sense, and the insertion of the article accords with the New Testament's usual objective stance rather than with contemporary subjectivism. So, my patient readers,

Grace be with you all.

APPENDICES

A
The Ordination of Women

Introduction

The Synod of 1976 of the Reformed Presbyterian Church, Evangelical Synod (R. P. C. E. S.) considered a *Report* advocating the ordination of women as deacons. Its non-controversial first half had been distributed some weeks in advance; but the second half was not made public until Synod convened. Since the commissioners had had no opportunity to study it, they wisely took no action on the second half.

After Synod adjourned, a paper was written analyzing the arguments of the *Report*. The committee prevented this paper from being included among the reports distributed before the Synod of 1977. To date no analysis of the controversial second half of the 1976 *Report* has been published. Therefore the author of the paper now makes it public on his own responsibility.

After Synod adjourned, a paper was written analyzing the arguments of the Report. The committee prevented this paper from being included among the reports distributed before the Synod of 1977.

The author of the paper now makes it public on his own responsibility.

Since the Synod of 1977 decisively rejected the ordination of women as deacons, some persons may think that the present publication is superfluous. The author disagrees.

First, shortly after the Synod of 1976, the *Presbyterian Journal*, without identifying its sources, reported that the advocates of ordination of women predicted that they would push their program through within four years. Hence, in spite of the 1977 action, future Synods may have to face the question again.

Second, before the 1977 Synod met, one minister, with the prior approval of the Midwestern Presbytery, the Presbytery within whose bounds Covenant Seminary is located, actually ordained one or more women. This, of course, was a deliberate violation of our *Form of Government*. It indicates that illegal actions are considered appropriate to attain the end in view.

Then third, since as yet no formal analysis of the original *Report* has been published, the present paper is not altogether superfluous, at least in the opinion of the author,

Gordon H. Clark.

THE ORDINATION OF WOMEN

The 154th Synod of the R. P. C. E. S. (May 1976) received and included in its minutes the *Report of a Study Committee on the Role of Women in the Church*. It recommends the ordination of women as deacons. The matter at hand is not a matter of deaconesses. For years the P. C. U. S. A. and the Reformed Church in America cooperated in supporting a Deaconess School in Philadelphia; and its graduates served in those denominations. The matter now at hand, however, is not to acknowledge this Presbyterian practice, but the quite different and novel proposal to ordain women as deacons.

Although the Study Committee does not advocate the ordination of women as elders, it advocates the ordination of women.

Although the Study Committee does not advocate the ordination of women as elders, it advocates the ordination of women. Because of our contemporary situation, most recently the actions of the Episcopal Church, it is unrealistic to think that a church which begins with ordaining women as deacons can long deny them ordination as elders. This paper will indeed consider the office of deacon, but the underlying question is the ordination of women, as the title of this paper indicates.

The Protestant Reformation, for all its opposition to Romanism, never questioned the practice of ordaining men only.

Since this is a modern proposal, the burden of proof falls on the innovators. A short note on history will clarify this point. *Hebrews* 5:1-4 shows that the Jewish High Priests were ordained: They were all men. A companion paper on "The Presbyterian Doctrine of Ordination"* will also mention the ordination, usually by anointing with oil, of lesser Old Testament officials. The Jewish restriction of such ordination to men has only recently been questioned by liberal Judaism. The Roman Catholic church ordains men only. One of the arguments of the high churchmen in the Episcopal Church, relative to its alteration of its government this year, was that the ordination of women would hinder ecumenical reunion with Rome. The Protestant Reformation, for all its opposition to Romanism, never questioned the practice of ordaining men only. Now, if this practice has continued from the time of Abraham down to 1960 or thereabouts, those who are innovators surely must bear the burden of proof. The *Westminster Confession* indeed says, "All Synods . . . may err, and many have erred." Therefore, it is theoretically possible that the Reformed Presbyterian Church is in error. But when the agreement is worldwide over 4,000 years, it is, I repeat, extremely improbable.

Therefore, a mountainous burden of proof rests on those who advocate the ordination of women. Suppositions of possible meanings of *gunaikas,* for example, even if "likely," are not enough. What the denomination needs, before it can have the authority to discard the historical concept of ordination, is compelling proof.

The present paper, in contrast with the *Report,* maintains that the historical Presbyterian procedure is required by Scripture. In con-

* See Appendix B.

formity with the third ordination vow of the R. P. C. E. S., our ministers "accept the Presbyterian form of Church Government *as derived from the Holy Scriptures*" (*Form of Government,* V, 1, 1). Therefore, the conclusion here will be that Scripture definitely forbids the ordination of women.

To this end, it would be possible to examine the *Report* paragraph by paragraph. But there may be a more orderly way. Of course, the readers of this paper should have the *Report* before them; and references to it will be frequent enough. But the outline, after these introductory lines will be:

I. The Question at Issue
II. The Basis of Debate
III. Peripheral Material
IV. The Main Passages.

The conclusion here will be that Scripture definitely forbids the ordination of women.

I. The Question at Issue

As the introductory remarks have already said, and as the *Report* makes clear, the issue is not that of unordained deaconesses. The issue is the ordination of women as deacons. Now, whether such is permissible depends on the doctrine of ordination. Is the Reformed Presbyterian doctrine of ordination Scriptural, or is it not, and should it therefore be changed?

It is strange that the *Report,* lengthy as it is, pays so little attention to the doctrine of ordination. Since the ordination of women depends on some view of ordination, a view in conflict with Reformed principles, the *Report* should have included a massive defense of its underlying premise. This it did not do.

Section F (132) is about the most the *Report* has to say. It begins with a statement relative to the official position of the R. P. C. E. S. However, it does not state that position correctly; and insofar as the *Report's* conclusions depend on this inaccuracy, they are to be rejected. The *Report's* statement is: "This denomination . . . has seen one of the distinctive elements of the elder's role *as distinguished from that of deacon* to be the possession of ecclesiastically binding authority." This statement contradicts the *Form of Government.* Since the immediate aim of the *Report* is to defend the *ordination of women* as *deacons,* three subject-matters need attention. Ordination is the inclusive one. It is the *Question at Issue.* The subordinate points are *deacons* and *women.* What does the *Form of Government,* in its authoritative definition of Reformed Presbyterian polity, say on these points?

To quote, *F. O. G.,* V, 5 says, "The formal steps by which a young man becomes an ordained minister. . . ." It does not say "a young person," and it does not say "a young man or woman." Since even a few years ago, no one advocated the ordination of women, this reference to a man rather than a woman was neither emphasized nor

Pastors, elders, and deacons all take the same vows.

Ordination is induction into an authoritative order.

repeated. At V, 8, *F. O. G.* simply says, "The qualifications of both teaching elders and ruling elders . . . ." "Laymen, ordained to the eldership" is another phrase. It is also said that these elders have "a certain ruling or governing authority." The section on deacons is not so explicit. Had women been envisioned as possible candidates it would have had to be explicit. The *Report* takes the position that Scripture allows the ordination of women as deacons but prohibits their ordination as elders. If this were the Reformed Presbyterian position, *F. O. G.* would have had to state the difference explicitly, clearly, and emphatically. It does not do so. What is explicitly said is, "The minister shall then propound to the elder- or *deacon*-elect the following questions: See Section 3 of this chapter."

Thus, pastors, elders, and deacons all take the same vows, with the one exception that pastors assent to question 8, while other ministers—not pastors—elders, and deacons, assent to question 9. None of these nine vows explicitly mentions authority to teach. But if this authority is assumed for an elder, it is also assumed for a deacon, because ruling elders, deacons, and non-pastoral ministers are treated as a single class. Then further, in V, 9, C, the minister makes the ordination prayer. Note that this is not an ordination of deacons-elect by previously ordained deacons, with the idea that elders are ordained by elders. Such might indeed greatly distinguish elders from deacons. *F. O.* G. does not make it clear who gives and who does not give the newly ordained deacon the right hand of fellowship.

But the clinching formula is that which the *Form of Government* imposes on the congregation: "Do you, the members of this church, acknowledge and receive the *brother* as a ruling elder (or *deacon*) and do you promise to yield him all that honor, encouragement, and *obedience* in the Lord to which . . . the Constitution of the Church *entitles* him?"

At this point, it seems proper to conclude that the *Report* bases its thesis on a mistaken view of Reformed Presbyterian government. The R. P. C. E. S. does not distinguish between an elder and a deacon by the latter's lack of ecclesiastical authority. On the contrary, it explicitly asserts this authority. The application to women—in the light of Scripture yet to be discussed—is automatic. Ignoring our constitution, the *Report* continues, "If this distinction is maintained, there need be no question of setting women in authority over men by ordaining them as deacons." But if this unconstitutional distinction were maintained, there would be no need or reason to *ordain* either men or women deacons. Ordination is induction into an authoritative *order*. This now returns the discussion from the ordination of *women* as *deacons* to the fundamental question of *ordination*.

There are several views as to the nature of ordination. The one acknowledged by the largest group of people is that of Romanism. At the Reformation Luther clearly, Calvin more clearly, and a great section of the European populace perceived that the elaborate Roman hierarchy with its awesome claims contrasted sharply with the simplicity of the church as the apostles had organized it. The Romish claims depended largely, perhaps almost entirely, on the premise that ordination confers a special rank of *priesthood* for the purpose of repeating Christ's sacrifice in the mass. In their opposition to the mass, all the Reformers abominated the papal hierarchy and rigorously defended the equal priesthood of all believers. Yet they did not for that reason abolish the ordained ministry.

There were some who did. The radical Anabaptists denounced all church government and civil government, too. Later, and continuing to the present, the Quakers and Plymouth Brethren rejected an official ministry. Even more recently, in opposition to organized religion, some groups would shut down the seminaries, close the church doors, sell the real estate, and, unlike the anarchism of the Anabaptists, spend the proceeds to establish socialism.

The European populace perceived that the elaborate Roman hierarchy with its awesome claims contrasted sharply with the simplicity of the church as the apostles had organized it.

Since the *Report* does not discuss these movements, since indeed it makes no effort to explain its new view of ordination, it is not possible to be sure of what direction this movement in our denomination may later take. It is clear, however, that the modern temper among religious people is rather inimical to "organized religion" and favors some form of pietism rather than the Presbyterian position.

Neither Luther nor Calvin accepted this left-wing position. Calvin *(Institutes,* IV, iii, 2) says,

> By the ministers to whom [Christ] has committed this office, and given grace to discharge it, he disperses and distributes his grace to the Church. Whosoever therefore studies to abolish the *order* and kind of government . . . or disparages it as a minor importance, plots the devastation, or rather the ruin and destruction of the churches.

These words show how highly Calvin esteemed ministerial order.

That this includes the deacons also a later paragraph (IV, iii) makes clear: "The qualifications of . . . bishops are stated at large by Paul in two passages. . . . The same rule is laid down for the deacons and governors."

There are other historical documents. The *French Confession of 1559* says, "We detest all fantastic people who greatly desire . . . to abolish the ministry" (Art. xxv).

The Second Book of Discipline of the Scottish Kirk says, "There are four ordinary functions or offices in the Kirk of God, the office of pastor, minister, or bishop; the doctor; the presbyter or elder; and the deacon." In Reformation days the main object was to reject the papal theory of hierarchy, and to insist on the priesthood of all believers. Our Scottish forebears also refused to acknowledge the Anglican ordination of deacons because this was part of the hierarchical scheme. But they ordained deacons, and they had strict views of the significance of ordination. They rejected the "indelible character" imposed by ordination as the Romanists understood it; but they did not object to an "indelible character," a life-long authority, as they themselves defined it.

It is strange, and perhaps one may be so bold as to say significant, that the *Report* in advocating the ordination of women has so little to say about ordination. Since the *Report,* in order to allow women to be ordained as deacons, excludes from ordination the conferring of authority, no one can be sure what theory of ordination the *Report* wishes to introduce into our denomination. One can be sure, however, that its view of ordination is destructive of Presbyterian polity.

Since the Report, in order to allow women to be ordained as deacons, excludes from ordination the conferring of authority, no one can be sure what theory of ordination the Report wishes to introduce into our denomination. One can be sure, however, that its view of ordination is destructive of Presbyterian polity.

During the Reformation the controversy centered chiefly on the ministry, less on the elders, and least on deacons. Yet the Reformers did not pass over the latter in complete silence. Luther in his *Address to the Christian Nobility of the German Nation,* June 1520, said,

> He [the minister] should have as assistants several priests [the term *priest* continued to be used for a time] and *deacons* who should help him to *govern* the people and congregations with sermons and the administration of the sacraments.

The *French Confession of 1559* (previously alluded to) also says, "It [the true church] ought to be *governed* according to the policy which our Savior Jesus Christ has established, that is, that there be pastors, supervisors, and deacons." Note that deacons form a part of the governing body. The Genevan *Ordinances* of 1541 state something similar: ". . . let the minister distribute the bread in good order and with reverence, and let no others give the cup except the ones appointed or the *deacons* with the ministers." The *Ordinances* of 1576 make the same statement about the deacons. Again, what Calvin says about women who perform baptism is surely applicable to women who might act as deacons. In his *Tracts* he says, "Even in the minutest matters, as meat and drink, whatever we attempt and dare with a doubtful conscience, Paul plainly denounces as sin. Now, in baptism by women, what certainty can there be, while a rule delivered by Christ is violated? For that office of the Gospel which he assigned to ministers, women seize for themselves." Further, Calvin's reply to the Synod of Lyons in 1563 (compare Quick, *Synodicon,* I, 53) says, "*Deacons* and elders, being the arms and hands of the Pastor, . . . may also distribute [the bread and cup] to those who are remote from [the pastor]."

In these passages the mention of deacons is noteworthy because there was a widespread disinclination to allow deacons and even elders to assist in the communion service. Calvin obviously regards deacons as having authority by virtue of ordination. They are no doubt subordinate to the minister. Ordination confers on the minister the authority to preach the Word, and, since the sacraments require the Word, ordination confers the authority to administer the sacraments, and also, in conjunction with other ordained men, the authority of the keys. But though the deacons are subordinate to the minister, they participate in that authority. The ordination questions are the same; the minister receives the deacon as taking "part of this office with us;" and the congregation promises obedience to the deacon.

II. The Basis of the Debate

The issue has now been clearly stated. It is the Reformed doctrine of ordination. This doctrine is not the prelatic and hierarchical theory of Rome, nor is it the anarchical chaos of the Anabaptists. But which of the three views is correct? Obviously the Reformed Presbyterian Church forbids the ordination of women. Since, however, "All Synods and councils since the apostles' times . . . may err, and many have erred," it is theoretically possible that Reformed Presbyterian government is in error. But it is highly unlikely that Presbyterianism is in error on this particular point. The believing Jews before the coming of Christ, as well as the unbelieving Jews afterward, had no women as priests. Neither does Romanism. Neither does Lutheranism. Among these groups there are differences regarding the nature of ordination, its validity, its authority, and more; but all agree that it is wrong to ordain women. Now, where Rabbis Eliezer and Agiba; Popes Leo and Gregory; and Luther, Calvin, and Knox agree on a particular point, it requires overwhelming argument to prove them wrong. On what basis could anyone construct such an argument? There is only one such basis, the Bible.

Where Rabbis Eliezer and Agiba; Popes Leo and Gregory; and Luther, Calvin, and Knox agree on a particular point, it requires overwhelming argument to prove them wrong. On what basis could anyone construct such an argument? There is only one such basis, the Bible.

The *Report,* be it not only cheerfully but also gratefully acknowledged, appeals to Scripture alone. Were it otherwise, they and we would have no common basis of argument. However much the present paper regards the *Report's* exegesis poor and its argument invalid, the *Report* is to be highly commended for its repeated rejection of the idea that parts of Scripture are not binding today because they were culturally conditioned. Since this rejection is not the contemporary stance of the religious community, a short paragraph or two stressing the contrast is pertinent.

Dr. Paul King Jewett is a particularly good example, for he has recently argued for the ordination of women. He has no trouble with the Scriptural material; he even agrees substantially that the view defended in this paper is Scriptural; but he simply rejects the Apostle Paul's mistakes as culturally conditioned. The seminary, too, in which Dr. Jewett teaches, is also a good example. Several of its members have publicly engaged in controversy against Scriptural inerrancy. The more conservative faculty members resigned and left the seminary some years ago. Yet the seminary claims to be evangelical. They should call themselves modernists, for their position is very much the same as that of the modernists early in this century. Their tactics are also similar, for in debasing the language so as to empty the term *evangelical* of its historic meaning, they repeat the earlier modernists' debasing of the term, the *divinity of* Christ, to accommodate Homer and Shakespeare, if not the divine Sarah. This pervasive influence of liberalism is most clearly seen in the large apostate denominations. In them a minister can be ejected or a candidate can be refused ordination because he disapproves of women's ordination. But liberalism's influence can also be seen, though it may be in modified form, in more conservative churches. Even in our church we must regard it as short-sighted to discuss an issue such as ordination without taking into consideration the conditions that press upon us from every side. Since liberal ideas pervade the entire religious community, Reformed Presbyterians will do well to combat them even in their incipient forms. Too many seminaries and denominations slip into apostasy almost imperceptibly. Let not the heirs of Covenanters meet this fate.

The seminary claims to be evangelical. They should call themselves modernists, for their position is very much the same as that of the modernists early in this century. Their tactics are also similar, for in debasing the language so as to empty the term evangelical of its historic meaning, they repeat the earlier modernists' debasing of the term, the divinity of Christ, to accommodate Homer and Shakespeare, if not the divine Sarah.

One recent, small, but encouraging sign on the horizon was the 135 to 74 vote against women's ordination in the 1976 General Synod of the Associate Reformed Presbyterian Church. They even voted down a motion to distribute the advocates' *Report* to the session "for prayerful consideration."

The successful introduction of the ordination of women into liberal churches is one with the general outlook of women's liberation. Apart from the excesses of left-wing philosophy, the permissiveness of parents and society, and the stress on women's alleged rights even to permitting a teenage girl to get an abortion in defiance of her parents—apart from this sort of thing it is doubtful that anyone would have agitated for the ordination of women. The mention of women's lib and the exceeding great immorality of our times is not intended to cast aspersions on the authors of the *Report*. No one accuses them of sitting enthralled at the feet of Bella Abzug. On the contrary, the procedure of the *Report* explicitly and throughout appeals to Scripture. In this it differs completely from the usual procedures. Is there any instance, in any denomination, of this sort of agitation on strictly Scriptural grounds? The present *Report* seems unique. For its reliance on Scripture, we are grateful. Nevertheless, the present sociological propensities tend to produce a more favorable reception of this proposal than the Scriptures warrant. With the *Report's* explicit basis this paper fully agrees and urges all readers to consult the Scripture alone.

Many seminaries and denominations slip into apostasy almost imperceptibly.

III. Peripheral Material

Some Scriptural material, however, bears on the main topic only to a small degree. Other passages relate more directly. And a few may be decisive. The first class cannot be completely omitted, for the *Report* contains a considerable amount of it, but perhaps in this reply brevity will be acceptable.

One such peripheral point is the matter of women praying in the public church service. The *Report* discusses this at some length. The reason is clear. If Paul has actually forbidden women to pray in public, he certainly would not have permitted them to be ordained. Hence the *Report* must combat this interpretation. On the other hand, if Paul permitted women to pray in public, it by no means follows that he would have ordained them.

This point of logic is sufficient to show the futility of several pages of the *Report*. However, a word in favor of the more obvious interpretation will count against ordination. The verses read, "Let your women keep silence in the churches, for it is not permitted unto them to speak. . . . It is a shame for women to speak in church" (*1 Corinthians* 14:34-35). The *Report* (116) notes an "apparent conflict between the prayer of women in chapter 11 and their silencing in chapter 14."

Can ordination solve this apparent conflict? Is it not possible, and much easier, to use another method? Since the later Corinthian reference commands silence, and hence rules out ordination, the only problem is that of contradiction. On this point two things may be said. First, as the *Report* itself acknowledges, the prayers of women that Paul permits may have taken place in informal prayer meetings. Or, what the *Report* does not consider, the prayers may have been made in women's own homes. Of course, as the *Report* says at the bottom of page 115, "These texts clearly presume that women did pray and prophesy." But the point at issue is where and when? The text does not say, "in the church." Therefore, these words should not be inserted. Then, when another text says explicitly, Let women keep silence in the church, it follows that *1 Corinthians* 11 *cannot* mean "in the church." It must refer to some informal gatherings, such as one of our women's missionary societies. The *Report* acknowledges that this solves the problems of alleged contradiction. But it rejects the solution because "it is doubtful that the case can be sustained exegetically" (116).

If Paul has actually forbidden women to pray in public, he certainly would not have permitted them to be ordained.

Philip's daughters prophesied, like Agabus, when no church service was in progress.

Doubtful? Not very. The clarity of chapter 14 and the absence from chapter 11 of the words "in the church," seem to be exegetically sufficient. Furthermore, so far as the main question of ordination goes, it is not necessary to sustain this interpretation exegetically. The immediate point is the solution of an apparent contradiction, and even the *Report* agrees that the interpretation given here is satisfactory. On the other hand, the *Report's* interpretation cannot be sustained exegetically. How can one extract from the verse the words that are not there? Yet the *Report* should provide exegetical certainty because it bears the burden of proof.

But that there were, actually and historically, occasions of prayer and prophecy other than the regular church service, and that therefore the present interpretation does not depend on unsupported assumptions, is clear, if not from *Acts* 11:28, at least from *Acts* 21:9-11. What Agabus did hardly fits into a worship service; and exegesis cannot deny that Philip's daughters prophesied, like Agabus, when no church service was in progress.

The result of this analysis is (1) that pages 115-117 of the *Report* hardly bear on the question at all; (2) that the solution rejected on page 116 remains satisfactory; and (3) that the *Report's* "Conclusion: I Corinthians 11:5 probably refers to public worship services" is not more than possible, and probably less compelling than what the *Report* rejects as a "weak possibility." It must be insisted that the advocates of women's ordination, not those who defend the official Reformed Presbyterian principles, must produce the "compelling external evidence." The burden of proof rests on the innovators, not on those who maintain the actual standards.

Another peripheral matter concerns Paul's stylistic abilities. In order to substitute its interpretation for the more obvious one, the *Report* argues in several places that there cannot be a "violent break" in the subject matter between the two verses in question. There must be a smooth transition. Now, admittedly, most verses connect logically with their preceding and succeeding verses. Otherwise there could be no continuous discussion. Nonetheless, paragraph breaks occur; and sometimes there are two or more sudden shifts within a very few lines.

It must be insisted that the advocates of women's ordination, not those who defend the official Reformed Presbyterian principles, must produce the "compelling external evidence." The burden of proof rests on the innovators, not on those who maintain the actual standards.

A major example is the well known passage, *Romans* 5:12-19. There, the passage has a single theme; but Paul mixes together many strands of a complex subject. There are parentheses within parentheses; and the sentence becomes so complicated that Paul breaks it off and begins over again in verse 18.

Active minds like Paul's are apt to write intricate sentences, including parenthetical remarks. And they jump back and forwards as their thoughts come in profusion. Note, therefore, another example: 1 Timothy 5:17 and the following verses, an epistle if not a chapter that occupies many pages in the *Report.* After discussing the plight of widows in the first half of the chapter, Paul turns to the Old Testament admonition that congregations should support their pastors. Then come directions concerning judicial cases. Then a warning against ordaining young men, or newly converted Christians. Then some medicinal advice to Timothy. Finally two verses, which do not connect with medicinal advice, are vague enough to make any connection uncertain. In view of such examples as these, and there are others, this paper will not relinquish its interpretation when the argument for its alternate depends so heavily on the assumption that Paul must write as smoothly as the *Report* expects. In fact, the *Report* itself (83) has to adjust itself to an "abrupt transition."

Under the rubric of "Peripheral Matters" there are distinctions in degree. A not so peripheral matter is the use of the term *deacon* in the New Testament.

If the New Testament contained even a single instance of the election and apostolic ordination of a woman as a deacon, the fact would be conclusive. Without an example, however, the argument can never be conclusive. The best that can be done is to refer to *Romans* 16:1, where Phoebe is called *diakonon,* and from this infer that the church members had elected her and that the apostles thereupon ordained her.

Such an inference is invalid. Note that in *Acts* 6:1 there was a daily *diakonia* before "deacons" were elected and ordained. The word originally was not the name of an ordained officer, but designated anyone who served the needs of others. In *John* 2:5, 9 it refers to those who were serving the marriage banquet. Compare *Matthew* 22:13. In *John* 12:26 it refers to any faithful servant of Christ. Thence the term can be applied to Phoebe, or to any other Christian, without implying ordination.

In fact, so far as the term itself goes, it even refers to servants of Satan (*2 Corinthians* 11:15).

In *1 Timothy* 4:6 Timothy is called a servant, a *diakonos;* though he was an elder or bishop and not a "deacon." So, too, the apostles themselves are called servants: *Acts* 6:2 says that the apostles had been serving (*diakonein*) tables, but henceforth they must drop this task and give themselves to the ministry of the Word *(diakoinia tou logou)*. When it is noted that the seven chosen were not called "deacons" in this passage, and that the verb *diakonein* applies to the apostles, must we conclude that Phoebe was an apostle?

Quite the contrary: The term *diakonos* was a name given to any servant. Its application to Phoebe in *Romans* 16:1 carries no implication of ordination.

The *Report* tries to dispose of this contention on page 134:

> Because the word *diakonos* can be translated either "deacon" or "servant" it is important to note that Paul *did not choose to use the feminine form of the word but rather broke gender to identify Phoebe with the masculine form of the noun* [italics in *Report*]. This very strongly suggests that he was not simply calling her a servant . . . but was rather using a formal term identifying her as a deacon.

But where in Greek literature does such a feminine form of the word occur? Neither Liddell and Scott nor Arndt and Gingrich lists any feminine form. On the contrary, they both cite passages in which the masculine form applies to women.

With respect to the masculine and feminine forms of Greek nouns, another point deserves mention. The *Report* is unique in that it recommends women for deacons but forbids their ordination as elders. Proposals and their adoption in other denominations include and indeed stress ordination as ministers. This is because these other denominations have little regard for Scripture, while the *Report* desires to follow the Bible. The *Report* has no inclination to argue that the Bible allows women to be ordained as pastors. Nevertheless, one can wonder whether or not the ordination of women as pastors can be prevented once the momentum has begun in their ordination as deacons. Indeed, it is possible to guess a part of the future

The term diakonos was a name given to any servant.

One can wonder whether or not the ordination of women as pastors can be prevented once the momentum has begun in their ordination as deacons. Indeed, it is possible to guess a part of the future argument. It will be pointed out that if we now ordain women as deacons, although there is no such form as diakone in the New Testament (or elsewhere?), we ought all the more to ordain women as pastors because 1 Timothy 5:1, 2 explicitly mention presbuterai (women elders) as well as presbuteroi (men elders).

argument. It will be pointed out that if we now ordain women as deacons, although there is no such form as *diakone* in the New Testament (or elsewhere?), we ought all the more to ordain women as pastors because *1 Timothy* 5:1, 2 explicitly mention *presbuterai* (women elders) as well as *presbuteroi* (men elders).

The words *diakonos* and *presbuteros* are not the only examples of words used colloquially, which we almost without exception use technically. The word *church* (*ecclesia*) is another example. In *Acts* 2:47 the Lord added converts to the "church" daily; and the context shows what church was meant. But the tumultuous assembly of heathen in Ephesus is thrice called the *ecclesia* (*Acts* 19:32, 39, 40). Hence the term *diakonos,* applied to Phoebe, is no evidence that she was ordained.

The verse itself says that Phoebe was a prostatis to Paul himself. Thus Paul must have been an inferior member of the order over which Phoebe was president and ruler.

But it is said that Phoebe was not merely a servant of the Lord, she was also a *prostatis* of many. The argument is that *prostatēs* (masculine) and therefore *prostatis* (feminine) meant ruler, authority, defender, guardian, presiding officer, patron, etc. Thus Phoebe was a regularly ordained officer with authority over many people.

Unfortunately, the masculine form does not occur in the New Testament, and the feminine form only this once. The verb, however, occurs about seven times and certainly indicates authority and command. To those who advocate the ordination of women, this one word seems to be strong evidence, and perhaps conclusive. But surely one ought to have more than a hapax legomenon to overturn thousands of years of ecclesiastical procedure. Nor is this all that can be said. For the verse itself says that Phoebe was a *prostatis* to Paul himself. Thus Paul must have been an inferior member of the order over which Phoebe was president and ruler. Contrary to these unacceptable inferences, this paper concludes that Phoebe was a faithful servant who had been of great help to many people and to Paul himself, as Peter's mother-in-law served (*diakonei*) Christ in *Matthew* 8:15.

This section on "Peripheral Material" has now canvassed the topic of women praying in church, Paul's stylistic peculiarities, and the usage of the term *deacon.* But as the discussion now continues, the material bears more and more directly on the main issue.

The chapter goes further than forbidding such ordinations: It even forbids women to pray in the public services.

IV. The Main Passages

1 Timothy 2 is surely one of major importance. Upon first reading it seems definitely to rule out the ordination of women. Indeed, a second and a third reading confirm this impression. In fact, the chapter goes further than forbidding such ordinations: It even forbids women to pray in the public services.

Against this clear statement the *Report* struggles at some length (pages 79-90). It first notes that the subject of the chapter is "prayer in the church." This, of course, is true; but it can lead to a misunderstanding. Chapter two is a subdivision of the epistle as a whole, the subject of which is broader than prayer. *1 Timothy* covers the general subject of worship, and hence Paul can pass from prayer to other phases of worship. By narrowing the subject to prayer, the *Report* wishes to avoid an alleged violent break supposedly required by the usual interpretation. The *Report* is extremely detailed and should be consulted. It would be unreasonably burdensome here to examine every line. But in general the *Report* argues that on the usual interpretation, there would be an impossible break "because it does not actually present Paul's intended contrasts but treats v. 8 (men praying with holy hands) as if it stood next to vv. 11ff. . . ." (80). The *Report's* argument seems to depend on the assumption that Paul could not have considered, in the same verse, two related subjects, here in fact one main subject and a subordinate part.

The prohibition of public prayer by women is not "unspoken."

The argument of the *Report* is defective at several points. Paragraph (1) on page 80 says, "If the intended comparison is the sex roles, the comment on holy hands . . . seriously obscures Paul's central but *unspoken* point that women should not pray." To this one can reply that there is not just one "central" point in the passage, unless it be the general topic of orderly worship. Many verses in Scripture contain several distinguishable points. Here, in addition to *holy hands* and *modest apparel,* the "sex roles" can hardly escape notice. Far from being "unspoken," as the *Report* strangely repeats three times over, verse 12 says, "she must be silent." This silence is consonant with the progression of thought in verses 8 and 9: Men are to pray [in the church], women are to dress modestly, and learn in silence and subjection. Verse 10, not verse 9, may be a parenthetical aside, for such are not absent from Paul's style, but there is no violent break or "parenthetical aside which seriously obscures Paul's central . . . point."

The *Report* makes much of the word *hosautos* in verse 9. The *Report* admits that it would be wrong to translate the verse as "Similarly also I want the women to pray" (80). This is a welcome admission, but the *Report* apparently fails to see how it undercuts its own continuation. First, it must be insisted upon that the prohibition of public prayer by women is not "unspoken." The *Report* at least three times asserts that it is unspoken; and upon this erroneous assertion builds part of its argument. Second, *hosautos kai* admittedly draws some kind of parallel. But the *Report* has already admitted that the parallel is not "I want men to pray . . . I also want women to pray." For this reason the parallel can as little be, "I want men to pray with holy hands and I want women to pray in modest dress." And for this reason the argument of pages 80-82 ought to be adjudged a failure.

Someone now is sure to ask, But then what is the parallel? This is a legitimate question, but it is permissible to decide that the *Report's* view is impossible without being able to answer this question. The *Report's* view is impossible because of the *spoken* (written) command of silence. However, a plausible answer to the question is at hand, which the *Report* itself vaguely hints at (page 82, last paragraph of the section). Briefly it is this: Paul's ideas came to him in profusion, the general subject here is public worship and not prayer alone; therefore, one may accept the words, if not the intention of the *Report* (page 82 end): "a continuation of Paul's discussion of prayer . . . understood as discussing . . . worship." If so, Paul has said, "Men are to worship by lifting holy hands in prayer; *likewise also,* women are to worship by dressing modestly and remaining silent."

Such is the conclusion proposed here. But a further point is that the wording of the *Report* is most misleading when it says, "we must question whether it is at all a tenable inference that women were silent at all times in the Pauline assemblies" (82). Of course it is not a tenable inference. The inference is exactly the opposite: Women were not always silent in the Pauline assemblies; that is why Paul wrote to correct the disorder. A similar peculiarity occurs on the next page also: "Why did the problems of prayer, prophecy, and teaching arise, if he never permitted women to speak in the churches?" (page 83, last line). One might as well ask about *1 Corinthians* 7, Why did the problem of incest arise, if Paul had never permitted incest in his churches?

Women were not always silent in the Pauline assemblies; that is why Paul wrote to correct the disorder.

Since the remainder of Part I (pages 84-90) is interesting, instructive, and substantially acceptable; in fact, since this material agrees more with the Reformed Presbyterian position and less with the *Report's* conclusions; and again, since its firm rejection of "cultural limitations" is so gratifying, it may not be altogether improper to skip to pages 132ff. on *1 Timothy* 3:8-13. That the *Report* on this page does not accurately state the Reformed Presbyterian position has already been made clear. But the "exegetical debate over I Tim. 3:11," on which "hangs the demonstration of biblical warrant" for the ordination of women, "centers on the meaning of the word *gunaikas."* Therefore, the *Report* must *demonstrate,* by strictly valid implication, or as the *Confession* says, "by good and *necessary* consequence," that *gunaikas* must mean "women deacons," and cannot possibly mean wives of deacons or elders.

Far from being a necessary deduction, the *Report's* argument is deficient both in premises and procedure. Note its starting point on page 133: "We may *confidently* dismiss [the view that *gunaikas* means either women in general or that it means wives of elders and deacons]." This confidence, however, is based on the assertion "that it would not be *probable* that Paul would break his train of thought. . . ." But, first, probability is not demonstration. Second, we have already seen how frequently Paul "breaks his train of thought." And third, he does not really break his train of thought, though he may put a coach or dining car between two Pullmans. Hence the *Report's* "probable" and "unlikely" (page 133) have no force in proving its conclusion.

It is here true that if Paul had inserted a *tas* (article) or an *autōn* (pronoun), there could have been no doubt as to the translation *wives.*

But then Paul frequently enough omits the article where English requires it. The *Report* asserts that the *King James* translation "gratuitously" supplies the word *their.* But if neither Paul nor the congregation had any idea of ordaining women, the article or pronoun was unnecessary. The *Report's* argument tends to circularity: *Their* is gratuitous because Paul meant women deacons, and he meant women deacons because *gunaikas* does not mean wives, and *gunaikas* does not mean wives because the *King James their* is gratuitous. Hence Paul approved the ordination of women.

The *Report* next reverts to what is "unlikely": "It is unlikely that he would carefully comment on deacons' wives and neglect those of the elders." But this, too, is rather circular. How does the *Report* prove that Paul neglected to speak of elders' wives, if he actually spoke of deacons' wives? Only on the ground stated above that "it would not be *probable* that Paul would break his train of thought concerning deacons." On the contrary, it is quite possible, and by the text quite probable that, after Paul had spoken of elders (3:1) and deacons (3:8) he inserted a parenthetical remark (3:11) concerning their wives, elders' wives as well as deacons' wives.

The office of deacon is an office which involves the exercise of ecclesiastical authority. In the Pauline churches it was closed to women. It therefore must be closed to women in our churches.

The *Report* takes notice of this latter interpretation. But it claims that its own view is "more likely." Now aside from the fact that the present article does not think the *Report's* interpretation is more likely, in fact considers it less likely and even quite improbable, one must insist that the *Report's* conclusion requires necessary consequence and valid argument. A doubtful likelihood about a single verse is not sufficient to overturn the Presbyterian view of ordination.

The *Report* continues with an argument about Phoebe; but this was disposed of a few pages ago. Phoebe was never "Madame President" (page 134) to Paul.

This is the end of the *Report's* argument. "Conclusions and Recommendations" follow. This is also the end of this paper's argument. Its conclusion can easily be anticipated.

Using the wording of the *Report (Diakonate,* page 135), but contradicting its sense by switching positives and negatives, the conclusion is:

The office of deacon is an office which involves the exercise of ecclesiastical authority. In the Pauline churches it was closed to women. It therefore must be closed to women in our churches.

And furthermore, with the pope, John Knox, the Scottish Kirk, and all Christendom, we believe that the position of the Reformed Presbyterian Church in refusing to ordain women is solidly Biblical, against which likelihoods have no logical force.

B

The Presbyterian Doctrine of Ordination

The examples of Saul and Uzziah, as well as the directions for anointing partially explained in Exodus 30:30-33, show that something was conferred on the recipient that he had not possessed before. This something was in one case the authority to act as a priest, and in another case the authority to act as a king. God prohibited anyone from so acting without being anointed.

In 1976 a *Report* to the Reformed Presbyterian Church, Evangelical Synod advocated the ordination of women to the diaconate. It failed, however, to consider the meaning of ordination. This strange omission should be remedied, for it would be most unfortunate, were the synod to decide to ordain women without considering what ordination is. A previous paper contested the view of the diaconate which the above mentioned *Report* held forth. Here the subject is ordination. The following material is roughly divided into three sections. The first section takes up the Scriptural teaching and includes arguments from the works of George Gillespie. The second and shortest section of the three briefly disposes of the liberal ecumenical movement. Third, because it comes from a sister church, a *Report* to the Synod of the Christian Reformed Church will be examined.

1

The Scriptural material can well begin with some Old Testament anticipations. Frequently in the Old Testament an anointing with oil was the method of inducting someone into a particular office. Anyone not so anointed was guilty of a grave offense, if he dared to execute that office. Saul and Uzziah are two examples. If, now, the New Testament provides some means for inducting a person into an office, the Old Testament ceremony must be regarded as an anticipation of the New Testament requirements. Hence it is profitable to glance at the Old Testament method and its significance.

The examples of Saul and Uzziah, as well as the directions for anointing partially explained in *Exodus* 30:30-33, show that something was conferred on the recipient that he had not possessed before. This something was in one case the authority to act as a priest, and in another case the authority to act as a king. God prohibited anyone from so acting without being anointed.

In the New Testament, anointing has no place. To be sure the Messiah is the Lord's anointed, but Jesus never had holy oil poured on his head. Paul in *2 Corinthians* 1:21 also refers to a figurative non-literal anointing. In this verse Paul may have had only the apostles in mind; but it is possible, because of the following verse, that he meant an anointing of every believer. That such a figurative development of the idea of anointing should have occurred is not surprising. In fact, the figurative use is quite clear in *1 John* 2:27.

Nevertheless, since the New Testament also speaks of inducting elders into their office, it would be perverse to limit the anticipation of the Old Testament to Jesus as Messiah plus a general anointing of all believers. Since there are distinct offices both in the Old Testament and in the New Testament, the anointing in the Old Testament is best understood as anticipating New Testament ordination. This would help to support the idea that ordination confers authority upon the ordained.

In the New Testament, anointing has no place.

The Old Testament also provides for induction into office by the laying on of hands. In the case of Jacob and the two sons of Joseph, the laying on of hands is not an induction into office, but the bestowal of a blessing. *Numbers* 8:10, however, inducts the Levites into office by this rite. Similarly in *Numbers* 27:18-23 Moses appointed Joshua as his successor by the laying on of hands. By so doing, Moses "put some of [his] honor upon him . . . and gave him a charge." That God may have given the Holy Spirit to Joshua before Moses ordained him is irrelevant to the point at issue. The point is that there was a public ceremony of induction, without which Joshua could not have officiated. The induction may not have given him the Spirit, but it surely gave him the authority to act. Someone may boggle at the anointing with oil, but who can fail to see here an anticipation of the ordination of New Testament elders?

The one man who most fully worked out the New Testament doctrine of ordination was the Scottish commissioner to the Westminster Assembly, George Gillespie.

It is the New Testament that most concerns us. The one man who most fully worked out the New Testament doctrine of ordination was the Scottish commissioner to the Westminster Assembly, George Gillespie. The argument will now show considerable dependence on *Aaron's Rod Blossoming, Dispute Against the English Popish Ceremonies,* and *Miscellany Questions.* The pagination comes from the 1844 Edinburgh edition of Gillespie's works.

At the climax of the Reformation, the age of the Westminster Assembly, this young man exhaustively examined the Scriptures and applied them to refute Romanism, Erastianism, and Socianism alike. It is to be feared that Gillespie's scriptural analysis is not well known in this present decadent century.

Since it is the Socinian view of ordination, rather than the Romish or Erastian view, that troubles us today, only short references to the latter two will be made. For example, against the Erastianism of a certain Mr. Hussey, Gillespie writes, "Civil governors cannot be the elders mentioned by the apostle Paul, except Mr. Hussey make them bishops and invest them with the power of ordination" *(Aaron's Rod*

Blossoming, II, ix, 124/2). Aside from the application to Erastianism, the sentence quoted refers to a certain power of ordination, that is, a power conferred by ordination. What this power is must be ascertained if one is to understand the Presbyterian doctrine of ordination.

On the following page Gillespie denies that elders are "without any power or authority of government." The source of that authority and its conferral are matters that must be determined. Gillespie at the place indicated continues for a column or so to show that elders have authority to rule. He adduces *Hebrews* 13:7, "Remember them that have the rule over you, men that spoke unto you the Word of God." The idea of ruling can be supported by other verses, such as *1 Timothy* 3:4-6, 12, and 5:17. But as these will be more carefully examined later, there is no need to quote them here.

Christ's kingdom is not of this world; nor is justice administered by swords and staves and torches. But it is a kingdom nonetheless. To deny laws and officers is to deny the kingdom, and to deny the kingdom is to deny the King.

Prior to the assertion that elders have authority to rule, it is logically necessary to show that the New Testament identifies something for the elders to rule over. That something is the visible, organized church. "The Scripture is plain that a visible, ministerial church is the body of Christ" (136/2). Scriptures supporting this are: *Romans* 12:4, 5, "Even as we have many members in one body, . . . so we who are many are one body in Christ"; *1 Corinthians* 10:17, "Seeing that we, who are many, are one bread, one body"; and similarly *1 Corinthians* 12:12-28. To which may be added *Luke* 19:14, 27, "His citizens hated him . . . saying, We will not have this man reign over us. . . . But these mine enemies, which would not that I should reign over them, bring hither and slay them before me." This passage, which may at first puzzle a person studying ordination and church government, Gillespie uses as the answer to the rhetorical question, "Dare any say that the Lord Jesus shall not govern the Church of England and reign over the same?"

More obvious in their reference to an organized church over which Christ reigns through his stewards are *Acts* 2:36; *1 Corinthians* 15:24; *2 Corinthians* 10:4-6; and *Ephesians* 1:21-23; all of which assert Christ's lordship over his church and kingdom. A kingdom requires laws, officers, and courts. Since this is true of earthly kingdoms, how much more so of Christ's kingdom! Christ's kingdom is not of this world; nor is justice administered by swords and staves and torches. But it is a kingdom nonetheless. To deny laws and officers is to deny the kingdom, and to deny the kingdom is to deny the *King.* Mr. Hussey, on the contrary, had said that the visible church is not the body of Christ, nor is Christ its head, nor does the kingdom have any officers except the Holy Spirit. Against Mr. Hussey Gillespie appeals to *Romans* 12:4, 5; *1 Corinthians* 10:16, 17; and *1 Corinthians* 12:12-28. But since the kingship of Christ is not questioned in the present controversy, it is hardly necessary to quote these additional verses.

If now it be admitted that elders are rulers in the organized church, one of *The Sins of the Ministry of Scotland* is "Entering the ministry without trials and receiving ordination . . . sometimes without or against the mind of presbytery." Since exercising the office without ordination is a sin, it is important to understand the significance and proper method of ordination. With his view of an established religion, Gillespie wants "Princes . . . to provide that men of those ecclesiastical orders, and those only which are instituted in the New Testament by divine authority, have vocation and office in the church." This includes deacons, as is clear in the context, for on the next page he says, "Deacons were instituted by the apostles [to help the poor], besides which employments the Scripture hath assigned neither preaching nor baptizing nor any other ecclesiastical function" *(Dispute Against the Ceremonies,* Chapter VII, Digression 1, pages 160/1, and 161/2).

Some exception may be taken to Gillespie's denial that deacons should neither preach nor baptize, for although the activities of five of the original seven are not described, the other two did in fact preach and baptize. However, with respect to ordination, Gillespie on these pages says, "Now, beside the apostles, prophets, and evangelists, which were not ordained to be ordinary and perpetual offices in the church, there are but two ecclesiastical orders or degrees instituted by Christ in the New Testament viz., elders and deacons."

Some exception may be taken to Gillespie's denial that deacons should neither preach nor baptize, for although the activities of five of the original seven are not described, the other two did in fact preach and baptize.

Again, speaking of the prince (162/1) Gillespie says that the prince "should cause, not one disdainful prelate [to examine and ordain], but a whole Presbytery or company of elders to take trial of" the candidate. That is to say, an election of a candidate by the congregation, which Gillespie is strong to enforce, is nonetheless insufficient. There must also be Presbyterial action; and this seems to apply to deacons as well.

With the threat of Rome on his mind, and with the episcopal policy of Charles I before his eyes, Gillespie is anxious to maintain the Presbyterian principle of congregational election. For this reason he sometimes seems to lessen the emphasis on ordination, or at least on the imposition of hands. Because of this anti-prelatical concern, which might have induced him to abandon ordination altogether, as was the result in the Reformation's left-wing, Gillespie's insistence on ordination, as in the preceding quotation, is all the more important to us today.

Gillespie is anxious to maintain the Presbyterian principle of congregational election.

Thus, in spite of his Reformation opposition to Romish ordination, Gillespie asserts its necessity as well as the necessity of election. The *Ceremonies* (162/2) states, "The outward calling is made up of election and ordination. . . . Let the Acts of the Apostles and the epistles of Paul be read, how ministers were elected and ordained. . . ." *Acts* 1:15, 23 show election by the congregation; and *Acts* 6:2, 3 show the same in the case of deacons.

Acts 1:15, 23 show election by the congregation; and Acts 6:2, 3 show the same in the case of deacons.

Whether Presbytery's doing something with its hands refers to ordination or to raising their hands in a voting procedure has occasioned some confusion. The participle in *2 Corinthians* 8:19 is almost surely an election; yet the same verb in *Acts* 14:23 rather clearly refers to ordination, for its subject is Paul and Barnabus, who certainly would not have elected local elders. But this confusion does not arise in some other verses because they use a different verb.

To explain: Neither *leinein* nor *anateinein* occur in the New Testament. In classical Greek these verbs mean *stretch* or *strain*. There is no hint of *raising* hands, though *anateinein* can sometimes mean to vote. Hence *cheirotonetheis* in *2 Corinthians* 8:19 can mean a show of hands in voting. But *Acts* 6:6, 8:17, and 13:3 have a completely different verb: The phrase is *epithentes tas cheiras*. Clearly this is not hands *raised* in voting, but hands *laid upon* the candidate for ordination. Ordination therefore was not election by the congregation, but an act of the apostles.

Gillespie shows little enthusiasm for the Presbyterian act of the laying on of hands.

Gillespie is right in supporting election and prohibiting patronage, prelatic assignment, and any ignoring of the desires of the congregation. While so arguing he may seem to cast a shadow on ordination itself. Nevertheless he says clearly,

> The act of ordination standeth in the mission to the deputation of a man to an ecclesiastical function with power and authority to perform the same; and thus are pastors ordained when they are *sent* to a people with power to preach the Word, minister the sacraments, and exercise ecclesiastical discipline among them. For "How shall they preach except they be *sent*" (*Ceremonies,* 165/1).

Note well that ordination confers authority to preach, administer the sacraments, and exercise discipline. A presbyterial or congregational rite that does not convey this authority is not an ordination service, and should not be so called. Or, conversely, persons chosen for non-authoritative functions are not to be ordained.

Presumably in an over-reaction against Romish superstitions, Gillespie shows little enthusiasm for the Presbyterian act of the laying on of hands. After the preceding quotation he adds, "Unto which mission or ordination neither *prayer nor the imposition of hands,* nor any other of the church's rites is essential." Today few Reformed presbyters would approve of omitting prayer. But perhaps in a time of insurrection or riot, an ordination by presbyterial vote only would be considered valid. But the omission of the laying on of hands could be excused only by reason of some great disaster that would also excuse the omission of prayer. In this light one may accept his statement, "The essential act of ordination [is] a simple deputation and application of a minister to his ministerial function with power to perform it. This may be done . . . by word alone, without any other ceremony. . . ." The example of Christ sending out the seventy is given as evidence.

While one may guess, from silence, that Christ did not ordain the seventy by laying his hands on them, the instance is irrelevant because it occurred before the resurrection. Christ and the original twelve observed the Mosaic rituals, which are not binding upon us;

and negatively they were not baptized with the Trinitarian formula, nor did they observe the Lord's Supper before its institution, both of which of course oblige us today. The normative example for this age, with respect to ordination, is the apostolic action of the laying on of hands. Gillespie says this rite is "permissible," but not necessary. "This rite," he says, "shall with our leave be yet retained in the church." Unfortunately, he adds that although the rite may be retained "with our leave," the Church "hath full liberty either to use any other decent rite . . . or else to use no rite at all."

Surely this is not the Reformed view or the Puritan principle. The Bible teaches that we should do all that God requires and no more: We should neither add to nor subtract from the prescribed elements of worship. Surely a Reformed theologian must deny that the church can do anything or omit anything by its own leave. If the laying on of hands is to be omitted, it would have to be during riot or insurrection, or other circumstance when the Lord's Supper also would have to be omitted.

The Bible teaches that we should do all that God requires and no more.

In admitting that the laying on of hands is proper, decent, and permissible, Gillespie refers to *1 Timothy* 4:14—a passage which says more than he desires to say. Paul's instructions here, which, if not wholly concerned with the organization of churches, are at least the apostolic norm for ministerial conduct, not only mention the laying on of hands, but assert further that the grace of preaching authority, by the prophetic act of election, was given to Timothy with the presbytery's laying its hands on him. There may be some doubt whether or not the prophecy mentioned was the presbyterial election, but there can be no doubt about the presbyterial ordination with the laying on of hands. The verb does not mean a raising of hands in voting, but the laying of hands upon (*epi*) Timothy.

If Gillespie, in our judgment, does not sufficiently esteem the laying on of hands, he most emphatically supports ordination. *The Miscellany Questions* (III, 16/1) says,

> if it were an intolerable usurpation, in a man's own family, if any man should take on him the steward's place to dispense meat to the household, not being thereunto appointed, how much more were it an intolerable usurpation in the church. . . . Suppose they be well gifted, yet they may not preach except they be sent. . . . This sending needs be ordination, not the church's election; a people may choose to themselves, but they cannot send to themselves.

In the next column he continues,

> There are five necessary means and ways which must be had and used by those who look to be saved: (1) calling on the name of the Lord; (2) believing on him; (3) hearing his Word; (4) a preaching ministry; (5) mission or ordination. If the first four

> be perpetually necessary to the end of the world, so must the fifth be; for the Apostle layeth almost as great necessity on this last as on the rest. . . . There can be no ministerial office without a mission or ordination.

One of Gillespie's opponents had argued that no ministerial or ecclesiastical sending was in view in the New Testament, "for then none could be an instrument to convert another but a minister or preacher sent . . . therefore . . . the Apostle speaks of a providential sending, by giving men gifts, and working with them in their use and exercise." To which Gillespie answers,

Ordination therefore is not simply an apostolic function to cease with the first century.

> in Christ himself . . . his having the Spirit of the Lord upon him was not his mission, but is plainly distinguished from his mission and ordination to his office which he had from God; Luke 4:18, "The Spirit of the Lord is upon me because he hath anointed me to preach the gospel to the poor; he hath sent me. . . ." The *dunamis* or ability of gifts to the office is one thing; the *exousia* or authority to it is another thing (page 17, and the argument continues for another column on page 18).

Ordination therefore is not simply an apostolic function to cease with the first century. Preaching is ordinary and regular. Therefore mission or sending is too. The Great Commission of*Matthew* 28:19-20 shows that mission is perpetual, and thus sending likewise. To the same effect is *Luke* 12:42. Since the illustration describes the work of a steward, its lesson is not applicable to all Christians. The immediate application is to the disciples or apostles themselves. The extended application is to future stewards. They are to be held more responsible than lesser servants. Verse 43 shows that the warning remains in effect until Christ returns. The steward of the parable and the minister of a church have therefore been appointed with authority. The connection between a steward and a bishop is made in *Titus* 1:7.

To this someone objects that since probationers preach, ordination is not necessary. The reply is that they do not preach regularly, ordinarily, or *ex officio*. They preach occasionally, without ministerial office. And even so, they must have been licensed. Note, too, that the seven deacons, after they were elected, were ordained by the apostles; and though we do not know much about their activities, those mentioned in Acts included evangelism.

That ordination is requisite to the preaching of the Gospel and that it confers authority may be inferred from *Hebrews* 5:1-4. "For every high priest taken from among men is ordained . . . that he may offer both gifts and sacrifices for sin. . . . And no man takes this honor unto himself . . . ." The Socinians, who took a low view of ordination, restricted the application of this passage to the apostles. But this low view, or, rather, denial of ordination, fails to note that the priesthood was ordinary and continuing. Therefore, the passage applies to the ordinary and continuing Christian ministry, an inference reinforced by the completely general statement of verse 4. When this verse says that no man takes this honor unto himself, it need not, it hardly can mean, "this Aaronic honor." There is no demonstrative pronoun here—just the article; and hence the meaning can be and likely is honor as an abstract noun, any ecclesiastical honor. Even if someone contentiously insists that the article serves as a demonstrative, and thus refers to the Aaronic honor, nevertheless, the whole passage applies to the New Testament ministry. Not only is the epistle addressed to Christians, but one may also argue that if the lesser Aaronic honor required ordination, then *a fortiori* the greater honor of the New Testament minstry cannot be had without ordination. Scriptural analogy also is given in *Romans* 13:7, *1 Timothy* 3:1, and more pointedly in *1 Timothy* 5:17, "Let the elders that rule well be counted worthy of double honor."

The deacons in Acts 6:3, 6 were first perceived to be full of the Holy Ghost, second elected, and third ordained.

Another passage in *Hebrews* also advances the argument. Chapter 6:1-2 lists some elementary teachings, such as might be required of catechumens before baptism or even before a church was organized. One of these elementary points is ordination, clearly necessary to the organization of a church. Thus in addition to repentance and faith, ordination ranks as an elementary doctrine.

Ordination should be distinguished from the bestowal of the Holy Ghost as described in *Acts* 8:17-19. The deacons in *Acts* 6:3, 6 were first perceived to be full of the Holy Ghost, second elected, and third ordained. Later *1 Timothy* 4:14 shows that ordination is an act of presbytery. *1 Timothy* 5:22 warns against laying hands suddenly on some attractive neophyte. And *Titus* 1:5, by the words "in every city," shows that ordination is regular and ordinary. Such was not the case when Simon Magus wanted to buy apostolic power with money.

That ministers are the regular and ordinary officers of the church bears emphasis. Ministers of the Gospel are called shepherds, entering by the door and not breaking in; they are called angels, ambassadors, and rulers. But men do not give themselves the position of ambassador or even of shepherd. They must be appointed and sent. *Luke* 12:42 has already made this point with reference to stewards. Paul calls himself a steward in *1 Corinthians* 4:1, and calls all bishops so in *Titus* 1:7. Ministers are therefore servants; they invite guests to the wedding feast. But clearly no one can properly invite guests to a lord's wedding feast, unless the lord had previously appointed him. Paul was so appointed: "Whereunto I am ordained a preacher and an apostle" (*1 Timothy* 2:7), in which phrase we note that Paul was ordained a preacher as well as an apostle. He repeats this in *2 Timothy* 1:11. Preachers, therefore, are to be given authority to preach by ordination.

Preachers are permanent and regular officers of the church. Paul and the New Testament refute the position of the Socinians and

Anabaptists because *2 Timothy* 2:2 commands generation after generation to appoint faithful teachers. Paul does not refer to any and all Christians; he does not even have all gifted Christians in mind. Aptitude is one thing; calling and authority are something else. There is more to the calling of pastors than the church's electing them, for, as Gillespie says, "Those unto whom the power of ordination belongeth do also *commit* unto them that which they are entrusted with: 'the same commit thou' " (*Luke* 12:48).

Ordination confers authority to teach, and therefore the New Testament is violated if women are ordained.

Ordination, authority, and the submission of the congregation go hand in hand. The latter, the submission of the congregation, presupposes an authority in the pastors. That the Scripture requires submission is clear in *1 Thessalonians* 5:12, 13: "And we beseech you, brethren, to know them which labor among you, and are over you in the Lord, and admonish you; and to esteem them very highly in love for their work's sake. And be at peace among yourselves"; and in *Hebrews* 13:17, "Obey them that have the rule among you and submit yourselves. . . ." The same submission is implied in the ministers' right to receive remuneration (*1 Corinthians* 9:7, 9, 11, 13). What will the Socinians and Anabaptists do? If ordination is not necessary, will they pay salaries to all who preach; or, to avoid such Scripturally enjoined expense, will they prohibit preaching altogether?

There are other passages which reinforce these main lessons; but these are sufficient to conclude this Scriptural section by asserting that ordination confers authority to teach, and that therefore the New Testament is violated if women are ordained.

2

The second section of this paper may be made very brief because the ecumenical movement does not acknowledge the Bible as the infallible norm for either theological doctrine or ecclesiastical practice. Its procedures, however, may serve as a warning to any who may wish to disregard Scriptural restrictions.

Two periodicals only need be consulted: *The Churchman* (Volume 88, October-December 1974), and *The Journal of Ecumenical Studies* (Volume 10, 1973). Whatever authority *The Churchman* accords to the Bible in its defense of ordaining women, it also appeals to "the promptings of the Spirit" especially when a solemn synod is assembled, of which its first example is Vatican II. "Catholic bishops, under the guidance of the Spirit, could change this triadic order" and are today "in the process of recognizing other orders . . . of non-Roman and even nonepiscopal ministers as apostolic . . ." (262). The articles in their entirety place authority in the church, rather than in the Bible. The church changes itself. Thus, though *The Churchman* spends many pages advocating the ordination of women, I hope Reformed Presbyterians will remain unimpressed.

The Journal of Ecumenical Studies is more interesting. J. Massyngberde Ford guesses that "Luke 8:1-3, 10:38-42 . . . may reflect the role of deaconesses within the early church," and "whereas the twelve all appear to be male Jews . . . one cannot make the same assumption about the seventy or seventy-two disciples whom Jesus commissioned" (672-673). The role of Mary at the wedding in Cana "may be of symbolic and theological importance and may represent such behavior of Mary as typical." In fact, "it may well be that Jewish women converts [from paganism] rose to influential positions in the synagogue." And it may well be that J. M. Ford is highly imaginative.

She assures us that Phoebe was "a minister, *diakonos,* of the church at Cenchrea. . . . Most importantly, however, is the word *prostatis.* . . . Our Conclusion would be that the deacon Phoebe is in a position of authority and responsibility" (674-677). (On this point see the companion paper on "The Ordination of Women.")

Is the headship of Christ nothing more than a culturally conditioned personal opinion of Paul? Is it not rather authoritative theology?

Those who argue for the ordination of women give themselves the liberal benefit of any doubt. After discussing Priscilla, Dr. Ford writes, "it is *possible* that . . . the word *diakonos* alludes to both men and women deacons. One cannot *dogmatically* argue that only males are addressed." And, "Romans 16:1 very strongly suggests an active and *authoritative* position of women ministers" (678). Why not say, Romans 16:1 hardly even suggests authority and one cannot *dogmatically* argue that *diakonos* refers to ordained women deacons?

More frequently, however, not even this much authority is accorded to Scripture. On *1 Corinthians* 11 Dr. Ford says, "Firstly, one notes that the teaching contained in I Cor. 11 is the personal opinion of Paul, not dominical teaching; e.g. *thelo* (I wish, v. 3)." In opposition to such lax exegesis, consider the very verse she mentions: "I would have you know," or "I want you to know that the head of every man is Christ." Is the headship of Christ nothing more than a culturally conditioned personal opinion of Paul? Is it not rather authoritative theology?

Again, "I Cor. 11 must be based on a literal interpretation of Gen. 3, which exegetes could not accept nowadays. . . . Paul gives no indication whatsoever that women are precluded from any of these [gifts in I Cor. 12-14], even apostleship or administration" (680). No indication whatsoever? How about *1 Corinthians* 14:34, "Let your women keep silence in the churches, for it is not permitted unto them to speak; but they are commanded to be under obedience, as also saith the law"?

This verse, which should settle the whole matter, causes Dr. Ford no difficulty whatsoever: "These verses are placed after verse 40 in D, G. . . . There is therefore some justification for arguing that they are an interpolation" (681). Some justification? How much? For arguing? Where is the argument? Dr. Ford seems to think that a transposition of verses in two uncials, against *p 46, Aleph, A, B, K, Psi*, and plenty of cursives, so conclusively proves this to be spurious that the church is authorized to abandon its agelong practice of ordaining men only. Could it not better be argued, that if Christ had wanted women to be ordained, he would have chosen at least one woman as a disciple? Or, after the resurrection, one woman as an apostle? Or even one woman as a deacon?

On a passage that corroborates *1 Corinthians* 14:34, Dr. Ford writes, "With regard to I Tim. 2:9-15, one may note again . . . the fact that Paul expresses his own wish *(boulomai,* v. 8, and 'I do not permit', *epitrepo,* in v. 12), *not* that of the Lord" (682).

Must we then say that "I wish men to pray" is merely a personal wish? And when Paul says "I do not permit a woman to teach," does he lack apostolic authority?

The demand for women's ordination is just one more element in the apostasy of the large denominations and the decline of our civilization.

To make this poor argument a bit more palatable, Dr. Ford mistranslates the verse, as "I do not permit a woman to teach or to have supreme authority, but to be modest." The verse actually says, "I do not permit a woman to teach nor have authority over a man, but to keep quiet."

Dr. Ford, by inserting the word *supreme,* wants to allow women an authority, though less than supreme. But if, as has been shown, she allows for women *apostles,* how can she deny them supreme authority? Then she tries to make the word *teach* mean *formulate doctrine.* The women can teach, but only the bishops can make creedal decisions.

But let us say sharply against all this baseless imagination that the verses contain no such ideas.

Finally in her *Summary* Dr. Ford delivers this astounding assertion: "Even if Jesus were a male by his incarnation . . . the Spirit of God is thought of as the feminine principle in the Deity" (691).

The conclusion of this second section may well be that the demand for women's ordination is just one more element in the apostasy of the large denominations and the decline of our civilization. It was certainly not initiated by any reverent and scholarly study of the Biblical text. No one would even have thought it up apart from the liberal women's movement.

Wherever this new idea occurs in relatively conservative churches, it must be explained by the influence around us, most viciously exemplified in drug addiction and the murder of babies, seriously enough exemplified in crimes of violence, sexual abominations, and disregard of property rights, and least disturbingly but more profoundly exemplified in the rejection of Biblical inerrancy by hitherto conservative scholars and seminaries: This moral collapse engulfs all church members and infects their opinions, however slightly and unwittingly. The demand for the ordination of women is one result.

3

The third section of this paper now considers an example of this deleterious influence in a denomination that has boasted loudly of its Reformed theology. It is *Report 44* to the 1969 Synod of the Christian Reformed Church. On page 643 the *Report* gives a curious argument relative to the ordination of deacons in Acts 6:1-6. Quoting verse 6 the *Report* says, "The way the passage reads in the original makes it appear that the entire congregation did the laying on of hands, though there are interpreters who hold that only the apostles did the laying on of hands. We shall not try to settle this question."

But it is of some use to settle this question; nor is it hard to do so. The *Report* quoted only verse 6. In this verse the praying and the laying on of hands are immediately dependent on the word *apostles.* It is grammatically possible, though rather forced, to take the participle *praying* and the verb *laid* as referring to the congregation. What settles the matter, however, is verse 3, which the *Report* failed to mention. The verse says, "Then the Twelve . . . said . . . you select seven men . . . whom we may appoint over this business." The multitude of disciples were to choose seven men; but the multitude could not ordain them; it was "we" the apostles who delegated authority to the seven.

Ordination confers the gift of authority to use the gifts of wisdom and eloquence in the preaching of the Gospel.

Acts 13:3 is something else again. Here certain prophets and teachers, explicitly inclusive of Barnabas in verse 1, obviously inclusive of Saul in verse 2, are commanded by the Holy Ghost to lay hands on Barnabas and Saul. Since all of these, especially Saul, had already been ordained, the passage describes, not an ordination service, but a commissioning to a particular task. It is repeated today whenever a mission board prays and lays hands on an already ordained man as they send him out to Africa or Asia. This passage is therefore irrelevant for establishing the doctrine of ordination.

The passages in *1 Timothy* 4:14 and *2 Timothy* 1:6 have occasioned debates that are more ingenious than instructive. That the presbytery laid hands on Timothy is not inconsistent with Paul's being present and having done so with them. Whether it was the presbytery of Lystra or of Ephesus, and in particular what deep theological difference it makes, is all a matter of guesswork. The important point is that this presbyterial ceremony conferred a gift on Timothy, which Paul now exhorts Timothy to exercise. This gift can be no other than the authority "to rule well . . . especially . . . in the word and doctrine" (*1 Timothy* 6:17). Nothing in these two epistles permits reduction of this event to a mere commissioning for a limited missionary tour.

The *Report* to the Christian Reformed Synod (647-648) urges that God gave Timothy gifts of wisdom, eloquence, or whatever characteristics are useful in the ministry, before he was ordained, and that the ceremony did not confer these gifts. So be it. But why suppose that ordination confers wisdom and eloquence? And if it does not, why suppose that it confers nothing? The *Report's* argument is defective, for ordination confers the gift of authority to use the gifts of wisdom and eloquence in the preaching of the Gospel. The *Report* misses the issue. Therefore one must disagree with at least one of the *Report's* conclusions, namely, "The gift must not be understood as some indelible character conveyed to Timothy by the imposition of hands, since Timothy is told too that he must use and cultivate his gift." The logic of the since-clause is doubly faulty.

First, an exhortation to use a gift does not imply that it cannot have been given by the imposition of hands. Indeed, the opposite is the case: "Now that you have received the gift at my hands, Timothy, make use of it." Then second, giving a gift by the laying on of hands does not preclude it from being "indelible." If anyone dislikes the historical origin of the term *indelible,* we can more literally call it a permanent possession, no doubt withdrawable on account of great sin, but otherwise a life-long authority to preach. Contrary to the position of the *Report* that "There is no indication in Scripture that an authorization or appointment symbolized and confirmed by the laying on of hands was necessarily to be for the life-time of the person appointed" (649), one must ask, was Paul's gift of apostleship and Timothy's ordination to preach intended to be valid for only eighteen months or two years?

Was Paul's gift of apostleship and Timothy's ordination to preach intended to be valid for only eighteen months or two years?

The *Report* contains other peculiar assertions. For example, in arguing that Christian ministers are not an exclusive priesthood, and that the kingship in Israel does not convey political authority on contemporary elders—all of which is true—the *Report* states, "If the Lord found it necessary to warn against a coercive authority on the part of Old Testament kings, how much more sensitive ought we not to be concerning coercive authority today?" (652). There is considerable confusion here. For one thing, although God charged the Israelites with sin for rejecting the system of judges and desiring a king, he nonetheless gave the kings coercive authority; and this was reaffirmed in the New Testament. But any application of such material to elders, whether to support or deny authority, is mistaken, for elders are not civil rulers. Nor does the priesthood of all believers militate against the prerogatives of the ministry. What seems to be operative several times in this *Report* is an over-reaction against Romanism. The papacy may be the Antichrist, as the *Westminster Confession* says; but nonetheless, most of what Romanism says about the Trinity, the two natures of Christ, and even some things about ordination are true.

The apparent intent of the Christian Reformed *Report*, not exactly to abolish, but at least to minimize orderly church administration, depends here and there on obviously bad logic. Consider: "Does the fact that a 'disciple' in the broader sense was permitted to baptize, according to Acts 9, imply that all the 'disciples' in the broader sense could likewise administer baptism? . . . There is nothing in the book of Acts which would rule out an affirmative answer to these questions." The reference to *Acts* 9 indicates that the *Report* has Ananias in mind. Although the text does not explicitly say that Ananias baptized Paul, it is so likely that it may be taken for granted. But was Ananias a "disciple in the broader sense"? To be sure, all

Christians could be called disciples, but it by no means follows that Ananias was not an elder or deacon. The fact that God spoke directly to him is enough to conclude that nothing in the chapter "would rule out a *negative* answer to these questions." The *Report's* arguments from silence do not support its assumptions and conclusions. Yet there are two more arguments from silence on the same page (666).

Even the conclusion on the following page attacks a straw man. It says, "We may well agree with G. R. Beasley-Murray when he says, 'To insist that the Apostles personally conducted every baptism in the primitive Church is an absurdity that no one, so far as I am aware, has asked us to believe.'" Beasley-Murray is quite right; and for that very reason the *Report is* quite wrong. No one asserts that the Apostles personally baptized every first century convert. Our contention is that baptism is to be administered by ordained officers.

A further silence the *Report* brings up is in *1 Timothy* 4:13 and *2 Timothy* 4:1, 2. The *Report* notices that among the duties Paul enjoins, baptism "is conspicuous by [its] absence." True enough, baptism is not mentioned in these verses. But should the absence be called "conspicuous" or significant? Note that the Lord's Supper is absent too. The Lord's Supper is conspicuous by its presence in *1 Corinthians* 10:16-17, 11:20ff, and one would think that baptism is sufficiently conspicuous in *Matthew* 28:19, not to mention *Acts* 2:38 et passim.

A priest was not the only person who circumcised infants, nor did every family need a priest to celebrate the Passover.

It must be conceded that the *Report* uses something better than silence when it appeals to Jewish customs. A priest was not the only person who circumcised infants, nor did every family need a priest to celebrate the Passover. It is another matter, however, whether this implies that unordained laymen should baptize and administer the Lord's Supper. The *Report* itself, under the subhead, "The Fluid New Testament Situation with Regard to Office," acknowledges that *1 Thessalonians* 5:12, 13 and *1 Corinthians* 16:15, 16 speak of men who had some degree of prominence, to whom, Paul says, the church members should submit. Submission certainly gives the impression that such men, and others who labored with Paul, had received authority.

We particularly object to the accusation that Scripture contradicts itself.

The New Testament period may have been "fluid," in the sense that the many congregations established developed at different speeds, and to different degrees of organization. It is certainly true that the evidence and even the instruction relative to administration in the New Testament is "scanty" (674) in comparison with the theological content of *Romans*, or even with the moral problems in Corinth. But we totally reject the *Report's* poorly disguised suggestion that the New Testament "includes such a variety of obscure, ambiguous, and even contradictory statements." We particularly object to the accusation that Scripture contradicts itself. One need not, however, hesitate to say that the "tunnel period," that is, the formative period in the first century, exhibits diversity and the "the later epistles reflect some changes in emphasis as compared with the early ones" (674). This would be normal, as Paul's early successes in evangelization led to a subsequent amount of instruction in organizing particular congregations. One can even acknowledge that "up to the year 100 A.D. the organization of the local church was not a matter of paramount concern." Several times the *Report* uses the word *necessarily,* or here *paramount,* to obtain a degree of plausibility while evading the main question. Ordination may not have been a matter of "paramount" concern; but it was a matter of concern, even at the date of the epistle to the *Romans*, for the idea, if not the word, occurred in *Romans* 10:15. Because of a verse like this, and a certain number of others, elsewhere exegeted, one can hardly approve the *Report's* assertion that "the changes in the concept of office which occurred during the ancient period were often subtle and obscure. What is beyond dispute is that a major change did take place during that period" (647). That there were changes in the actual organizations of local congregations is indeed beyond dispute; but that there was any *major* change in the *concept* of ordination must repudiated. Paul may have added details to his earlier instruction on ordination, but he never contradicted himself. An inspired writer, through whom God breathes out his words on the written page, does not assert falsehoods. But if two assertives contradict, one must be false. For the rest, a paragraph on the fifth century (675) is irrelevant to the matter now under discussion.

Paul may have added details to his earlier instruction on ordination, but he never contradicted himself. An inspired writer, through whom God breathes out his words on the written page, does not assert falsehoods. But if two assertives contradict, one must be false.

More to the point are the remarks concerning the Reformation's opposition to sacerdotalism. The *Report* correctly stresses and condemns the popish claim that ordination confers the power of performing the miracle of transubstantiation. Rejection of this claim, however, does not entail rejection of an indelible character conferred by ordination, nor even of a "second class citizenship in the Church of Christ," no matter how repulsive this phraseology is; for no one can deny that the laity lack ministerial authority. The *Report* also correctly notes that the Reformers were preoccupied with the doctrine of grace, and not with the nature of ordination. "Yet in spite of these difficulties, it is possible, by way of implication, to draw . . . some conclusions" (679). Indeed, though the *Report is* not overly optimistic at this point, it is possible to draw some implications relative to the office of deacon. At any rate, it is possible to contradict the *Report's* assertion that "all believers are 'ordained' priests, prophets, and kings" (681). Clearly not all believers have been elected by the congregation and installed in office by laying on of hands.

The Report is once more correct in stating that the Reformers aimed to avoid both the Romish view and that of the Anabaptists and Socinians. But it seems to dismiss Luther's and Calvin's later more conservative position as chiefly an historical reaction against left-wing chaos. True, the *Report* acknowledges that the two Reformers appealed to Scripture, but its emphasis is on "fear of the Anabaptists as disturbers of civil and ecclesiastical peace." It would be better to say that these disturbers forced Calvin to study material in the Scriptures to which previously, and because of the major concern with Romanism, he had paid little attention. Action in an historical context (681) does not imply non-scriptural norms of action.

The authors of the *Report* may reject these criticisms on the ground that they explicitly recognize the assertions of Zwingli and the *Second Helvetic Confession*. Granted, granted; but some of the phraseology seems to minimize the "conservative" thrust of the "later" Luther and Calvin.

This minimizing is again found in the words "functional or instrumental" (682). One could say that the Romish priesthood also was functional and instrumental. The two words have an extensive application. But if the *Report* means that ordination is merely a pragmatic happenstance, rather than a divine command, a New Testament student must disagree. The wording of the *Report* is disturbing: "Although such division of labor is necessary for good order and efficiency, it does not create an essentially different order or hierarchy in the church that may be regarded as an end in itself' (682). But even the Romish priesthood is not "an end in itself." And Protestant or Biblical ordination does indeed create an "order" on which the laity must not encroach. Laymen may bring charges against an elder, but the session is the judicatory. Whether this authority is called "status" or "function" or "office" is merely semantics. By any name it is a divine ordinance, reserved to those only who are so elected. The language of the *Report* and of R. G. Johnson, whom it quotes, raises a false disjunction: "Although Calvin views the ministry as an institution of God, he still speaks of it in strongly functional terms." How else could anyone describe the office of King, President, or Senator except in "functional" terms, strongly or not? To use such terms does not deny the honor of the position. The *Report* embarrasses us by quoting Calvin's *Institutes,* IV, iii, 4, where he seems to say that the office of apostle and prophet continues sporadically to the present day, even though "Paul gives the appellation of 'prophets,' not to all interpreters of the Divine will, but only to those who were honored with some special revelation." In view of Calvin's and all the Reformers' stress on *sola Scriptura,* one cannot believe that Calvin, when he said, "the Lord . . . still raises up [apostles and prophets] on particular occasions, when required by the necessity of the times," meant what the words seem to say.

Because of the great doctrines of grace, for which the Protestants were being martyred and massacred, Calvin did not produce too detailed a doctrine of ordination.

Because of the great doctrines of grace, for which the Protestants were being martyred and massacred, Calvin did not produce too detailed a doctrine of ordination. In his *Ecclesiatical Ordinances* he recommends that the ordaining presbytery should abstain from laying on of hands "because of the infirmity [i.e. the superstitions] of the times." Yet in the *Institutes,* IV, iii, 16, he alleges that the example of the apostles should not be abandoned for "their very observance ought to serve in lieu of a precept." This latter consideration surely outweighs the dangers of superstition. The Reformers did not abolish baptism, even though several superstitious rites had been attached to it; and none of them ever dreamed of abolishing the Lord's Supper, though the mass was an idolatrous abomination. Considerations of normal routine, pragmatic usefulness, or something so vague as to be called functionalism, are inadmissible. (Compare the *Report,* page 686, Summary, the first paragraph.)

Ordination is a Scriptural ceremony by which the presbytery confers authority to preach the Gospel and to rule the church.

In conclusion, therefore, we assert, that ordination is a Scriptural ceremony by which the presbytery confers authority to preach the Gospel and to rule the church. The offices involved are those of elder and deacon. Since Scripture explicitly forbids women to teach or exercise authority, it is a violation of divine law to ordain a woman.

Bibliography

Henry Alford. *The Greek Testament.* Revised by E. F. Hanson. 4 vols. Chicago: Moody Press.

C. K. Barrett. *The Pastoral Epistles.* Oxford at the University Press, 1963.

J. A. Bengel. *Gnomon of the New Testament.* 5 vols. Revised and edited by Andrew R. Fausse. Edinburgh: T. and T. Clark, 1857-1895.

John Henry Bernard. *The Pastoral Epistles.* Cambridge Greek Testament. Cambridge at the University Press, 1922.

F. Blass and A. DeBrunner. *A Greek Grammar of the New Testament,* translated and edited by Robert W. Funk. The University of Chicago Press, 1961.

John Calvin. *Commentaries on I and II Timothy and Titus.* Grand Rapids, Michigan: Baker Book House, 1979.

John Calvin. *Institutes of the Christian Religion.* Philadelphia: Presbyterian Board of Publication, 1844.

Gordon H. Clark. *First John.* The Trinity Foundation, 1980.

Gordon H. Clark. *Predestination in the Old Testament.* Presbyterian and Reformed Publishing Company, 1978.

Hans Conzelman and Martin Dibelius. *The Pastoral Epistles.* Philadelphia, 1972.

Charles J. Ellicott. *The Pastoral Epistles of St. Paul.* London: Longmans, Green, Reader and Dyer, 1869.

Patrick Fairbairn. *Commentary on the Pastoral Epistles.* Grand Rapids, Michigan: Zondervan, 1956.

Patrick Fairbairn. *An Exposition of Ezekiel.* Grand Rapids, Michigan: Sovereign Grace Publishers, 1960.

John Gill. *A Body of Divinity.* Grand Rapids, Michigan: Sovereign Grace Publishers, 1971.

John Gill. *The Cause of God and Truth.* Evansville, Indiana: Sovereign Grace Book Club, 1971.

Donald Guthrie. *The Pastoral Epistles.* Grand Rapids, Michigan: Wm. B. Eerdmans Publishing Company, 1964.

William Hendriksen. *New Testament Commentary: The Pastoral Epistles.* Grand Rapids, Michigan: Baker Book House, 1965.

Charles Hodge, *Systematic Theology.* Grand Rapids, Michigan: Wm. B. Eerdmans Publishing Company, 1970.

John Edward Huther, *Meyer's (H. A. W. Meyer) Commentary on the New Testament.* 10 vols. Vol. 9. New York: Funk and Wagnalls, 1885.

George William Knight III. *The Faithful Sayings in the Pastoral Letters.* Kampen, 1968.

R. C. H. Lenski. *Interpretation of the New Testament.* 14 vols. Minneapolis: Augsburg Publishing House, 1946.

Bruce Metzger. *A Textual Commentary on the Greek New Testament.* London: United Bible Societies, 1971.

William Robertson Nicoll, editor. *The Expositor's Greek Testament.* 5 vols. Grand Rapids, Michigan: Wm. B. Eerdmans Publishing Company, 1951.

Alfred Plummer. *The Pastoral Epistles. The Expositor's Bible.* New York: A. C. Armstrong & Son, 1908.

Friedrich Schleiermacher. *Uber den Sogenannen Brief von Paulus an den Timotheus.* 1807.

Edmund Kidley Simpson. *The Pastoral Epistles.* London: Tyndale Press, 1954.

Helmut Thelicke. *The Evangelical Faith.* Grand Rapids, Michigan: Wm. B. Eerdmans Publishing Company, 1974.

John W. Walvoord, editor. *Inspiration and Interpretation.* Grand Rapids, Michigan: Wm. B. Eerdmans Publishing Company, 1957.

Scripture Index

Index

The Crisis of Our Time

Historians have christened the thirteenth century the Age of Faith and termed the eighteenth century the Age of Reason. The twentieth century has been called many things: the Atomic Age, the Age of Inflation, the Age of the Tyrant, the Age of Aquarius. But it deserves one name more than the others: the Age of Irrationalism. Contemporary secular intellectuals are anti-intellectual. Contemporary philosophers are anti-philosophy. Contemporary theologians are anti-theology.

In past centuries, secular philosophers have generally believed that knowledge is possible to man. Consequently they expended a great deal of thought and effort trying to justify knowledge. In the twentieth century, however, the optimism of the secular philosophers has all but disappeared. They despair of knowledge.

Like their secular counterparts, the great theologians and doctors of the church taught that knowledge is possible to man. Yet the theologians of the twentieth century have repudiated that belief. They also despair of knowledge. This radical skepticism has filtered down from the philosophers and theologians and penetrated our entire culture, from television to music to literature. *The Christian in the twentieth century is confronted with an overwhelming cultural consensus–sometimes stated explicitly but most often implicitly: Man does not and cannot know anything truly.*

What does this have to do with Christianity? Simply this: If man can know nothing truly, man can truly know nothing. We cannot know that the Bible is the Word of God, that Christ died for his people, or that Christ is alive today at the right hand of the Father. Unless knowledge is possible, Christianity is nonsensical, for it claims to be knowledge. What is at stake in the twentieth century is not simply a single doctrine, such as the virgin birth, or the existence of Hell, as important as those doctrines may be, but the whole of Christianity itself. If knowledge is not possible to man, it is worse than silly to argue points of doctrine–it is insane.

The irrationalism of the present age is so thoroughgoing and pervasive that even the Remnant–the segment of the professing church that remains faithful–has accepted much of it, frequently without even being aware of what it was accepting. In some circles this irrationalism has become synonymous with piety and humility, and those who oppose it are denounced as rationalists–as though to be logical were a sin. Our contemporary anti-theologians make a contradiction and call it a Mystery. The faithful ask for truth and are given Paradox. If any balk at swallowing the absurdities of the anti-theologians, they are frequently marked as heretics or schismatics who seek to act independently of God.

The Crisis of Our Time

There is no greater threat facing the true church of Christ at this moment than the irrationalism that now controls our entire culture. Totalitarianism, guilty of tens of millions of murders–including those of millions of Christians–is to be feared, but not nearly so much as the idea that we do not and cannot know the truth. Hedonism, the popular philosophy of America, is not to be feared so much as the belief that logic–that "mere human logic," to use the religious irrationalists' own phrase–is futile. The attacks on truth, on revelation, on the intellect, and on logic are renewed daily. But note well: The misologists–the haters of logic–use logic to demonstrate the futility of using logic. The anti-intellectuals construct intricate intellectual arguments to prove the insufficiency of the intellect. The anti-theologians use the revealed Word of God to show that there can be no revealed Word of God–or that if there could, it would remain impenetrable darkness and Mystery to our finite minds.

Nonsense Has Come

Is it any wonder that the world is grasping at straws–the straws of experientialism, mysticism, and drugs? After all, if people are told that the Bible contains insoluble mysteries, then is not a flight into mysticism to be expected? On what grounds can it be condemned? Certainly not on logical grounds or Biblical grounds, if logic is futile and the Bible unintelligible. Moreover, if it cannot be condemned on logical or Biblical grounds, it cannot be condemned at all. If people are going to have a religion of the mysterious, they will not adopt Christianity: They will have a genuine mystery religion. "Those who call for Nonsense," C.S. Lewis once wrote, "will find that it comes." And that is precisely what has happened. The popularity of Eastern mysticism, of drugs, and of religious experience is the logical consequence of the irrationalism of the twentieth century. There can and will be no Christian reformation–and no reconstruction of society–unless and until the irrationalism of the age is totally repudiated by Christians.

The Church Defenseless

Yet how shall they do it? The spokesmen for Christianity have been fatally infected with irrationalism. The seminaries, which annually train thousands of men to teach millions of Christians, are the finishing schools of irrationalism, completing the job begun by the government schools and colleges. Some of the pulpits of the most conservative churches (we are not speaking of the apostate churches) are occupied by graduates of the anti-theological schools. These products of modern anti-theological education, when asked to give a reason for the hope that is in them, can generally respond with only the intellectual analogue of a shrug–a mumble about Mystery. They have not grasped–and therefore cannot teach those for whom they are responsible–the first truth: "And you shall know the truth." Many, in fact, explicitly deny it, saying that, at best, we possess only "pointers" to the truth, or something "similar" to the truth, a mere analogy. Is the impotence of the Christian church a puzzle? Is the fascination with pentecostalism and faith healing among members of conservative churches an enigma? Not when one understands the sort of studied nonsense that is purveyed in the name of God in the seminaries.

The Trinity Foundation

The creators of The Trinity Foundation firmly believe that theology is too important to be left to the licensed theologians–the graduates of the schools of theology. They have created The Trinity Foundation for the express purpose of teaching the faithful all that the Scriptures contain–not warmed over, baptized, secular philosophies. Each member of the board of directors of The Trinity Foundation has signed this oath: "I believe that the Bible alone and the Bible in its entirety is the Word of God and, therefore, inerrant in the autographs. I believe that the system of truth presented in the Bible is best summarized in the *Westminster Confession of Faith*. So help me God."

The ministry of The Trinity Foundation is the presentation of the system of truth taught in Scripture as clearly and as completely as possible. We do not regard obscurity as a virtue, nor confusion as a sign of spirituality. Confusion, like all error, is sin, and teaching that confusion is all that Christians can hope for is doubly sin.

The presentation of the truth of Scripture necessarily involves the rejection of error. The Foundation has exposed and will continue to expose the irrationalism of the twentieth century, whether its current spokesman be an existentialist philosopher or a professed Reformed theologian. We oppose anti-intellectualism, whether it be espoused by a neo-orthodox theologian or a fundamentalist evangelist. We reject misology, whether it be on the lips of a neo-evangelical or those of a Roman Catholic charismatic. To each error we bring the brilliant light of Scripture, proving all things, and holding fast to that which is true.

The Primacy of Theory

The ministry of The Trinity Foundation is not a "practical" ministry. If you are a pastor, we will not enlighten you on how to organize an ecumenical prayer meeting in your community or how to double church attendance in a year. If you are a homemaker, you will have to read elsewhere to find out how to become a total woman. If you are a businessman, we will not tell you how to develop a social conscience. The professing church is drowning in such "practical" advice.

The Trinity Foundation is unapologetically theoretical in its outlook, believing that theory without practice is dead, and that practice without theory is blind. The trouble with the professing church is not primarily in its practice, but in its theory. Christians do not know, and many do not even care to know, the doctrines of Scripture. Doctrine is intellectual, and Christians are generally anti-intellectual. Doctrine is ivory tower philosophy, and they scorn ivory towers. The ivory tower, however, is the control tower of a civilization. It is a fundamental, theoretical mistake of the practical men to think that they can be merely practical, for practice is always the practice of some theory. The relationship between theory and practice is the relationship between cause and effect. If a person believes correct theory, his practice will tend to be correct. The practice of contemporary Christians is immoral because it is the practice of false theories. It is a major theoretical mistake of the practical men to think that they can ignore the ivory towers of the philosophers and theologians as irrelevant to their lives. Every action that the "practical" men take is governed by the thinking that has occurred in some ivory tower–whether that tower be the British Museum; the Academy; a home in Basel, Switzerland; or a tent in Israel.

In Understanding Be Men

It is the first duty of the Christian to understand correct theory–correct doctrine–and thereby implement correct practice. This order–first theory, then practice–is both logical and Biblical. It is, for example, exhibited in Paul's epistle to the Romans, in which he spends the first eleven chapters expounding theory and the last five discussing practice. The contemporary teachers of Christians have not only reversed the order, they have inverted the Pauline emphasis on theory and practice. The virtually complete failure of the teachers of the professing church to instruct the faithful in correct doctrine is the cause of the misconduct and cultural impotence of Christians. The church's lack of power is the result of its lack of truth. The *Gospel* is the power of God, not religious experience or personal relationship. The church has no power because it has abandoned the Gospel, the good news, for a religion of experientialism. Twentieth-century American Christians are children carried about by every wind of doctrine, not knowing what they believe, or even if they believe anything for certain.

The chief purpose of The Trinity Foundation is to counteract the irrationalism of the age and to expose the errors of the teachers of the church. Our emphasis–on the Bible as the sole source of truth, on the primacy of the intellect, on the supreme importance of correct doctrine, and on the necessity for systematic and logical thinking–is almost unique in Christendom. To the extent that the church survives–and she will survive and flourish–it will be because of her increasing acceptance of these basic ideas and their logical implications.

We believe that the Trinity Foundation is filling a vacuum in Christendom. We are saying that Christianity is intellectually defensible–that, in fact, it is the only intellectually defensible system of thought. We are saying that God has made the wisdom of this world–whether that wisdom be called science, religion, philosophy, or common sense–foolishness. We are appealing to all Christians who have not conceded defeat in the intellectual battle with the world to join us in our efforts to raise a standard to which all men of sound mind can repair.

The love of truth, of God's Word, has all but disappeared in our time. We are committed to and pray for a great instauration. But though we may not see this reformation of Christendom in our lifetimes, we believe it is our duty to present the whole counsel of God because Christ has commanded it. The results of our teaching are in God's hands, not ours. Whatever those results, his Word is never taught in vain, but always accomplishes the result that he intended it to accomplish. Professor Gordon H. Clark has stated our view well:

> There have been times in the history of God's people, for example, in the days of Jeremiah, when refreshing grace and widespread revival were not to be expected: The time was one of chastisement. If this twentieth century is of a similar nature, individual Christians here and there can find comfort and strength in a study of God's Word. But if God has decreed happier days for us and if we may expect a world-shaking and genuine spiritual awakening, then it is the author's belief that a zeal for souls, however necessary, is not the sufficient condition. Have there not been devout saints in every age, numerous enough to carry on a revival? Twelve such persons are plenty. What distinguishes the arid ages from the period of the Reformation, when nations were moved as they had not been since Paul preached in Ephesus, Corinth, and Rome, is the latter's fullness of knowledge of God's Word. To echo an early Reformation thought, when the ploughman and the garage attendant know the Bible as well as the theologian does, and know it better than some contemporary theologians, then the desired awakening shall have already occurred.

In addition to publishing books, the Foundation publishes a monthly newsletter, *The Trinity Review*. Subscriptions to *The Review* are free to U.S. addresses; please write to The Foundation to become a subscriber and receive a list of books currently available. The Trinity Foundation is a non-profit foundation, tax exempt under section 501 (c)(3) of the Internal Revenue Code of 1954. You can help us disseminate the Word of God through your tax-deductible contributions to the Foundation.

John W. Robbins

The Works of Gordon Haddon Clark

Born in Philadelphia, Pennsylvania, in 1902 and interred near Westcliffe, Colorado, in 1985, Gordon Haddon Clark was one of the most profound and brilliant scholars God has ever given his Church. Even the eighteenth century American prodigy, Jonathan Edwards, must defer to Clark as the greatest American theologian and philosopher.

Clark was a college professor for 60 years, from the time he received his baccalaureate degree from the University of Pennsylvania in 1924 until his death in 1985. He was also the author of more than 40 books and hundreds of articles, essays, and book reviews, most of which are listed below. Despite his prolific writing, Clark's brilliant work remains little known and less admired in contemporary churches, seminaries, and colleges, for they have rejected the premise upon which the whole of Clark's work is based: The Bible alone, and the Bible in its entirety, is the Word of God. Rather than agreeing that Christianity claims to have a systematic monopoly on truth, contemporary churches and schools seek common ground with non-Christian faiths, philosophies, and traditions. Nevertheless, Clark's consistently Christian philosophy and theology are becoming more and more well-known and appreciated among Christians who have remained faithful to Scripture, and it is for these genuine Christians that The Trinity Foundation has undertaken the task of collecting, editing, and publishing Clark's writings.

Although he had descended from Presbyterian ministers, Clark was to choose a different path (although he, too, would eventually be ordained a Presbyterian minister in 1944). His interest was philosophy and his career was teaching, and both philosophy and teaching were acts of worship. After receiving his baccalaureate degree in 1924 from the University of Pennsylvania, Clark was inivited to teach at the University, and he was awarded his doctorate in philosophy in 1929, after writing his doctoral dissertation on Aristotle. During those years, Clark was active in the Presbyterian church, being ordained an elder in 1927, and he vigorously opposed modernism within that denomination. His energetic opposition to modernism was to cost him the chairmanship of the Department of Philosophy at the University of Pennsylvania in 1936.

While teaching at the University of Pennsylvania, from 1924 to 1936, Clark assisted J. Gresham Machen, the eminent Princeton theologian, in organizing a new seminary in 1929 and a new denomination in 1936, both in Philadelphia, after the board of Princeton Seminary had been re-organized to make modernism rather than Christianity its theology, and after the

Presbyterian church had expelled Machen for his defense of the Gospel, in violation of its own judicial procedure.

After leaving the University of Pennsylvania, Clark was invited to teach at Wheaton College in Illinois, where he became one of the college's most popular and admired instructors. But his experience at the University of Pennsylvania repeated itself, and his tenure at Wheaton was cut short by a change in administration. The new regime, Arminian rather than modernist, was offended by Clark's consistently Biblical Christianity and forced his resignation. Until a permanent appointment arrived, Clark temporarily taught at the Reformed Episcopal seminary in Philadelphia. While in Philadelphia, he was ordained a minister in the Orthodox Presbyterian Church, which he had helped organize in 1936. There he came under attack, again for his intransigent defense of consistent Christianity, but this time from a faction within the Orthodox Presbyterian denomination that had been influenced by neo-orthodox theology.

In 1944, Butler University in Indianapolis invited Clark to become chairman of its Department of Philosophy, and he joined the University in January 1945. There he remained for 28 years, until his retirement from the University in 1973. During this time, and despite both ecclesiastical and academic hostility, Clark produced a magnificent body of work. For forty more years, he continued his warfare against modernism, Arminianism, and neo-orthodoxy within the churches, as well as with secular philosophies in academia. No one in modern times has as competently defended the faith against both the world and the wolves as Gordon Clark. Indeed, one must return to the works of Augustine to find anything comparable in the history of Christian thought, and even Augustine did not see so clearly the implications of the Bible.

The following bibliography of Clark's works is incomplete. It lists all the known essays and articles he produced, but more essays come to light each year. Most of his books are now in print, far more than were in print at any time during his life. Some of his essays have been collected and put into book form (*Essays on Ethics and Politics* and *God's Hammer: The Bible and Its Critics*, for example), and more are scheduled to be published in this series of volumes titled *The Works of Gordon Haddon Clark*.

This new series of books is intended to provide a definitive and handsome collection of Clark's works, for the benefit of both those who have already studied and are familiar with his writings, and those who are just embarking on an intellectual adventure that will change their lives forever. It is our prayer that God will use these books to further his truth everywhere on Earth in the twenty-first century.

Books

Ancient Philosophy. The Trinity Foundation, 1997.
Atonement, The. The Trinity Foundation [1987, 1996].
Behaviorism and Christianity. The Trinity Foundation, 1982.
Biblical Doctrine of Man, The. The Trinity Foundation, 1984.
Biblical Predestination. The Presbyterian and Reformed Publishing Company, 1969. Reprinted in *Predestination*, 1987.
Christian Philosophy of Education, A. The Trinity Foundation [1946] 1988.
Christian View of Men and Things, A. The Trinity Foundation [1952, 1991] 1998.
Clark Speaks From The Grave. The Trinity Foundation, 1986.
Colossians: Another Commentary on an Inexhaustible Message. The Trinity Foundation [1979] 1989.

Concept of Biblical Authority, The. The Presbyterian and Reformed Publishing Company, 1979. Reprinted in *God's Hammer: The Bible and Its Critics* [1982, 1987] 1995.
Dewey. The Presbyterian and Reformed Publishing Company, 1960. Reprinted in *William James and John Dewey*, 1995.
Ephesians. The Trinity Foundation, 1985.
Essays on Ethics and Politics. The Trinity Foundation, 1992.
Faith and Saving Faith. The Trinity Foundation [1983] 1990.
First and Second Thessalonians. The Trinity Foundation, 1986.
First Corinthians: A Contemporary Commentary. The Trinity Foundation [1975] 1991.
First John. The Trinity Foundation [1980] 1992.
God and Evil. The Trinity Foundation, 1996.
God's Hammer: The Bible and Its Critics. The Trinity Foundation [1982, 1987] 1995.
Historiography: Secular and Religious. The Trinity Foundation [1971] 1994.
History of Philosophy, A. Seymour G. Martin, Gordon H. Clark, Francis P. Clarke, and Chester T. Ruddick. F. S. Crofts and Company, 1941.
Holy Spirit, The. The Trinity Foundation, 1993.
Incarnation, The. The Trinity Foundation, 1988.
In Defense of Theology. Mott Media, 1984.
Introduction to Christian Philosophy, An. The Trinity Foundation, 1993.
Johannine Logos, The. The Trinity Foundation [1972] 1989.
Karl Barth's Theological Method. The Trinity Foundation [1963] 1997.
Language and Theology. The Trinity Foundation, [1980] 1993.
Logic. The Trinity Foundation [1985, 1988] 1998.
Logical Criticisms of Textual Criticism. The Trinity Foundation [1986] 1990.
Lord God of Truth. The Trinity Foundation, 1994.
New Heavens, New Earth. The Trinity Foundation [1980] 1993.
Pastoral Epistles, The. The Trinity Foundation [1984] 1999.
Peter Speaks Today: A Devotional Commentary on First Peter. The Presbyterian and Reformed Publishing Company, 1969. Reprinted in *New Heavens, New Earth*.
I and II Peter. The Presbyterian and Reformed Publishing Company, 1980. Reprinted as *New Heavens, New Earth*.
II Peter, A Short Commentary. The Presbyterian and Reformed Publishing Company, 1972. Reprinted in *I and II Peter*, 1980.
Philippians. The Trinity Foundation, 1996.
Philosophy of Gordon H. Clark, The. Ronald H. Nash, editor. The Presbyterian and Reformed Publishing Company, 1968. Part 1 reprinted as *An Introduction to Christian Philosophy*, 1993.
Philosophy of Science and Belief in God, The. The Trinity Foundation [1964, 1987] 1996.
Predestination. The Presbyterian and Reformed Publishing Company, 1987.
Predestination in the Old Testament. The Presbyterian and Reformed Publishing Company, 1978. Reprinted in *Predestination*, 1987.
Readings in Ethics. Gordon H. Clark and T. V. Smith, editors. F. S. Crofts and Company, first edition, 1931; second edition, 1935 (chapter on Spinoza added).
Religion, Reason and Revelation. The Trinity Foundation [1961, 1986] 1995.
Sanctification. The Trinity Foundation, 1992.
Selections from Early Greek Philosophy. M. C. Nahm. (Translations of Democritean material). F. S. Crofts and Company, 1934.
Selections from Hellenistic Philosophy. Appleton-Century-Crofts, 1940.
Thales to Dewey: A History of Philosophy. The Trinity Foundation [1957, 1989] 1997.

Three Types of Religious Philosophy. The Trinity Foundation [1973] 1989.
Trinity, The. The Trinity Foundation [1985] 1990.
What Christians Believe. The Trinity Foundation, 1999.
What Do Presbyterians Believe? The Presbyterian and Reformed Publishing Company [1965] 1985.
What Presbyterians Believe. The Presbyterian and Reformed Publishing Company, 1956.
William James. The Presbyterian and Reformed Publishing Company, 1963. Reprinted in *William James and John Dewey*.
William James and John Dewey. The Trinity Foundation, 1995.

Articles

Abelard. *Encyclopedia of Christianity* (National Foundation for Chrisian Education), 1964.
Activism. *Baker's Dictionary of Christian Ethics* (Carl F. H. Henry, editor), Washington, D. C.: Canon Press, 1973. Reprinted in *Essays on Ethics and Politics*.
Adoption. *The Southern Presbyterian Journal*, January 5, 1955.
Agnosticism. *Encyclopedia of Christianity* (National Foundation for Christian Education), 1964.
Alexandrian School. *Collier's Encyclopedia*. New York: P. F. Collier and Son, 1949.
Altruism. *Baker's Dictionary of Christian Ethics* (Carl F. H. Henry, editor), Washington, D. C.: Canon Press, 1973. Reprinted in *Essays on Ethics and Politics*.
Anarchism. *Baker's Dictionary of Christian Ethics* (Carl F. H. Henry, editor), Washington, D. C.: Canon Press, 1973. Reprinted in *Essays on Ethics and Politics*.
Anselm. *Encyclopedia of Christianity* (National Foundation for Christian Education), 1964.
Antithesis. *Baker's Dictionary of Christian Ethics* (Carl F. H. Henry, editor), Washington, D. C.: Canon Press, 1973.
Apologetics. *Contemporary Evangelical Thought* (Carl F. H. Henry, editor), Grand Rapids, Michigan: Baker Book House, 1957.
Apologetics. *Encyclopedia of Christianity* (National Foundation for Christian Education), 1964.
Appeal to Fundamentalists, An. *The Presbyterian Guardian*, March 10, 1943.
Aquinas. *Baker's Dictionary of Christian Ethics* (Carl F. H. Henry, editor), Washington, D. C.: Canon Press, 1973.
Art and the Gospel. *The Trinity Review*, Number 24, March/April 1982.
Assault Upon the Living God (Contributor). *Christianity Today*, March 15, 1968.
Assurance. *The Southern Presbyterian Journal*, January 19, 1955.
Atheism. *Baker's Dictionary of Christian Ethics* (Carl F. H. Henry, editor), Washington, D. C.: Canon Press, 1973.
Atheism. *The Trinity Review*, Number 32, July/August 1983.
Augustine. *Baker's Dictionary of Christian Ethics* (Carl F. H. Henry, editor), Washington, D. C.: Canon Press, 1973.
Augustine of Hippo. *Encyclopedia of Christianity* (National Foundation for Christian Education), 1964.
Baptism. *The Southern Presbyterian Journal*, March 16, 1955.
Barth's Critique of Modernism. *Christianity Today*, January 5, 1962.
Barth's Turnabout from the Biblical Norm (excerpt from *Karl Barth's Theological Method*). *Christianity Today*, January 4, 1963.
Beginnings of Greek Philosophy, The. *A History of Philosophical Systems* (Vergilius Ferm, editor), New York: The Philosophical Library, 1950. Reprinted in *Ancient Philosophy*.
Behaviorism. *Baker's Dictionary of Christian Ethics* (Carl F. H. Henry, editor), Washington, D. C.:

Canon Press, 1973.
Bible As Truth, The. *Bibliotheca Sacra*, April 1957. Reprinted in *God's Hammer: The Bible and its Critics*.
Bonaventura. *Encyclopedia of Christianity* (National Foundation for Christian Education), 1964.
Bultmann's Historiography. *Jesus of Nazareth: Saviour and Lord* (Carl F. H. Henry, editor), Grand Rapids, Michigan: Eerdmans, 1966.
Bultmann's Three-Storied Universe. *Christianity Today*, March 2, 1962.
Calvinistic Ethics. *Baker's Dictionary of Christian Ethics* (Carl F. H. Henry, editor), Washington, D. C.: Canon Press, 1973. Reprinted in *Essays on Ethics and Politics*.
Can Moral Education Be Grounded in Naturalism? (Paper presented to the fourth annual meeting of the Evangelical Theological Society, Wheaton, Illinois, 1952), *Bulletin of the Evangelical Theological Society*, Fall 1958. Reprinted in *Essays on Ethics and Politics*.
Capital Punishment. *Baker's Dictionary of Christian Ethics* (Carl F. H. Henry, editor), Washington, D. C.: Canon Press, 1973. Reprinted in *Essays on Ethics and Politics*.
Capital Punishment and the Bible. *Christianity Today*, February 1, 1960. Reprinted in *Essays on Ethics and Politics*.
Carneades. *Collier's Encyclopedia*, New York: P. F. Collier and Son, 1949.
Censures and Councils. *The Southern Presbyterian Journal*, April 13, 1955.
Christ the Mediator. *The Southern Presbyterian Journal*, December 1, 1954.
Christendom's Key Issue: 25 Scholars' Views. *Christianity Today*, October 12, 1959.
Christian Aesthetics. *The Trinity Review*, Number 67, May/June 1989.
Christian and the Law, The. *HIS*, October 1957. Reprinted in *The Trinity Review*, Number 1, March 1979. Reprinted in *Essays on Ethics and Politics*.
Christian Liberty. *The Southern Presbyterian Journal*, February 16, 1955. Reprinted in *Essays on Ethics and Politics*.
Christian Philosophy of Education, A. *The Trinity Review*, Number 61, May/June 1988.
Church, The. *The Southern Presbyterian Journal*, March 23, 1955.
Civil Magistrate, The. *The Southern Presbyterian Journal*, March 30, 1955. Reprinted in *Essays on Ethics and Politics*.
Clark Speaks from the Grave. *The Trinity Review*, Number 46, November/December 1985.
Classical Apologetics. *The Trinity Review*, Number 45, September/October 1985.
Cleanthes. *Collier's Encyclopedia*, New York: P. F. Collier and Son, 1976.
Comments on Mr. Verduin's Essay. *Christianity Today*, May 21, 1965.
Concerning Free Will. *Reformed Presbyterian Advocate*, August-September, 1961. Reprinted in *Essays on Ethics and Politics*.
Concerning Justification. *Christianity Today*, March 16, 1973.
Cosmic Time: A Critique of the Concept in Herman Dooyeweerd. *The Gordon Review*, September 1956.
Cosmological Argument, The. *The Trinity Review*, Number 7, September 1979.
Covenant, The. *The Southern Presbyterian Journal*, November 24, 1954.
Creation. *The Southern Presbyterian Journal*, November 10, 1954.
Creeds. *The Southern Presbyterian Journal*, October 6, 1954.
Cynicism. *Baker's Dictionary of Christian Ethics* (Carl F. H. Henry, editor), Washington, D. C.: Canon Press, 1973.
Democritus. *American People's Encyclopedia*, Chicago: The Spencer Press, 1948.
Destiny. *Zondervan Pictorial Encyclopedia of the Bible* (Merrill C. Tenney, editor), Grand Rapids, Michigan: Zondervan Publishing House, 1975.
Determinism. *Baker's Dictionary of Christian Ethics* (Carl F. H. Henry, editor), Washington, D. C.:

Canon Press, 1973. Reprinted in *Essays on Ethics and Politics*.
Determinism and Responsibility. *The Evangelical Quarterly* (London), January 1932. Reprinted in *Essays on Ethics and Politics*.
Diogenes. *Collier's Encyclopedia*, New York: P. F. Collier and Son, 1950.
Dispensationalism. *The Trinity Review*, Number 12, March/April 1980.
Divine Attributes, The. *Baker's Dictionary of Theology* (Everett F. Harrison, editor), Grand Rapids, Michigan: Baker Book House, 1960.
Eclecticism. *Collier's Encyclopedia*, New York: P. F. Collier and Son, 1949.
Effectual Calling. *The Southern Presbyterian Journal*, December 29, 1954.
Egoism. *Baker's Dictionary of Christian Ethics* (Carl F. H. Henry, editor), Washington, D. C.: Canon Press, 1973. Reprinted in *Essays on Ethics and Politics*.
Emanation. *American People's Encyclopedia*, Chicago: The Spencer Press, 1948.
Empedocles and Anaxagoras in Aristotle's *De Anima*. Doctoral dissertation. Reprinted in *Ancient Philosophy*.
Empiricism. *Encyclopedia of Christianity* (National Foundation for Christian Education), 1968.
Enlightenment, The. *Encyclopedia of Christianity* (National Foundation for Christian Education), 1968.
Epictetus. *Collier's Encyclopedia*, New York: P. F. Collier and Son, 1949.
Epicureanism. *Encyclopedia of Christianity* (National Foundation for Christian Education), 1968.
Epicureans. *Zondervan Pictorial Encyclopedia of the Bible* (Merrill C. Tenney, editor), Grand Rapids, Michigan: Zondervan Publishing House, 1975.
Epistemology. *Encyclopedia of Christianity* (National Foundation for Christian Education), 1968.
Eriugena, John Scotus. *Encyclopedia of Christianity* (National Foundation for Christian Education), 1968.
Eternity. *Zondervan Pictorial Encyclopedia of the Bible* (Merrill C. Tenney, editor), Grand Rapids, Michigan: Zondervan Publishing House, 1975.
Ethics. *Zondervan Pictorial Encyclopedia of the Bible* (Merrill C. Tenney, editor), Grand Rapids, Michigan: Zondervan Publishing House, 1975. Reprinted in *Essays on Ethics and Politics*.
Ethics, History of. *Baker's Dictionary of Christian Ethics* (Carl F. H. Henry, editor), Washington, D. C.: Canon Press, 1973. Reprinted in *Essays on Ethics and Politics*.
Ethics of Abortion, The. *The Trinity Review*, Number 25, May/June 1982. Reprinted in *Essays on Ethics and Politics*.
Evangelicalism. *Encyclopedia of Christianity* (National Foundation for Christian Education), 1968.
Evangelical Theological Society Tomorrow, The. *Bulletin of the Evangelical Theological Society*, Winter 1966. Reprinted in *God's Hammer: The Bible and Its Critics*.
Existence of God, The. *Encyclopedia of Christianity* (National Foundation for Christian Education), 1968.
Faith. *Baker's Dictionary of Christian Ethics* (Carl F. H. Henry, editor), Washington, D. C.: Canon Press, 1973.
Faith and Prayer. *Reformed Presbyterian Adovcate*.
Faith and Reason. *Christianity Today*, February 18 and March 4, 1957.
Faith Without a Focus Is Also Dead. *Christianity Today*, December 5, 1968.
Fate. *Baker's Dictionary of Christian Ethics* (Carl F. H. Henry, editor), Washington, D. C.: Canon Press, 1973.
Feuerbach, Ludwig A. *Encyclopedia of Christianity* (National Foundation for Christian Education), 1968.
Foreknowledge. *Encyclopedia of Christianity* (National Foundation for Christian Education), 1968.
Foreordination. *Encyclopedia of Christianity* (National Foundation for Christian Education), 1968.

Free Will. *The Southern Presbyterian Journal*, December 22, 1954. Reprinted in *Essays on Ethics and Politics.*

Fresh Look At the Hypothesis of Evolution, A. *Christianity Today*, September 1, 1958.

Fruits of the Reformation in Philosophy and Ethics . . . 'A Complete Reversal of Scholasticism'. *Christianity Today*, October 22, 1965. Reprinted in *Essays on Ethics and Politics.*

Gnosticism. *Encyclopedia of Christianity* (National Foundation for Christian Education), 1968.

God. *Baker's Dictionary of Theology* (Everett F. Harrison, editor), Grand Rapids, Michigan: Baker Book House, 1960.

God and Logic. *The Trinity Review*, Number 16, November/December 1980.

God's Countdown: 1960 (Contributor). *Christianity Today*, December 21, 1959.

Good Works. *The Southern Presbyterian Journal*, February 9, 1955. Reprinted in *Essays on Ethics and Politics.*

Greek Ethics. *Baker's Dictionary of Christian Ethics* (Carl F. H. Henry, editor), Washington, D. C.: Canon Press, 1973. Reprinted in *Essays on Ethics and Politics.*

Greek Religion and Philosophy. *Zondervan Pictorial Encyclopedia of the Bible* (Merrill C. Tenney, editor), Grand Rapids, Michigan: Zondervan Publishing House, 1975. Reprinted in *Ancient Philosophy.*

Guest Editorial. *Journal of the Evangelical Theological Society*, Spring 1969.

Hamilton's Theory of Language and Inspiration. *Journal of the Evangelical Theological Society*, 1972. Reprinted in *God's Hammer: The Bible and Its Critics.*

Happiness. *Baker's Dictionary of Christian Ethics* (Carl F. H. Henry, editor), Washington, D. C.: Canon Press, 1973. Reprinted in *Essays on Ethics and Politics.*

Hard Saying, A. *The Southern Presbyterian Journal*, October 27, 1954.

Healthy, Sick, or Dead? *The Southern Presbyterian Journal*, November 17, 1954. Reprinted in *Essays on Ethics and Politics.*

Hedonism. *Baker's Dictionary of Christian Ethics* (Carl F. H. Henry, editor), Washington, D. C.: Canon Press, 1973. Reprinted in *Essays on Ethics and Politics.*

Hellenistic and Roman Schools of Philosophy. *A History of Philosophical Systems* (Vergilius Ferm, editor), New York: The Philosophical Library, 1950. Reprinted in *Ancient Philosophy.*

Heritage of Irrationalism, A (excerpt from *Karl Barth's Theological Method*). *Christianity Today*, October 9, 1964.

Holy Scripture. *Bulletin of the Evangelical Theological Society*, Winter, 1963. Reprinted in *God's Hammer: The Bible and Its Critics.*

How Do We Learn? *The Trinity Review*, Number 34, November/December 1983.

How Does Man Know God? *The Trinity Review*, Number 68, July/August 1989.

How May I Know the Bible Is Inspired? *Can I Trust the Bible?* (Howard Vos, editor). Chicago: Moody Press, 1963. Reprinted in *God's Hammer: The Bible and Its Critics.*

Human Nature and Political Theory. Reprinted in *Essays on Ethics and Politics.*

Humanism. *Baker's Dictionary of Christian Ethics* (Carl F. H. Henry, editor), Washington, D. C.: Canon Press, 1973. Reprinted in *Essays on Ethics and Politics.*

Idealistic Ethics. *Baker's Dictionary of Christian Ethics* (Carl F. H. Henry, editor), Washington, D. C.: Canon Press, 1973. Reprinted in *Essays on Ethics and Politics.*

Image and Likeness of God, The. *The Trinity Review*, Number 33, September/October 1983.

Image of God. *Baker's Dictionary of Christian Ethics* (Carl F. H. Henry, editor), Washington, D. C.: Canon Press, 1973.

Image of God in Man, The. *Journal of the Evangelical Theological Society*, Fall 1969.

Immutability. *Wycliffe Bible Encyclopedia.* (Howard Vos, Charles Pfeiffer, John Rea, editors) Chicago: Moody Press, 1975.

In the Beginning. *The Trinity Review*, Number 40, November/December 1984
Incarnation: Fact or Theory? *Christianity Today*, December 10, 1956.
Intuition. *Baker's Dictionary of Christian Ethics* (Carl F. H. Henry, editor), Washington, D. C.: Canon Press, 1973.
Irrationalism. *Baker's Dictionary of Christian Ethics* (Carl F. H. Henry, editor), Washington, D. C.: Canon Press, 1973.
Is Christianity Unique? *Christianity Today*, December 21, 1959.
James, William. *Baker's Dictionary of Christian Ethics* (Carl F. H. Henry, editor), Washington, D. C.: Canon Press, 1973.
Jesus Christ: Fact or Fantasy? *Reformed Presbyterian Advocate*, Parts 1-3.
John Dewey. *Baker's Dictionary of Christian Ethics* (Carl F. H. Henry, editor), Washington, D. C.: Canon Press, 1973. Reprinted in *Essays on Ethics and Politics*.
Justification. *The Southern Presbyterian Journal*, December 8, 1954.
Kant. *Baker's Dictionary of Christian Ethics* (Carl F. H. Henry, editor), Washington, D. C.: Canon Press, 1973. Reprinted in *Essays on Ethics and Politics*.
Kant and Old Testament Ethics. *The Evangelical Quarterly*, July 1935. Reprinted in *Essays on Ethics and Politics*.
Know, Knowledge. *Zondervan Pictorial Encyclopedia of the Bible* (Merrill C. Tenney, editor), Grand Rapids, Michigan: Zondervan Publishing House, 1975.
Knowledge. *Baker's Dictionary of Theology* (Everett F. Harrison, editor), Grand Rapids, Michigan: Baker Book House, 1960.
Knowledge and Ignorance. *The Southern Presbyterian Journal*, October 13, 1954.
Language and Logic. *The Gordon Review*, January 12, 1955.
Law of God, The. *The Southern Presbyterian Journal*, January 12, 1955.
Legalism. *Baker's Dictionary of Christian Ethics* (Carl F. H. Henry, editor), Washington, D. C.: Canon Press, 1973. Reprinted in *Essays on Ethics and Politics*.
Liberalism. *Wycliffe Bible Encyclopedia*. (Howard Vos, Charles Pfeiffer, John Rea, editors) Chicago: Moody Press, 1975.
Logic and Language. *The Gordon Review*, February 1956.
Logical Criticisms of Textual Criticism. *The Trinity Review*, Number 36, March/April 1984.
Lord God of Truth. *Ambitious To Be Well-Pleasing* (Allen Guelzo, editor). Jefferson, Maryland: The Trinity Foundation, 1986.
Lord's Supper, The. *The Southern Presbyterian Journal*, April 6, 1955.
Mindless Men: Behaviorism and Christianity. *The Trinity Review*, Number 14, July/August 1980.
Miracles. *Zondervan Pictorial Encyclopedia of the Bible* (Merrill C. Tenney, editor), Grand Rapids, Michigan: Zondervan Publishing House, 1975.
Miracles, History, and Natural Law. *The Evangelical Quarterly* (London), January 1940.
Modal Spheres and Morality. Reprinted in *Essays on Ethics and Politics*.
Modern Christianity's Crucial Junctures. *Christianity Today*, October 11, 1963.
Modern Science and Belief in God (excerpt from *The Philosophy of Science and Belief in God*). *Christianity Today*, August 27, 1965.
Moon Shot: Its Meaning to 25 Scholars (Contributor). *Christianity Today*, October 13, 1958.
More Questions on Barth's Views (Contributor). *Christianity Today*, January 5, 1962.
Natural Law and Revelation (Anonymous guest editorial). *Christianity Today*, June 24, 1957. Reprinted in *Essays on Ethics and Politics*.
Naturalism. *The Southern Presbyterian Journal*, March 7, 1962.
Nature of the Physical Universe, The. *Christian Faith and Modern Theology* (Carl F. H. Henry, editor), New York: Channel Press, 1963.

Neoorthodoxy. *Wycliffe Bible Encyclopedia*. (Howard Vos, Charles Pfeiffer, John Rea, editors) Chicago: Moody Press, 1975.

New Discovery in the Quest of the Historical Jesus, A. *Christianity Today*, January 15, 1971. Reprinted in *The Trinity Review,* Number 60, March/April 1988.

Next Ten Years, The (Contributor). *Christianity Today*, October 9, 1964.

Number of the Beast, The. *The Trinity Review*, Number 38. July/August 1984.

Oaths. *Baker's Dictionary of Christian Ethics* (Carl F. H. Henry, editor), Washington, D. C.: Canon Press, 1973. Reprinted in *Essays on Ethics and Politics*.

On the Primacy of the Intellect. *Westminster Theological Journal*, May 1943.

Ordination of Women, The. *The Trinity Review*, Number 17, January/February 1981. Reprinted in *The Pastoral Epistles* and in *Scripture Twisting in the Seminaries, Feminism* (John W. Robbins).

Perseverance. *The Southern Presbyterian Journal*, February 23, 1955.

ΦΑΝΤΑΣΙΑ in Plotinus. *Philosophical Essays in Honor of Edgar A. Singer, Jr.* (F. P. Clarke and M. L. Nahm, editors), University of Pennsylvania Press, [1942] 1969. Reprinted in *Ancient Philosophy*.

Philo Judeus. *Zondervan Pictorial Encyclopedia of the Bible* (Merrill C. Tenney, editor), Grand Rapids, Michigan: Zondervan Publishing House, 1975.

Philosophy. *Zondervan Pictorial Encyclopedia of the Bible* (Merrill C. Tenney, editor), Grand Rapids, Michigan: Zondervan Publishing House, 1975.

Philosophy in the Sixties. *Christianity Today*, May 9, 1960.

Plotinus. *Collier's Encyclopedia*, New York: P. F. Collier and Son, 1949.

Plotinus on the Eternity of the World. *The Philosophical Review*, March 1949. Reprinted in *Ancient Philosophy*.

Plotinus' Theory of Empirical Responsibility. *The New Scholasticism*, January 1943. Reprinted in *Ancient Philosophy*.

Plotinus' Theory of Sensation. *The Philosophical Review*, July 1942. Reprinted in *Ancient Philosophy*.

Pragmatism. *Baker's Dictionary of Christian Ethics* (Carl F. H. Henry, editor), Washington, D. C.: Canon Press, 1973.

Problem of Motion, The. *The Gordon Review*, Winter 1958.

Protestant World View, A. *The Trinity Review*, Numbers 2 and 3, April and May, 1979.

Protestant-Roman Unity: 25 Scholars' Views (Contributor). *Christianity Today*, October 10, 1960.

Providence. *The Southern Presbyterian Journal*, November 3, 1954.

Puritans and Situation Ethics, The. *The Trinity Review*, Number 65, January/February 1989. Reprinted in *Essays on Ethics and Politics*.

Questions on Barth's Theology (Contributor). *Christianity Today*, July 3, 1961.

Reference to Plotinus in Liddell and Scott, A. *The American Journal of Philology*, July 1944.

Relationship of Public Education to Christianity, The. *The Trinity Review*, Number 43, May/June 1985.

Repentance. *The Southern Presbyterian Journal*, February 2, 1955.

Responsibility. *Baker's Dictionary of Christian Ethics* (Carl F. H. Henry, editor), Washington, D. C.: Canon Press, 1973. Reprinted in *Essays on Ethics and Politics*.

Resurrection, The. *Christianity Today*, April 15, 1957.

Resurrection and Judgment. *The Southern Presbyterian Journal*, April 20, 1955.

Revealed Religion. *Christianity Today*, December 17, 1965. Reprinted in *God's Hammer: The Bible and Its Critics*.

Romans. *The Biblical Expositor* (Carl F. H. Henry, editor), Philadelphia, Pennsylvania: A. J.

Holman Company, 1960.

Sacraments, The. *The Southern Presbyterian Journal*, March 9, 1955.

Sanctification. *The Southern Presbyterian Journal*, December 15, 1954. Reprinted in *Essays on Ethics and Politics*.

Saving Faith. *The Southern Presbyterian Journal*, January 26, 1955.

Saving Faith. *The Trinity Review*, Number 10, December 1979.

Scholars' Panel Identifies Contemporary Idols (Contributor). *Christianity Today*, October 13, 1961.

Science and Truth. *The Trinity Review*, Number 19, May/June 1981.

Sighting the Final Third of the Twentieth Century . . . The Church and the Nation (Contributor). *Christianity Today*, January 20, 1967.

Situational Ethics. *Baker's Dictionary of Christian Ethics* (Carl F. H. Henry, editor), Washington, D. C.: Canon Press, 1973. Reprinted in *Essays on Ethics and Politics*.

Skepticism. *Baker's Dictionary of Christian Ethics* (Carl F. H. Henry, editor), Washington, D. C.: Canon Press, 1973.

Sovereignty of God, The. *The Trinity Review*, Number 28, November/December 1982.

Special Divine Revelation as Rational. *Revelation and the Bible* (Carl F. H. Henry, editor), Grand Rapids, Michigan: Baker Book House, 1959. Reprinted in *God's Hammer: The Bible and Its Critics*.

Spontaneity and Monstrosity in Aristotle. *The New Scholasticism*, January 1934. Reprinted in *Ancient Philosophy*.

Stoicism. *Collier's Encyclopedia*, New York: P. F. Collier and Son, 1949.

Stoics. *Zondervan Pictorial Encyclopedia of the Bible* (Merrill C. Tenney, editor), Grand Rapids, Michigan: Zondervan Publishing House, 1975.

Textual Criticism. *The Trinity Review*, Number 37. May/June 1984.

Theism. *Zondervan Pictorial Encyclopedia of the Bible* (Merrill C. Tenney, editor), Grand Rapids, Michigan: Zondervan Publishing House, 1975.

Theory of Time in Plotinus, The. *The Philosophical Review*, July 1944. Reprinted in *Ancient Philosophy*.

Thomas Aquinas. *Encyclopedia of Christianity* (National Foundation for Christian Education), 1964. Reprinted in *Essays on Ethics and Politics*.

Timaeus or Plato? *The New Scholasticism*, October 1934. Reprinted in *Ancient Philosophy*.

Time and Eternity. *The Trinity Review*, Number 21, September/October 1981. Reprinted in *God's Hammer: The Bible and Its Critics*.

I and II Timothy. *The Trinity Review*, Number 30, March/April 1983.

Toronto School, The. *The Trinity Review*, Number 6, August 1979.

Traducianism. *The Trinity Review*, Number 26, July/August 1982.

Trinity. *Wycliffe Bible Encyclopedia*. (Howard Vos, Charles Pfeiffer, John Rea, editors), Chicago: Moody Press, 1975.

Trinity, The. *The Southern Presbyterian Journal*, October 20, 1954.

Trinity, The. *The Trinity Review*, Number 9, November 1979.

Trouble with Humanism, The. *Christianity Today*, May 12, 1967. Reprinted in *Essays on Ethics and Politics*.

Truth. *Baker's Dictionary of Theology* (Everett F. Harrison, editor), Grand Rapids, Michigan: Baker Book House, 1960.

Two Religions. *Christianity Today*, April 9, 1965.

Two Translations of Plotinus. *The New Scholasticism*, January 1938.

Utilitarianism. *Baker's Dictionary of Christian Ethics* (Carl F. H. Henry, editor), Washington, D. C.:

Canon Press, 1973. Reprinted in *Essays on Ethics and Politics*.
Values. *Baker's Dictionary of Christian Ethics* (Carl F. H. Henry, editor), Washington, D. C.: Canon Press, 1973. Reprinted in *Essays on Ethics and Politics*.
Variety of Versions, The. *The Trinity Review*, Number 35. January/February 1984.
Verbal Inspiration: Yesterday and Today. *The Southern Presbyterian Journal*, September 12, 1956. Reprinted in *God's Hammer: The Bible and Its Critics*.
What Is Truth? *Presbuterion*, Fall 1980. Reprinted in *God's Hammer: The Bible and Its Critics*.
Wisdom in First Corinthians, *Journal of the Evangelical Theological Society*, Fall 1972.
Word of God, The. *The Southern Presbyterian Journal*, September 29, 1954.
Worship and Vows. *The Southern Presbyterian Journal*, March 2, 1955.
Zeno. *Collier's Encyclopedia*, New York: P. F. Collier and Son, 1949.

Book Reviews

Act and Being. Dietrich Bonhoeffer. *Christianity Today*, June 22, 1962.
After Fundamentalism: The Future of Evangelical Theology. Bernard Ramm. *Fundamentalist Journal*, June 1983.
Albert Schweitzer. Jacques Feschotte. *Christianity Today*, September 1, 1958.
Anselm: Fides Quaerens Intellectum. Karl Barth. *Christianity Today*, June 5, 1961.
Aristotle's Theory of the Infinite. Abraham Edel. *The New Scholasticism*, January 1935.
The Catechism, A Review of *The School of Faith* by Thomas F. Torrance. *Reformed Presbyterian Advocate*.
Challenge of Our Age, The. Hendrik Hart. *Blue Banner Faith and Life*, October-December 1974.
Christ and Christian. Nels F. S. Ferré. *Christianity Today*, January 5, 1959.
Christian Commitment: An Apologetic. Edward John Carnell. *Christianity Today*, September 2, 1957.
Christianity and World Issues. T. B. Maston. *Christianity Today*, October 14, 1957.
Classical Apologetics. R. C. Sproul, John Gerstner, and Arthur Lindsley. *The Trinity Review*, Number 45, September/October 1985.
Coming World Civilization, The. William Ernest Hocking. *Christianity Today*, May 26, 1958.
Conflict with Rome. G. C. Berkouwer. *Christianity Today*, February 17, 1958.
Conscience and Its Rights to Freedom. Eric D'Arcy. *Christianity Today*, April 27, 1962.
Defence of Theological Ethics, A. G. F. Woods. *Christianity Today*, September 16, 1966.
Deliverance to the Captives. Karl Barth. *Christianity Today*, June 5, 1961.
Divine Perfection: Possible Ideas of God. Frederick Sontag. *Christianity Today*, April 13, 1962.
Enforcement of Morals, The. Patrick Devlin. *Christianity Today*, October 8, 1965.
Essays in Applied Christianity. Reinhold Niebuhr. *Christianity Today*, January 4, 1960.
Essence of Plotinus, The. Grace H. Turnball. *The New Scholasticism*, January 1935.
Ethics and Science. Henry Morgenau. *Christianity Today*, December 18, 1964.
Experience and God. John E. Smith. *Christianity Today*, November 8, 1968.
Fabric of Paul Tillich's Theology, The. David H. Kelsey. *Christianity Today*, June 23, 1967.
History of Religions, Essays in Methodology, The. Edited by Eliade and Kitagawa. *Christianity Today*, February 15, 1960.
Humanity of God, The. Karl Barth. *Christianity Today*, April 25, 1960.
Idea of Transcendence in the Philosophy of Karl Jaspers, The. R. D. Knudsen. *The Gordon Review*, Summer 1959.
In the Beginning, God. William M. Logan. *The Gordon Review*, Winter 1958.
In the Twilight of Western Thought. Herman Dooyeweerd. *Christianity Today*, August 29, 1960.
Issues in Science and Religion. Ian G. Barbout. *Christianity Today*, October 28, 1966.

Karl Barth on God. Sebastian A. Matczak. *Christianity Today*, March 1, 1963.
Karl Barth's Doctrine of Holy Scripture. Klaas Runia. *Christianity Today*, July 6, 1962.
Late Medieval Mysticism. Edited by Ray C. Petry. *Christianity Today*, May 12, 1958.
Limits of Reason, The. George Boas. *Christianity Today*, May 8, 1961.
Many-Faced Argument, The. Edited by John Hick and Arthur C. Magill. *Christianity Today*, January 5, 1968.
Myth and Truth. John Knox. *Bulletin of the Evangelical Theological Society*, Summer 1967.
Persons in Relation. John Macmurray. *Christianity Today*, December 22, 1961.
Perspectives in 19th and 20th Century Protestant Theology. Paul Tillich. *Christianity Today*, June 23, 1967.
Philosophical Study of Religion, A. David Hugh Freeman. *Christianity Today*, October 23, 1964.
Philosophy of St. Bonaventure, The. Etienne Gilson. *Westminster Theological Journal*, November 1938.
Platonic Legend, The. Warner Fite. *The New Scholasticism*, January 1935.
Principles of Christian Ethics, The. Albert C. Knudson. *Westminster Theological Journal.*
Relativism, Knowledge and Faith. Gordon D. Kaufman. *Christianity Today*, June 20, 1960.
Revolt Against Heaven. Kenneth Hamilton. *The Gordon Review*, Spring 1966.
Sacra Doctrina: Reason and Revelation in Aquinas. Per Eric Persson. *Christianity Today*, October 9, 1970.
Scepticism and Historical Knowledge. Jack W. Meiland. *The Gordon Review*, Spring 1966.
Scholastic Miscellany: Anselm to Ockham, A. Edited by Eugene R. Fairweather. *Christianity Today*, January 21, 1957.
School of Faith, The. Thomas F. Torrance. *Christianity Today*, July 4, 1960.
Sense and Nonsense in Religion. Sten H. Stenson. *Christianity Today*, July 4, 1969.
Social Ethics of Reinhold Niebuhr, The. Theodore Minnema. *Christianity Today*, January 4, 1960.
Social Responsibilities of Organized Labor. John A. Fitch. *Christianity Today*, June 22, 1959.
Speculation in Pre-Christian Philosophy. Richard Kroner. *Christianity Today*, March 18, 1957.
Tennant's Philosophical Theology. Delton Lewis Scudder. *Westminster Theological Journal.*
Theological Ethics. James Sellers. *Christianity Today*, July 22, 1966.
Theories of Revelation. H. C. McDonald. *Christianity Today*, September 13, 1963.
To Prod the Slumbering Giant (Association for the Advancement of Christian Scholarship). ("Toronto Scholarship"), *Blue Banner Faith and Life*, July-September, 1975.
Understanding the Scripture. A. H. DeGraaff and C. G. Seerveld. ("How to Let the Bible Confuse You"), *Episcopal Recorder*, February 1972.
Varieties of Christian Apologetics. Bernard Ramm. *Christianity Today*, July 20, 1962.
Vision of Paul Tillich, The. Carl J. Armbruster. *Christianity Today*, June 23, 1967.
What About Speaking in Tongues? Anthony A. Hoekema. *The Gordon Review*, Winter 1967.
Words and Images. E. L. Mascall. *Christianity Today*, August 18, 1958.
Words and the WORD. Kenneth Hamilton, ("Hamilton's Theory of Language and Inspiration"). *Journal of the Evangelical Theological Society*, Winter 1972.

Letters

(Agape). *Christianity Today*, March 2, 1959.
(Biblical separation). *Christianity Today*, December 9, 1957.
(Biblical separation). *Christianity Today*, May 26, 1958.
(Causality and mechanism). *Christianity Today*, April 27, 1952.
(Church property grab). *Christianity Today*, September 28, 1962.

(Government and ethics). *Christianity Today*, December 21, 1962.
(Greek views of God). *Christianity Today*, September 10, 1971.
(Liberalism). *Christianity Today*, January 7, 1957.
(Liberalism). *Christianity Today*, March 18, 1957.
(Liberalism). *Christianity Today*, June 18, 1964.
(Malcolm X, Stokely Carmichael, and Eldridge Cleaver). *Christianity Today*, January 16, 1970.
(The order of salvation). *Present Truth*, June 1973; September 1976.
(The problem of evil). *Christianity Today*, May 21, 1971.
(Roman Catholicism). *Christianity Today*, March 27, 1964.
(Scholasticism and the Reformation). *Christianity Today*, November 19, 1965.
(Social engineering). *Christianity Today*, May 11, 1959.